Waves of Upheaval

GENDERING ASIA
A Series on Gender Intersections

Gendering Asia invites book proposals on gender issues in Asian societies, including Asia in the world. The series is multidisciplinary and concerned with the wide range of understandings, practices and power relations in Asian societies. It explores theoretical, empirical and methodological gender issues in the social sciences and the humanities.

Series Editors: Wil Burghoorn, Monica Lindberg Falk and Pauline Stoltz.

NIAS Press is the autonomous publishing arm of NIAS – Nordic Institute of Asian Studies, a research institute located at the University of Copenhagen. NIAS is partially funded by the governments of Denmark, Finland, Iceland, Norway and Sweden via the Nordic Council of Ministers, and works to encourage and support Asian studies in the Nordic countries. In so doing, NIAS has been publishing books since 1969, with more than two hundred titles produced in the past few years.

norden
Nordic Council of Ministers

UNIVERSITY OF COPENHAGEN

Waves of Upheaval

Political Transitions and Gendered Transformations in Myanmar

Edited by

Jenny Hedström
Elisabeth Olivius

 niasPRESS

Waves of Upheaval
Political Transitions and Gendered Transformations in Myanmar
Edited by Jenny Hedström and Elisabeth Olivius

Nordic Institute of Asian Studies
Gendering Asia, no. 17

First published in 2023 by NIAS Press
NIAS – Nordic Institute of Asian Studies
Øster Farimagsgade 5, 1353 Copenhagen K, Denmark
Tel: +45 3532 9503 • Fax: +45 3532 9549
E-mail: books@nias.ku.dk • Online: www. niaspress. dk

A CIP catalogue record for this book is available from the British Library

ISBN 978-87-7694-322-6 Hbk

Typeset in 11.5 pt Arno Pro by Don Wagner
Printed and bound in the United States by Maple Press, York, PA
Cover design: NIAS Press
Cover image: women protesting the military takeover in Myanmar
(photo: Women's League of Burma 2021)

Contents

Figures

Foreword

Chie Ikeya

The complex nature of the path that women in Myanmar tread in negotiating gendered relations of power amidst profound political and economic transformations – the topic explored in this book – was highlighted poignantly for me in 2014. In that year, I co-organized an international conference on 'New Approaches to Myanmar History' with Dr Margaret Wong, the Chair of the History Department at the University of Yangon, Myanmar, intended as a small step towards reviving scholarly ties. In what I read as a sign of how much had changed in Myanmar since 2011, the conference took place without much ado. Organized around four themes – Buddhism, art and architecture, transnational and intra-Asian history, and women's and gender history – it attracted over 180 attendees and generated lively translingual exchanges in Burmese and English. However, there was a moment in the late afternoon panel on women's and gender history that crystallized what had *not* changed. Presenting on the topic of 'Women in Myanmar History', Dr Wong spoke favourably about relations between men and women in the country. Women in Myanmar, she emphasized, had historically enjoyed autonomy, freedom and a social standing as the complementary counterpart, not the inferior, of men. Marriage and motherhood were not institutions of oppression but domains in which true partnership between men and women was forged and the full potential of women was actualized.

Now this was, in my view, an idealized rather than historicized portrayal of women in Myanmar. And it was not, by any measure, a novel way of understanding the history of the country. In fact, it was an abiding trope seeded by the encounter with British imperialism. British colonial authorities praised Burmese women as the freest women in the Orient, unencumbered by the patriarchal practices such as polygamy, veiling, and child marriage that were presumed to be endemic to other Oriental civilizations. The teachings of the Buddha had made Burma an exceptional society that conferred upon its women independence and social equality, they insisted. British imperialists deployed this image of Burmese women, which constituted Burma and its population as essentially Buddhist, to 'otherize' Muslims, as despotic, degenerate and fanatic, and to conjure fear and panic about the dangers of Muslim empires and domination. This colonial form of knowledge was appropriated and propagated enthusiastically by colonized subjects who considered the Buddhist Burman the heart and soul – and the rightful master – of a sovereign Burmese nation in the making.

The purported liberty of Burmese women is not just a matter of national pride. Its imperilment, imagined and otherwise, has served to authorize the detention, displacement, and dispossession of those who are rendered foreign and domestic enemies of the nation, as we have recently witnessed in the persecution of the Rohingya as 'Bengali terrorists'. It is a foundational national myth that has underwritten a system of discrimination and differential inclusion that consigns racial and religious minorities to second-class status. It is a sacrosanct belief that has harmed and marginalized the very women it ostensibly celebrates and honours. The idea that Myanmar has never needed feminism because it does not suffer from sexism – confirmed by official pronouncements by the government that discrimination against women does not exist in the country – has banished from collective memory the contentious history of women agitating, organizing, and mobilizing to address the penalties of being a woman or a girl in Myanmar. It is a deceptive narrative that has suppressed public discussions of, and attempts at redressing, the complex and diverse experiences and legacies of systemic gender inequality.

What compelled Dr Wong to deliver such a conservative talk on women in Myanmar? My guess is that it was a calculated decision, one that speaks to the constraints and challenges that women in Myanmar face. Few women, not least those belonging to an ethnic minority, as does Dr Wong, who is Sino-Burmese, had risen to the position at the university that she then occupied. The historical profession, as with academia more generally, in Myanmar is a male-dominated world. Ministers of education, rectors of universities and directors of research centres are almost exclusively men. No doubt she anticipated that a women-organized event such as our conference, publicized as a rethinking of the way in which Myanmar history had been told and taking place at a 'historic' moment of Myanmar's liberalization, might hurt egos and stoke anxieties among her male colleagues. Tellingly, she had invited three honoured guests to the conference, all of whom were male emeritus professors. Throughout the day, they were seated, in turns, at the head of the conference table flanked by a handful of junior male faculty. While they played the ceremonial role of masters of the event, the cadre of women faculty, senior and junior, who handled all the preparations for the conference, sat at a remove in a corner of the room, in a symbolic self-deprecation of their intellect. The gendered labour and performance of the Burmese women at the conference served to affirm their fidelity to their nation, to their men and to the normative values of their nation in a time of transition.

The gendered dynamics of the political transformation in Myanmar are probed and unravelled with care and clarity in this volume, which represents a new generation of feminist scholars, researchers, teachers, and activists working on, and often in, Myanmar. The contributions not only dispel the national myth and belief about gender equality in Myanmar; they also disrupt the nationalist 'move to innocence': the strategy of blaming British colonialism and capitalism for any traces of gender oppression (along with virtually all forms of social strife, not least racial and religious). As the volume shows, over the last decade of transition out of military rule to quasi-civilian rule, the powerful and the privileged in Myanmar have consistently dismissed opportunities to tackle gendered structures of inequality, insecurity, and violence, not just reinstating but in fact enhancing male privilege and patriarchal institutions.

Many of the contributors to this book were beneficiaries of the military-led political and economic liberalizations that began in 2011, which enabled local and international researchers and students to conduct in-person, on-site fieldwork in locations, over durations, on topics and materials and with funding and freedom that had all been unthinkable for many decades. As a result, they were afforded an intimate exploration of Myanmar's transition and its impact. Together, they have forged a community of talented and determined interrogators and interlocutors of a kind that I could have only dreamed of when I began researching modern Burmese history 20 years ago. They stand as proof that women's and gender studies is no longer a lonely, neglected corner of Burma-Myanmar studies but a force to be reckoned with.

In the following pages, they offer richly textured accounts and analyses of the meanings and implications of the political developments of the last decade for women in Myanmar. Based on micro-level studies of everyday life, they foreground the analytic frameworks of gender and intersectionality – that is, the intersection of gender with other categories of difference and systems of power such as ethnicity, class and religion. All contributions underscore the differential positioning of people in Myanmar and their different experiences of and perspectives on the political transition, even as they highlight broad, persistent patterns in gender inequality and insecurity across and beyond the period of transition. Even as those closer to the elites, namely Buddhists and Burmans, gained economic mobility and security, historically minoritized groups became more marginalized, widening disparities. In some parts of the country, such as in Kachin state or in Rakhine state, attacks, displacement and human rights violations by the Myanmar military intensified. Elsewhere, ceasefire deals, development agendas and business investments in former conflict zones deepened familiar forms of precarity such as forced labour conscription by the military, land grabbing, and heroin and methamphetamine epidemics. Only in the aftermath of the 2021 military coup in which the Myanmar army weaponized itself against the ethnic and religious majority Burmans and Buddhists was there widespread reckoning with the fact that the regime change had done little to dismantle the violent political economy that has prevailed in Myanmar. Political and economic liberalization had proceeded without demilitarization.

The 'transition' has therefore made feminist organizing and mobilizing against militarized, masculinist regimes of governance more, not less, urgent. At the same time, it has presented women with new opportunities and pathways for bargaining with patriarchal, militarist authorities and institutions. Many, though not all, women who had once devoted their lives to armed struggles against the Myanmar government have become leaders, brokers and supporters of peacebuilding movements. Their participation in the peace process, as the volume demonstrates, is not attributable to some intrinsic feminine inclination to peace. They are motivated into action by their embodied knowledge of the disproportionate burdens and repercussions of armed conflict on women and children. They have borne the brunt of inhabiting and repairing spaces of unrelenting destruction and dispossession. Long after wars have officially ended and ceasefires have been concluded, women have continued to perform the everyday work of rehabilitating bodies, lands, livelihoods, families and communities that have been tortured, mutilated, and plundered.

Writing almost three decades ago, the feminist scholar Anne McClintock observed that 'nowhere has a national or socialist revolution brought a full feminist revolution in its terrain', nor has 'feminism in its own right been allowed to be more than the maidservant to nationalism'. Myanmar has been no exception. Nevertheless, the last decade has brought visibility to women's political engagement and participation in unprecedented ways. Women in Myanmar are shaping public debates and collective narratives more powerfully than they did in the past. Their efforts to name and challenge systems of gender-based exclusion, exploitation, and violence have made the public denial and erasure of these problems and injustices more difficult, but not impossible or implausible. Indeed, the history of Myanmar, as elsewhere, teaches us that periods of upheaval – whether they be wars, revolutions, economic crises, or military coups – are always watershed moments for women in both material and symbolic ways. They invariably entail political and social campaigns to control and regulate the lives and bodies of women in the name of a greater cause, such as the controversial 'national race and religion protection laws' (2015), which outlaw polygamy and restrict interfaith marriages between Buddhist women and non-Buddhist men. The contributions assembled here illuminate the promises and perils of large-scale transformations and the vital importance of gender as an analytic category in understanding those transformations.

References

McClintock, Anne. 1993. 'Family feuds: Gender, nationalism and the family.' *Feminist Review* 44: 61–80, 78.

Acknowledgments

*T*his book would not have been possible without the people contributing to it in the most direct ways: all of the chapter authors, their research associates, and their research participants who shared their experiences and insights. The decade of political transition in Myanmar opened up possibilities to travel to and within the country, and to engage in fieldwork and research collaborations with scholars from Myanmar and elsewhere, activists, and interlocutors from diverse walks of life. Importantly, this opening enabled the emergence of a vibrant community of scholars of and from Myanmar, many of which are included in this book. Together, they have contributed to building more grounded and nuanced knowledge about the state of gender relations and the gendered dynamics of political change in the country.

We also want to extend our heartfelt thanks to the reviewers of individual chapters in the book, and to the reviewers of the collection as a whole, who gave us useful and generous feedback. At NIAS Press, Gerald Jackson has been a steadfast supporter, and the excellent copyediting undertaken by Monica Janowski was much appreciated.

While the kind of research that underpins this book is, at this time, no longer possible in Myanmar, the community of scholars and activists which this book represents will continue to critically analyse the political situation, draw attention to injustice, violence and oppression, and in various ways support ongoing struggles for a just, equal and democratic Myanmar.

Contributors

Aye Thiri Kyaw is a PhD student at the Gender, Violence and Health Centre, London School of Hygiene and Tropical Medicine. She holds an MSc from the London School of Economics and Political Science, and an MA from Mahidol University. Her research focuses on prevention and intervention research on violence against women and children, and the health and well-being of child domestic workers. Before commencing her PhD research, Aye Thiri Kyaw worked for the UN, INGOs, and civil society organizations for nearly ten years in various roles, such as researcher, gender specialist, and humanitarian officer.

Magda Lorena Cárdenas is a PhD candidate in Political Science at Umeå University, Sweden. Her research focuses on women's roles in conflict resolution and peacebuilding in different conflict settings, including Georgia, Myanmar, and Colombia. She has recently published in the *Women's Studies International Forum*, *Civil Wars*, and the *European Journal of Politics and Gender*. She has also worked as a consultant for UN Women on the themes of women's participation in peace efforts, mediation, and women's mobilization in non-violent movements.

Dan Seng Lawn is a political analyst and consultant focusing on Myanmar politics in general and Kachin State politics in particular. He holds a master's degree in politics from Jawaharlal Nehru University in India, and has been working as a researcher, lecturer and political analyst in Kachin State since 2015. He is currently the Director of Kachinland Research Centre, a leading regional Think Tank in Northern Myanmar. Dan Seng Lawn's recent publications include "Ethnicity and Great Power Politics: A Case of Transnational Ethnic Kachin of Myanmar and Singpho of Northeast India", in Charisma K. Lepcha & Uttam Lal (eds), *Communities, Institutions and Histories of India's Northeast*.

Hilary Faxon is a feminist political ecologist interested in environment, development and technology in Southeast Asia. She uses participatory methods and ethnography to investigate agrarian and political change in

Myanmar. She is an Assistant Professor of Environmental Social Science at the University of Montana. Hilary's work has most recently appeared in *Political Geography, Geopolitics* and the *Journal of Rural Studies.*

Shae Frydenlund is a human geographer concerned with the political economy of forced displacement. Her research examines the changing world of work and refugee livelihoods in Myanmar, Malaysia, and the United States. She is currently a National Science Foundation Postdoctoral Fellow in the Department of Geography at Indiana University, Bloomington, and is Co-PI on an NSF project entitled 'Essential Workers in the US Food System'. Shae is the author of articles published in Political Geography, Cultural Geography, and Journal of the Association of Nepal and Himalayan Studies.

Terese Gagnon is an environmental anthropologist and postdoctoral researcher at the Nordic Institute of Asian Studies and the Department of Political Science at the University of Copenhagen. She holds a PhD in anthropology from Syracuse University. Her current book project, a multi-sited ethnography, is about Karen food, seed, and political sovereignty across landscapes of home and exile. She is co-editor of the book *Movable Gardens: Itineraries and Sanctuaries of Memory* and is currently editing a second volume, *Embodying Biodiversity.* Terese incorporates creative forms, including ethnographic poetry and visual anthropology, in her scholarly work.

Jenny Hedström is an Associate Professor in War Studies at the Swedish Defence University. Her research concerns the relationship between households, gender and warfare; gender, transitions and peacebuilding; women's activism and resistance; and ethics and methods when researching war, often with a focus on civil wars in Myanmar. Her recent work has been published in journals such as the *European Journal of Gender and Politics, Peacebuilding,* the *International Feminist Journal of Politics,* and *Conflict, Security & Development.*

Hsa Moo has been an activist all her life. As a youth, she worked with the Karen Student Network Group. She is now the Media Coordinator for the Karen Environmental and Social Action Network. She also works for the Salween Peace Park, a Karen initiative dedicated to peacebuilding, biodiversity conservation, and preservation of Indigenous culture. Her writing has appeared in publications including *The Irrawaddy, Karen News,* and *The Transnational Institute.* A committed advocate on issues of gender, indigenous rights, and human rights, Hsa Moo has provided testimony to the

International Criminal Court to support charges of crimes against humanity brought against the Myanmar military. She is also a talented songwriter.

Khin Khin Mra is a consultant on gender, governance and development. She has more than ten years' experience and extensive knowledge of working in conflict affected areas and humanitarian settings and operating at a senior programme leadership level. Years of experience with different agencies has enabled her to leverage the important interplay between international and national commitments, and research and practice as it relates to women's rights, gender equality, and governance issues. She has an MA in Public Policy and a Graduate Diploma in Public Administration from the Australian National University.

Deborah Livingstone is an independent consultant specializing in gender equality and social inclusion, climate change, and governance. She has over 20 years' experience working with DFID/FCDO, the UN, World Bank and INGOs in Myanmar, Kenya, Malawi, Rwanda, South Sudan and Ethiopia. Deborah has worked in Myanmar for the past nine years integrating her specialist areas into research projects, policy work and programme areas such as community-based justice, peacebuilding, infrastructure, public financial management and health. She has an master's degree in Public Policy and another in English Literature from the University of Edinburgh.

Ma Khin Mar Mar Kyi (Dr Mar) is the first Burmese female Senior Gender Research Fellow and Research Associate in Anthropology at the University of Oxford. She is the producer of an acclaimed documentary, *Dreams of Dutiful Daughters* (2013), and her PhD thesis won the 'Excellence in Gender Research' award from the Australian Gender Institute, Canberra. She has founded the Oxford Thanakha International Gender Tekkatho, a knowledge platform for collaborating and working on social cohesion, gender equality and peace in Myanmar through anthropological research.

Rosalie Metro is an Assistant Teaching Professor in the College of Education and Human Development at the University of Missouri-Columbia. As an anthropologist of education, she is interested in in the conflicts that arise around history, identity, and language in the classroom. She holds a PhD in Learning, Teaching, and Social Policy from Cornell University, and she has been studying education in Myanmar and working with teachers on the Thai border since 2001.

Mi Sue Pwint was a young student leader of the 8888 uprising in Karenni State, and joined the armed revolution in 1988. As one of the founders of

Burmese Women's Union (BWU) and Women's League of Burma (WLB), she is a prominent leader in the women's movement in Myanmar. In this role, she has played a leadership role in the struggle for women's rights, peace and federal democracy in Myanmar for decades. As an Executive Committee member of the All Burma Student's Democratic Front, she is one of a handful of women in a leadership position in armed groups, and was one of a few women negotiators in the peace process up until 2021.

Henri Myrttinen is a visiting research fellow with the University of Bremen and has worked extensively with various NGOs and research institutions on issues of gender, peace and security, in particular from a critical masculinities perspective. He has been working in and on Myanmar for several years for a variety of local and international NGOs, and holds a PhD from the University of KwaZulu-Natal, South Africa.

Jana Naujoks is an experienced Conflict, Gender and Peacebuilding Advisor. Most recently she was the Head of Programmes and WPS Lead at Inclusive Peace, a think-and-do tank supporting peace and transition processes through evidence-based advice. Prior to this, she spent five years in Myanmar, working as Gender Adviser on peacebuilding, natural resource governance and inclusive private sector development projects, and later leading International Alert's Myanmar programme as Country Director. She has also worked on peacebuilding, gender in peace and security, international cooperation, project coordination and financial management for International Alert in London for nearly a decade.

Naw K'Nyaw Paw, a Karen woman and refugee, is the General Secretary of the Karen Women's Organization (KWO). This is a feminist, indigenous rights community-based organization that plays a leadership role in the struggle to bring democracy and human rights to Burma. She received the P'doh Mahn Sha Young Leader Award in 2013 and in 2019 she received the Women of Courage Award from the US Department of State. She is a women's right activist and works for gender justice, social justice, human rights, democracy and community ownership.

Elisabeth Olivius is an Associate Professor in Political Science at Umeå University. Her research explores peacebuilding, post-war development, women's activism, and migration and diaspora politics with a focus on Myanmar. She is a book reviews editor for the *International Feminist Journal* *of Politics* and coordinates the Varieties of Peace research network. Her recent work has been published in journals such as the *European Journal of Gender and Politics, Journal of Intervention and Statebuilding, Journal of Peacebuilding and Development*, and *Conflict, Security & Development*.

Maggi Quadrini is a feminist and human rights activist who works with community-based organizations along the Thai-Burmese border. Her work focuses on issues affecting women, refugees, internally displaced people, and children. Maggi also writes about her work and observations in outlets such as *The Diplomat, Southeast Asia Globe*, and *New Naratif*, where she offers a grassroots perspective of human rights issues in the region.

Wai Wai Nu is a former political prisoner and the founder and Executive Director of the Women's Peace Network in Myanmar. Through the Women's Peace Network, she works to build peace and mutual understanding between Myanmar's ethnic communities and to empower and advocate for the rights of marginalized women throughout Myanmar, and particularly in Rakhine State. Wai Wai Nu received her bachelor's degree in law from the University of Yangon in Myanmar and her master's degree in law from the University of Berkeley. Recently, she served as a fellow at the Simon-Skjodt Center for the Prevention of Genocide at the U.S. Holocaust Memorial Museum.

Matthew J. Walton is an Assistant Professor in Comparative Political Theory in the Department of Political Science at the University of Toronto. Previously, he was the inaugural Aung San Suu Kyi Senior Research Fellow in Modern Burmese Studies at St Antony's College, University of Oxford. His research focuses on religion and politics in Southeast Asia, with a special emphasis on Buddhism in Myanmar. Matt was a co-founder of the Burma/Myanmar blog *Tea Circle*, and is currently co-directing a pedagogical project with Melissa Williams at the University of Toronto focused on deparochializing teaching in political theory.

Zin Mar Phyo is a women's rights activist originally from Mon State in Myanmar, now based in Chiang Mai, Thailand. She speaks Burmese and English fluently, and has worked with local women's organizations in Myanmar since 2005. She is also a feminist journalist, and former editor of Honest Information online media, writing and publishing articles focusing on the situation of gender justice and women in conflict areas in Myanmar.

Introduction

Political Transitions and Gendered Transformations in Myanmar

Jenny Hedström and Elisabeth Olivius

*I*n the early hours of 1 February 2021, the Myanmar military seized power in a coup, arresting leading politicians and declaring a state of emergency. Min Aung Hlaing, the military commander-in-chief, quickly assumed office as the chairman of the newly-formed State Administration Council and abolished the mandatory retirement age previously in place for his position (Ardeth Maung Thawnghmung 2021; Sithu Aung Myint 2021). In the immediate aftermath of the coup, many observers referred to gender as a perspective through which to understand both the coup and the way public protests against it played out. Feminist scholars and activists argued that the coup was facilitated by the stubborn persistence of militarized, masculinized politics in Myanmar. They pointed to the fact that the 2008 Constitution grants the military 25 per cent of the seats in parliament, and that in the 2020 elections, a mere 17 per cent of elected representatives were women (Bjarnegård and Barall 2021; Khin Khin Mra 2021). Several commentators have also highlighted the prominent role played by women in the subsequent resistance campaigns against military rule (Aguilar and Quadrini 2021; Beech 2021; Khan 2021; Mimi Aye 2021). In the cities, young women from garment factories and student unions have led protest actions, and almost a third of people appointed to the National Unity Government, a political body contesting the junta's claim to legitimacy, are women (Anonymous 2021; Jordt, Tharaphi Than and Sue Ye Lin 2021). In ethnic minority areas, women have built upon previous experiences of surviving war and resisting oppression to mobilize against the coup and find ways to provide for everyday needs in the absence of a functioning state (Quadrini 2021), while on social media young female

1

activists are spearheading campaigns to raise awareness about sexual violence perpetuated against anti-junta protesters. As Mi Sue Pwint, veteran women's activist, resistance fighter and peace negotiator, argues in this volume, this extensive involvement of women in leadership positions, and the presence of political commitments to gender equality in resistance movements, sets the ongoing protests apart from previous popular uprisings against military rule in Myanmar, such as those in 1988.

Thus, in seemingly contradictory ways, the coup and its aftermath have been represented as revealing the state of gender relations in Myanmar, bringing into relief both what changed and what has stayed the same for women and men in Myanmar during the period prior to the coup. To understand the 2021 military coup and the current configuration of mas-culinized, military dictatorship, as well as the unprecedented role played by women in the on-going pro-democracy protests, we argue that it is necessary to examine the gendered dynamics and effects of the decade of political transition in Myanmar which came before it. This is the aim of this volume. In the pages that follow, the contributors to this book engage in a careful, comprehensive analysis of the gendered transformations, and persistent continuities, that characterized the reform period that started with U Thein Sein's ascendance to political office in 2011. This event ended decades of military rule and marked the beginning of a hybrid, semi-dem-ocratic regime (Tin Maung Maun Than 2014; Stokke and Soe Myint Aung 2020; Thant Myint-U 2019; Zin Mar Aung 2015), leading to the return of many exiled organizations and activists (Thin Thin Aye 2015; Bjarnegård 2020; Olivius 2019), and a nationwide ceasefire process which, for the first time ever, brought multiple armed actors together in a dialogue with the central state and its military (Ardeth Maung Thawnghmung 2017). However, the end of military rule did not mean an end to war, militari-zation, ethnic persecution and human insecurity in Myanmar. Indeed, in Kachin state armed conflict resumed, and in Rakhine state discrimination against the Rohingya population culminated in a genocide (Nyi Nyi Kyaw 2019; Sadan 2016). In contested border areas populated primarily by eth-nic minorities, state-led reform initiatives facilitated state expansion and militarization, unleashing significant public protests and unrest (Olivius and Hedström 2021; Meehan and Sadan 2017). In other words, unfolding transitional processes generated new tensions as well as opportunities for women and men living across the country.

As feminist scholars of peace and conflict studies, development studies and democratic transitions have long argued, periods of drastic political change are always conditioned by gender relations, hierarchies, and norms (Al-Ali and Pratt 2009; Tripp et al. 2009). At the same time, these processes of change and historic waves of upheaval also reshape gendered dynamics and lived realities (Marchand and Runyan 2010; Cockburn 2010). As elsewhere, this was the case with Myanmar's political transition between 2011 and 2020. As detailed by the contributors to this volume, this period saw a vast expansion of women's civil society activism, the adoption of pioneering gender equality legislation, and the arrival of an international peacebuilding and development industry promoting international gender equality norms in their support to Myanmar (Hedström, Olivius and Kay Soe 2020). However, the gendered dynamics and effects of Myanmar's transition have not yet received sustained scholarly attention, as we discuss further below. Providing a comprehensive account of the multifaceted processes of gendered transformation that have taken place in the past decade, this book contributes a much-needed historical corrective, and helps us make sense of the current political situation in Myanmar. This is because the changes that the transition brought about shape the way resistance is playing out now, and the ways in which Myanmar's political landscape might continue to be reshaped.

Gendered Transformations and Political Transitions

Myanmar gained independence from the British in 1948. During the era of parliamentary democracy that followed, the country was soon embroiled in civil war as political factions 'reflect[ing] every side of the political spectrum' took up arms demanding greater autonomy and rights (Smith 2007: 1). This included left-leaning, communist and a number of ethnic minority insurrections (Ardeth Maung Thawnghmung 2011) fighting against the central regime. In attempts to quell these rebellions, the military, led by General Ne Win, assumed power through a caretaker government between 1958 and 1960. Two years later, in 1962, General Ne Win again seized power. This military junta would rule until 1988, when thousands of people took to the streets to demand reforms. Aung San Suu Kyi emerged as the figurehead of this revolution, which led to multi-party elections being held in 1990. However, the military junta did not honour the election results but instead cracked down on presumed opponents and political dissidents. Military rule continued, albeit in new iterations.

As activists fled the cities in the aftermath of the 1988 uprising, they were received by ethnic minority insurgents who had fought the military for decades. Myanmar is a highly ethnically diverse country: a large percentage of the population belongs to communities that differ from the majority Bamar people in language, custom and religion, and the largest armed opposition groups are organized around ethnic belonging. In this context, military rule has in effect been employed as a response to demands for greater rights and autonomy from minority groups, ostensibly to prevent disintegration and disorder (Callahan 2003). It is therefore ethnic minority communities that have experienced the brunt of the conflict and oppressive policies on the part of successive military regimes. This included in particular the infamous 'four-cuts' counterinsurgency policy, first executed under General Ne Win's rule, which targeted ethnic minority communities by forcibly relocating or destroying entire villages, resulting in massive human suffering (Ardeth Maung Thawnghmung 2011). However, these ethnic communities, particularly in the border areas from which ethnic insurgencies emerged and operated, also became a key political space for the mobilization of women, and the formation of a range of women's organizations challenging gender inequality, both within oppositional movements as well as within Myanmar more broadly (Olivius and Hedström 2019).

While the primary focus of this book is on the period between 2011–2020, we situate our analysis of this period against this longer historical backdrop, and in relation to the current political landscape. However, most chapters in the book take events *after* 2011, when U Thein Sein took office, as their starting point. During the first few years of the transition, overall changes in the political and economic situation led to a significant influx of international donors, the establishment of a peacebuilding and development industry and the lifting of sanctions (Thant Myint-U 2019; Kyaw Yin Hlaing 2012). Foreign direct investments quadrupled, from US$1.9 billion in 2011/12 to US$8 billion in 2014/15 (World Bank Group 2013, 2015). A de-regulation of military-era draconian laws meant a return of political exiles, a rapid increase in media outlets and, for the first time in the nation's history, widespread and affordable access to the internet (Brooten 2016). The women's movement flourished, with the return of prominent female activists and the establishment of several large networks focused on women's rights across the country and within different political processes (Olivius and Hedström 2020). The transition from outright military rule to semi-civilian rule was further cemented in the 2015 elections, when the National League for Democracy (NLD), headed by Aung San Suu Kyi, won a landslide victory in the first openly contested, and respected, elections since 1960. Although the military was guaranteed a quarter of all seats in the parliament, as per the 2008 Constitution, the extent of NLD's win meant that they secured a majority. Women, alongside male civilian politicians, slowly began to replace the male, and often elderly, generals who had for long held all power (Shwe Shwe Sein Latt et al. 2017). Aung San Suu Kyi, unable to become president under rules that prevented anyone with foreign family members from holding that post, became State Counsellor, a new post created specifically for her by the parliament (Thant Myint-U 2019). Myanmar's transition was, to many observers, now firmly underway.

However, overarching reforms were not always progressive, and were unevenly experienced across the country. While more affluent urban households and communities saw an increase in living standards, political freedoms and rights, the rural poor often faced a decrease in living standards. Top-down development projects, the prevalence of illicit economies controlling access to markets, and the appropriation of over a million acres of land from rural households by corrupt officials and businessmen meant that the transition was understood differently depending on *who* experienced it (Doi Ra and Khu Khu Ju 2021; Hedström and Olivius 2020). Among Kachin communities, living close to the Chinese border with Myanmar, events after 2011 meant a return to outright war, and Rohingya, Arakanese and Hindu communities living in Rakhine state experienced both communal violence and genocide (Schissler, Walton and Phyu Phyu Thi 2017; Aye Thiri Kyaw 2020; Cheesman 2017; Sadan [ed.] 2016). Extensive land-grabbing led to an upsurge in urban slums, while increased poverty and the ready availability of cheap drugs resulted in widespread drug use, especially among younger men (Rehmonnya.org. 2013; Sai Lone and Renaud Cachia 2021)

As this overview makes clear, teleological models of transition as a linear progression toward liberal democracy, held both by policy makers and scholars on democratic transitions (Linz and Stephan 1996; Diamond 2012), do not neatly map on to events in Myanmar. Rather than applying this dominant conception of democratic transition, to help make sense of the country's recent history we argue that there is much to learn from

5

recent advances in peace studies on the concept of post-war transition (Klem 2018; Gusic 2019; Olivius and Hedström 2021). Critiquing the idea of war-to-peace transitions for employing linear assumptions similar to those in the democratic transition literature, Bart Klem (2018) suggests that the term 'post-war transition' can be used to describe the period of substantial, multidirectional societal changes that follow the end of war – but without assuming progress or a set direction, not least because these changes can be contradictory and unpredictable. While Myanmar's transitional years cannot generally be characterized as a post-war context, this way of thinking about the transition is useful. It allows us to conceptualize and approach Myanmar's transition as a period of intense, contradictory and multifaceted changes, without assuming either linear progress or a fixed end goal.

While these transitional changes are conditioned by, and contribute to reshaping, gendered relations and norms, surprisingly little attention has been paid to the gendered effects the transition has precipitated in different areas of Myanmar. With some important exceptions, much of the literature on Myanmar's transition has interpreted politics narrowly (see for example Egreteau 2016; Bünte 2014), focusing on the formal, public sphere and on the representatives of the armed forces, as opposed to looking at informal activities, movements, civilians and foot soldiers. This edited volume, bringing together academics and activists working in a variety of disciplines and across the country, contributes to a dynamic and growing conversation exploring the relationship between gender, conflict and transitional politics in Myanmar. Rather than employing a singular focus and theoretical framework, contributions to the volume employ gender as an analytical handle to draw on a number of different theoretical and methodological approaches to expand our collective understanding of transitional politics in the country, through attention to everyday situated experiences as well as to formal state processes and institutions. This breadth helps us better explore how notions of femininity and masculinity, and ideas about 'appropriate' gender roles, were deployed, negotiated, reproduced and/or resisted in the Myanmar transition.

Through this comprehensive analysis of many aspects of transitional change, the volume also contributes to advancing broader debates in feminist scholarship of relevance to understanding political transitions. Broader feminist scholarship has, to a significant extent, been characterized by disciplinary thinking and a resulting fragmentation between fields focusing on different aspects of societal change. As an illustration, feminist peace research tends to focus on the gendered dynamics of peace processes and peacebuilding efforts (Shepherd 2018; Krause, Krause, and Bränfors 2018; True and Riveros-Morales 2019); feminist political economy scholars explore issues relating to economic development interventions (Martin De Almagro and Ryan 2019; Pratt and Chilmeran 2019); and feminist security scholars examine the securitized and gendered effects of violence and upheaval that both shape and span the period from conflict to peace (Hansen 2001; Sylvester 2013; Wibben 2010). Given the interrelated nature of these processes of post-war and post-dictatorship transformation, this fragmentation prevents sustained analytical attention to the intersections between, and accumulated effects of, political, institutional, economic, social or cultural processes of change.

We therefore argue that a more consolidated, multi-disciplinary feminist approach to political transitions taking place in proximity to armed conflict and authoritarian rule is needed. Myanmar constitutes a timely and critical case for advancing this research agenda, generating theoretical insights with wider significance as well as new empirical knowledge about the multifaceted processes of change currently taking place in the country. In this book, we aim to break these silos down in order to gain a fuller understanding of the gendered dynamics of Myanmar's transitional period, and assess its implications for the future. This means that this project is necessarily inter-disciplinary, drawing on disciplines such as peace and conflict studies, development studies, gender studies, as well as Myanmar studies.

By using gender as a starting point for our analysis, we do not intend to fix or isolate gender from other forms of power and identity. Indeed, we understand gender to be a social – and fluid – construct that permeates all aspects of lives, from the household to the highest level of governance, and as existing in a dialectical relationship with the past. It is '[an] ordering principle' (Peterson 1998: 42) constructing differences between that and those deemed masculine and that and those deemed feminine. In other words, gender differences construct power differences. Understanding gender as a social construct does not relieve the term of its real-life impact: socially constituted differences shape peoples' experiences of, and access to, transitional politics in the everyday. We use the concept of gender to identify and analyse how these gender differences and hierarchies are reproduced or resisted through intersections of ethnicity, sexuality, religion and gendered identity, and in transitional politics and across time. This is particularly important as ideas about 'appropriate' gender roles in Myanmar tend to be justified through religious and cultural discourses, which mask the unequal distribution of power embedded in gender relations, regardless of ethnic or religious background, sexual preference, or class (Gender Equality Network 2015).

Further, in view of dominant liberal ideas situating the 2011 reforms as the beginning of gendered change and transformation in Myanmar, it is important to stress that while this book focuses on events taking place after 2011, we do not suggest that changes in gendered norms and relationships that occurred during the transitional years were somehow unique to that decade; rather, gendered transformations have been at the heart of political change and upheaval both before 2011 and after 2020. In Myanmar, gendered identities and transformations have been at the locus of broader political changes and upheavals since the fight for independence from the British in the late 1940s (Ikeya 2011; Tharaphi Than 2014). Representing the past decade of political transition as the beginning of women's political mobilization and women's empowerment would therefore be wrong, just as presenting the coup as the end of women's political resistance and political involvement would be incorrect. Instead – and as the discussions in this book make clear – transitional opportunities and openings were both predicated upon and interrupted by shifts in and contentions of gendered relations and identities related to political events and gendered transformations seemingly located in the past. While the transition created space for feminist mobilization and women-led civil society advocating for women's rights and equality in policy and decision-making, possibilities for real and substantial change were nevertheless limited by patriarchal and militarized politics. Several chapters in the book give detailed accounts of attempts during the period to change women's representation in politics as well as laws and policies, but also demonstrate the obstacles to and limits of such change. This suggests that the fact that there were not enough changes with regard to gender in politics and governance contributed to the reinstatement of military politics once again. This helps us reconsider the idea that the reforms of 2011 represented a definite break from earlier political and economic transformations, or that the coup in 2021 heralds a completely new era of political rule. The chapters included in this volume trace this complex mix of change and continuity, contributing to a nuanced and granular analysis of gendered transformations in relation to overarching political transitions and reforms.

Key Themes of the Book

This volume identifies and explores the gendered dynamics of Myanmar's transition in three interrelated political spheres. Firstly, a set of chapters interrogate the openings and obstacles for gendered change in formal politics and governance, demonstrating that while the transition did bring about significant institutional change, gendered inequalities and norms that upheld male superiority and excluded women persisted alongside, and continued to shape, formal changes. Secondly, a set of chapters explore the changing landscape of Myanmar women's feminist mobilization, capturing the expansion of women's movements both in terms of numbers and in terms of diversity during the period, and examining how women activists responded to a changing political context. Thirdly, a set of chapters analyze the gendered politics of everyday lives and struggles; of friendship, land, labour and love. Here, the interplay of change and continuity becomes especially visible. While transitional processes had a direct impact on the everyday lives of women and men, for example through economic investments and development projects, many forms of gendered marginalization and insecurity have remained across time and throughout macro-political waves of upheaval. Below, we introduce these three themes and the individual contributions to the book further.

Transitional Politics, Institutions and Policymaking

The first political sphere that is explored in this book is the sphere of formal political institutions and policymaking. The transition did not only mean that the generals exchanged their uniforms for civilian clothes. While democratization was undoubtedly always limited – or disciplined, as the military would have it – there were, nevertheless, significant changes to the rules of the political game after 2011. The representation of women in elected office remained low, however. In the 2010 election women candidates were largely absent, and while the number of women standing for election increased for the next general election in 2105, and again in 2020, the number of elected women remained the lowest in Southeast Asia. Norms and stereotypes about women's inherent incompatibility with politics ensured the preferential treatment of, as well as votes for, male candidates (Shwe Shwe Sein Latt et al. 2017: 3; Asian Development Bank 2016: 157). The military quota, functioning in effect as a quota for men, skewed the numbers further in favour of men. Thus, notions of male superiority carried over into transitional political institutions and the formal sphere of decision-making. Nevertheless, the transition did open up new opportunities for women's organizations to engage with the state and make a difference in formal policymaking processes (Hedström, Olivius and Kay Soe 2020; Faxon, Furlong and May Sabe Phyu 2015), not least with regard to the violence that women continued to experience (Aye Thiri Kyaw, this volume; Women's League of Burma 2014; Khin Chan Myae Maung 2018; Tanabe et al 2019; Phyu Phyu Oo and Davies 2021). This was a rather drastic change, which in tandem with the expansion of women's organizing led to the emergence of a new strand of women's activism that targeted their advocacy towards the Myanmar political system rather than towards international audiences. Moreover, various reform processes opened up space to challenge dominant gender norms from within the machinery of the state. The three chapters in the first section of the book reflect these transformations through analyses of the gender politics of specific institutional changes, policy processes and reforms.

In their chapter, Khin Khin Mra and Deborah Livingstone draw on a feminist institutionalist framework to interrogate the effects of local governance reforms on women's political participation and representation. While institutional change opened up formal opportunities for women, these were constrained by the persistent power of norms linking masculinity, politics, and leadership: new institutions were 'nested' within older ones. The authors thereby provide theoretical insights into the slowness of social and political change and into the interplay between formal and informal institutions. This means that the chapter has important implications for the current political situation, telling us that while formal democratic reforms can be rolled back, institutional and political change within the Myanmar state in the past decade has taken place at many levels, and will not be easily undone by the new military junta.

In her chapter, Aye Thiri Kyaw reflects on the efforts of women activists to exploit new political openings and arenas and push for the adoption of a law against violence against women, the PoVAW law. While there were partial successes that testify to the changing opportunities for women's organizations to advocate for policy change during the transition, the chapter also highlights the obstacles experienced by women's rights activists in politicizing men's violence against women. This pushes us to consider how gender informs recognition of what counts as a political problem, and demonstrates the pervasiveness of gender inequality and violence despite significant political changes. Thus, while the transitional period produced an opening for women activists to engage with policymaking processes, pervasive ideas about the formal political sphere being a male space, as well as actions taken by military leaders and politicians to materially ensure that this notion is realized, have constrained women's access to transitional policies and institutions.

The tension between change and the reproduction of existing norms and power relations is also foregrounded in the chapter by Rosalie Metro. In 2016, the Myanmar Ministry of Education (MOE) began working with international donors to revise basic education curricula. This type of partnership and international support was itself a new feature of the transitional period. In her chapter, Metro demonstrates how this process became a site of contestation of ideologies around gender. Whereas international development organizations prioritized globalized ideologies of 'social inclusion' and 'gender equality', existing textbooks presented local conceptions of what Metro terms 'gender harmony'. The curriculum revision process was characterized by both resistance to change and the translation and adaptation of new norms, reflecting the complexity of change in gender norms as well as the power dynamics between international development actors and the Myanmar government.

Feminist Mobilization, Resistance and Movement Building

In Myanmar, the English word 'feminism' is understood, at least in the mainstream, 'as an ideology to promote women domination rather than an idea to fight for women's rights' (Tharaphi Than, Pyo Let Han and Shunn Lei 2018; also see Zin Mar Aung 2015). As gender scholars from Myanmar note, feminist resistance and organizing for gender equality therefore come into direct conflict with the country's 'two most powerful institutions', the military and the *sangha* (Tharaphi Than, Pyo Let Han and Shunn Lei 2018; Ma Khin Mar Mar Kyi 2019). Both military and monastic institutions wield a great deal of (masculine) power, which they are loath to give up, as the 2021 coup effectively illustrates. Despite this, the transitional period saw an exponential increase in women's activism in Myanmar. Prior to 2011, limited space for civil society generally meant that an organized women's movement had primarily been able to form outside of Myanmar; in particular, in the Thai–Myanmar borderlands, where ethnic armed organizations as well as oppositional political movements had found a conducive political environment. This was the context in which a number of ethnic minority women's organizations mobilized and joined together under the umbrella of the Women's League of Burma (Women's League of Burma 2011; Olivius and Hedström 2019; Cárdenas and Olivius 2021).

This history of mobilization in exile, with its achievements and challenges, is explored by Mollie Pepper in her chapter. Here, Pepper situates women's diasporic activism as a form of grassroots peacebuilding, which was transforming conflict before the initiation of any formal peace process. Further, the chapter captures how the transition has reshaped the landscape for Myanmar women's activism, bringing a geographic shift back into Myanmar, along with the reorientation towards the state discussed above. This has opened up opportunities for engagement with the formal peace process, but has also brought new challenges for returning exile activists. However, as Pepper argues, focusing only on women's formal participation in peace and transitional processes 'obscures the highly active feminist peace and resistance politics being enacted by diverse women in the country'. Her emphasis on informal spaces enhances our understandings of women's peacebuilding outside of recognized and clearly demarcated political institutions, and demonstrates how women's activism around the nationwide peace process is part of a wider feminist movement in which women attempt to leverage their peace activism into gains for women's rights *beyond* the peace process.

In a related process, and due to the unevenness of transitional processes, the shift discussed above within women's mobilization and forms of activism had very different effects for – and was embraced to varying extents by – different women's organizations and activists. In her chapter, Magda Loréna Cárdenas provides an in-depth case study of one organization, the Kachin Women's Association Thailand (KWAT). In Kachin areas in Northern Myanmar, the onset of the transitional period did not bring increased freedom for civil society, but a resurgence of armed conflict (Sadan 2016). While many women's organizations in exile moved much of their work back into Myanmar, for KWAT the security and freedom of working in Thailand remained crucial. In her chapter, Cárdenas examines how KWAT has navigated the contradictions of this situation in relation to three key audiences and partners: the international community; the wider Myanmar women's movement; and the Kachin Independence Organization and their armed, ethno-nationalist struggle. In doing this, the chapter provides key insights into the tensions and disruptions brought by Myanmar's uneven transition, along with theoretical insights about the space for feminist mobilization within armed, nationalist movements. These have broader relevance for Myanmar women's activism, as many organizations have emerged in close relationship with male-dominated ethnic struggles, but also for feminist scholarship and activism beyond Myanmar as a case study.

The two conversation pieces between activists and scholars included in the book also illustrate, in a similar way, how the lack of formal recognition of women as leaders is in contrast to their actual lived experience and the labour they put into ensuring the survival both of their immediate families and of their broader communities, as well as into achieving revolutionary goals. In the first, Zin Mar Phyo and Mi Sue Pwint explore the many ways in which women's political participation is informed by their overwhelming reproductive responsibilities and care work for their families and their communities, as well as by dominant gender norms, which frame young women as being in need of protection. Sharing insights accumulated from over three decades of activism, Mi Sue Pwint reflects on the hard labour and the focus needed to keep working towards democratic change and gender justice, as well as on the strategies women use to overcome gender-specific challenges.

In the second conversation, Naw K'nyaw Paw and Maggi Quadrini discuss the nature of the participation of women in the resistance movement in Karen state. They explore how in Karen state, the region in south-east Myanmar where Naw K'nyaw Paw hails from and works in, women's leadership experiences have fluctuated in relation to changes in the dynamics of conflict: women have historically emerged as leaders during and in the aftermath of attacks by the Myanmar Army, when men have fled the areas – yet women have often been asked to step back upon cessation of outright hostilities (also see The Karen Women's Organization 2010; Zin Mar Oo and Kusakabe 2010). Thus, as Naw K'nyaw Paw explains, women have had to contend with three type of challenges: the violent, ethnic oppression of the Myanmar state targeting the Karen community; the patriarchal practices of the Karen revolution; and the military campaigns executed by the *Tatmadaw* (the Myanmar military). Despite these obstacles, women have played, and continue to play, a key role in resisting oppressive military regimes and contesting patriarchal leadership through their actions and activism, through both armed and non-armed means. Indeed, K'nyaw Paw concludes that the sustained inclusion of women in political activism and leadership is of paramount importance in ensuring a future in Myanmar that is not only free and fair, but also feminist.

Labour, Land and Everyday Lives

Feminist scholarship has a long tradition of foregrounding everyday lives and experiences as sites of knowledge production, emphasizing the political nature of mundane, embodied, everyday relationships and practices (Ruddick 1995, Enloe 1990, Das 2007, Sylvester 2012). Following this tradition, we argue that the everyday constitutes a key political sphere where we can examine the real-life, on the ground, gendered dynamics and effects of Myanmar's transition (Hedström 2021; Blomqvist, Olivius and Hedström 2021). We understand the everyday as a space permeated by gendered relations of power, where people's actions and experiences are shaped by gendered norms and hierarchies. It is a site of violence and oppression as well as of resistance, love and care (Berents 2015; Hedström 2021; Elias and Shirin Rai 2015, 2018; Marijan 2017; Väyrynen 2019; Agatha Ma and Kusakabe 2015; Rahman 2019). This is clearly visible in the chapters in the third section of the book, which provide a careful and granular analysis of the gendered everyday politics of the transition.

Hilary Faxon's chapter centres on rural women's perspectives and everyday practices as a key source of knowledge enabling us to understand Myanmar's agrarian transition. In the past decade, new land legislation has been passed as part of broader liberalization reforms, facilitating investment but at the same time dispossessing many rural people making a living from customary and communal land use. This has led to new rural dynamics, such as increased labour migration, primarily by men. Using a participatory methodology involving photography, and a feminist political ecology approach, Faxon demonstrates powerfully how rural women's own visual insights can ground our understanding of gender in the transition in lived relations of soil, struggle and care.

The chapter by Jenny Hedström, Elisabeth Olivius and Zin Mar Phyo explores everyday experiences conveyed through life history interviews and focus groups in Mon and Kayah states, two conflict-affected areas which at the time of the interviews enjoyed ceasefires and relative stability, to under-

14

stand how macro-processes of war, ceasefire, and post-war development efforts manifest in gendered everyday realities. The findings point to the complex co-existence of change and continuity, where reductions in armed violence and greater freedom and livelihood opportunities over time have been accompanied by new insecurities caused by transitional reforms and processes of change, and by the persistence of other insecurities such as an absence of welfare provisioning. These dynamics have affected men and women differently: for example, while armed violence, which primarily targeted men, decreased, structural violence, which disproportionally affected women, persisted. Among new insecurities has been an escalating drug epidemic, which saw men falling victim to abuse and women picking up the resulting burden of caring for them and keeping families alive. Moreover, life histories make clear how present realities cannot be disentangled from past experiences of violence and insecurity. These experiences continue to shape experiences of the present and expectations for the future, and complicate a conventional temporality of political transition.

Shae Frydenlund and Wai Wai Nu's chapter highlights memories of friendship and co-existence between Rakhine and Rohingya women, and provides an important antidote to simplistic readings of ongoing violence is Rakhine state. Shifting the scale of inquiry from the national to the intimate spaces of everyday life, they demonstrate that recent communal violence is not an expression of inherent ethnic animosity, but is linked to the intensified pursuit of Burman hegemony during the transitional period. Through this, the authors show how interethnic personal relationships and cultural practices are politically and economically significant activities, which are simultaneously impacted by and productive of broader transitional processes of political and economic change.

The chapter by Dan Seng Lawn, Henri Myrttinen and Janà Naujoks, provides a unique analysis of how the intersection between disabilities, gender and displacement have shaped people's lives since the resumption of conflict in Kachin state. This adds important insights from people whose perspectives on Myanmar's transition are rarely heard. Moreover, the chapter contributes new knowledge about how the impact of disabilities are mediated and compounded by gendered norms and expectations, not only to literature on Myanmar but also to wider literature on gender and disability – for example in relation to norms about men as providers and how his plays out in a context of armed conflict in particular.

15

In their conversation piece, Terese Gagnon and Hsa Moo discuss Karen women's work for peace and justice both during and after periods of armed conflict. As their dialogue makes clear, women's work in providing care and subsistence are important, yet overlooked, sites where transitional politics are felt, produced and contested. The chapter demonstrates how women's work often remains unrecognized by male allies, and how the everyday is a site where women constantly have to resist efforts to put them 'back in their place'. Despite this, through their everyday care work women carve out space to transform conflict and to shape visions for a gender-just peace.

Future Directions

The timely analyses offered by our authors' contributions provide important insights into the gendered dynamics and effects of transitional changes. As Ma Khin Mar Mar Kyi and Matthew Walton note in the afterword to this book, this represents a new generation of scholars doing robust gendered analysis of political events, providing a more complete picture of past and present transformations. For example, there are chapters in the book that consider how gender norms are defined and contested within transitional politics and across conflict-affected landscapes, and with what consequences. Several chapters pay attention to the relationship between ethnic minority identity and gender in the context of political reforms and peace negotiations, including in relation to land disputes, educational reforms and peacebuilding efforts. One chapter examines the relationship between masculinities, disability and everyday life; and yet others highlight the ways in which women's movements, non-state armed actors, state bodies and narratives shape the experiences of women and men during conflict and transitional periods. Drawing attention to the diverse ways in which gendered relations of power intersect with ethnic, religious and urban-rural inequalities, contributions to the book caution against homogenizing and simplistic readings of women and men's experiences of transitional politics. Through this, they capture the different socio-economic and political transformations leading up to, and shaping, the events that took place in early 2021, which helps to deepen our understanding of how gender relates to wider macro-level events such as coups, ceasefires and other types of political crises. This makes the insights provided by different contributions to this book critical for the development of comprehensive theoretical analyses – not only of the military coup, but also of its aftermath. In other words, to understand what is happening now we need to know what happened in the past.

This book, then, both broadens our knowledge base relating to gender and political transition and contributes a much-needed analysis of this; and it also identifies several new avenues for further research, by pointing to changes in gendered relations and norms that have occurred over the last decade. How do these shape the ways in which women and men mobilize and resist, or comply with, the demands of the military junta? For example, in what ways are developments in women's rights and in the ways in which they organize over the past decade informing women-led responses to the coup and to the policies of the National Unity Government and of other demo-cratically-aligned institutions? How and why are gendered superstitions and stereotypes employed and utilized in popular responses to the coup, such as in the sarong strike (*Htamain Alan Htu*)? As Ma Khin Mar Mar Kyi asserts in the afterword to this volume, the '2021 Spring Revolution is historic and for the first time, we see ideological and identity-oriented revolutions in Myanmar that include gender'. To understand why these gendered transfor-mations are occurring now, the insights of this book are crucial.

There are some research strands that are less explored in this book. In its exploration of the gendered dynamics of Myanmar's transition, many chapters in this book give particular priority to understanding women's experiences and their changing social and political position. This focus is motivated by the historic and academic exclusions that continue to render women and their lived realities invisible. However, future research should delve deeper into the interplay between norms associated with masculinity, violence and politics, and explore gendered experiences and politics beyond the male–female binary.

For example, there is a gap when it comes to the role of norms associated with masculinity in relation to the socialization and mobilization of soldiers within the Myanmar military, and also when it comes to understanding the experiences of both men and women in the armed forces of the state. While the conversation pieces touch on the experiences of female soldiers in non-state armed groups, there is no detailed or systematic discussion of this included in the volume. Applying a gendered lens to the behaviour of armed groups, whether state or non-state, would contribute analytical depth to theorizations of gender in ceasefire processes and in war. Moreover, with the notable exception of reports commissioned by International Alert

(Naujoks and Myat Thandar Ko 2018a, 2018b, 2018c) there is still a paucity of data when it comes to how and in what ways norms and ideas around masculinity have developed in relation to conflict and post-conflict processes in Myanmar. How do different ideas about masculinity affect peacebuilding processes; and how do they affect everyday life in conflict-affected areas? In what ways do notions of protection and the ideology of patriarchy shape the politics of the junta? What are the long-term effects of masculine gender roles on the physical and mental wellbeing of boys, men and people with other gendered identities? How do these gender norms affect security and access to rights, socio-economic opportunities and justice? A focus on these relationships would likely reveal an even higher level of complicity of gender in politics, conflict and transitional processes in the country, and identify important entry point for researchers interested in learning more about the varied gendered dimensions of communities and societies emerging from, or spiralling into, violent conflict and crisis.

Another gendered dimension that remains understudied is the effect of LGBTI and queer identities on transitional processes, and vice versa. Important exceptions to this silence includes Lynette Chua's study on the development of queer politics and activism in Myanmar (Chua 2019) and David Gilbert's work on gender, sexuality and everyday life in Yangon (Gilbert 2013; also see Chua and Gilbert 2015). Recent reports, blog posts and academic research exploring and localizing LGBTI, queer and same-sex experiences within and across Myanmar's borders have contributed important insights into issues of gender diversity, heteronormativity and queer lives, spaces and politics.[1] Several of these interventions are building on studies and contributing to conversations foregrounding the gendering of *nat* spirits, or *nat kadaw*, as a way to contextualize and explore gender and sexuality in Myanmar.[2] A deeper understanding of how this affects and is affected by macro-political changes would add much richness to how gender is practiced, experienced and performed in transitional societies.

These limitations notwithstanding, the insights provided within this edited collection contribute to our understanding of the gendered dynamics of the decade of transition, and of the recent military coup and its effects.

---

1   See, for example, Ferguson 2014; Colors Rainbow 2013, 2016, 2017, 2019; Ohnmar Nyunt and Muthoni Murage 2017; Ohnmar Nyunt 2020.

2   See, for example, Brac de la Perrière 2007; Ho 2009; Keeler 2015; Coleman, Pathy Allen and Ford 2018; and Jackson and Baumann (eds) 2022.

Especially given the new political landscape unfolding in Myanmar, knowledge about how we got here, and why, is crucial in exploring and explaining both overarching political transitions and everyday gendered transitions during times of upheaval and change. Such insights demonstrate the importance of gender to transitional dynamics and provide critical lessons, which are of relevance not just for Myanmar but also for transitional societies elsewhere.

References

Agatha Ma and Kyoko Kusakabe. 2015. 'Gender analysis of fear and mobility in the context of ethnic conflict in Kayah State, Myanmar.' *Singapore Journal of Tropical Geography* 36 (3): 1–15.

Aguilar, Macarena, and Maggi Quadrini. 2021. '"We're unstoppable": Meet the women leading Myanmar's protests.' *OpenDemocracy*. Blog post. 24 February 2021. Accessed at: www.awid.org/news-and-analysis/were-unstoppable-meet-women-leading-myanmars-protests

Al-Ali, Nadje and Nicole Pratt. 2009 (eds). *Women and War in the Middle East: Transnational Perspectives*, London: Zed Books.

Anonymous. 2021. *Recommendations for Effective International Support to Gender Equality and Women's Rights in Myanmar*. June. Unpublished.

Ardeth Maung Thawnghmung. 2011. *The 'other' Karen in Myanmar: Ethnic minorities and the struggle without arms*. Washington: Lexington Books.

———. 2017. *Signs of Life in Myanmar's Nationwide Ceasefire Agreement?* Finding a way forward. *Critical Asian Studies*, 49(3): 379–395.

———. 2021. 'Back to the future? Possible scenarios for Myanmar.' *ISEAS Perspective* 2021/30, 12 March 2021. Available at: www.iseas.edu.sg/articles-commentaries/iseas-perspective/2021-30-back-to-the-future-possible-scenarios-for-myanmar-by-ardeth-maung-thawnghmung/

Asia Development Bank. 2016. *Gender Equality and Women's Rights: A Situation Analysis*. Manila: Asian Development Bank, United Nations Development Programme, United Nations Population Fund and the United Nations Entity for Gender Equality and the Empowerment of Asian Women.

Aye Thiri Kyaw. 2020. *Can We Take You as a Bride? – The Stories of Eight Hindu Women*. London School of Economics and Political Science. 11 February 2021. Accessed: blogs.lse.ac.uk/socialpolicy/2021/02/11/now-in-myanmar-the-military-coup-and-implications-for-women-rights/

Beech, H. 2021. '"She is a hero": In Myanmar's protests, women are on the front lines.' *The New York Times*, 4 March 2021. Available at: www.nytimes.com/2021/03/04/world/asia/myanmar-protests-women.html

Berents, Helen. 2015. 'An embodied everyday peace in the midst of violence.' *Peacebuilding* 3 (2): 1–14.

Bjarnegård, Elin. 2020. 'Introduction: Development challenges in Myanmar: Political development and politics of development intertwined.' *The European Journal of Development Research*, 32 (2): 255–273.

Bjarnegård, E. and G. Barall. 2021. 'The exclusion of women helped fuel the military coup.' *The Conversation*. Blog post. 21 February 2021. Available at: theconversation.com/the-exclusion-of-women-in-myanmar-politics-helped-fuel-the-military-coup-154701

Blomqvist, Linnéa, Olivius, Elisabeth, and Hedström, Jenny. 2021. 'Care and silence in women's everyday peacebuilding in Myanmar.' *Conflict, Security & Development*, 21(3), 223–244.

Brac de la Perrière, Bénédicte. 2007. '"To marry a man or a spirit." Women, the spirit possession cult, and domination in Burma.' In M. Skidmore and P. Lawrence (eds), *Women and the Contested State: Religion, Violence and Agency in South and Southeast Asia*, pp. 208–228. Notre Dame IN: University of Notre Dame Press.

Brooten, Lisa. 2016. 'Burmese media in transition.' *International Journal of Communication* 10 (1): 182–99.

Bünte, Marco. 2014. 'Burma's transition to quasi-military rule: From rulers to guardians?' *Armed Forces and Society* 40 (4): 742–64.

Callahan, Mary P. 2004. *Making enemies: War and state building in Burma*. Singapore: NUS Press.

Cárdenas, Magda Lorena and Olivius, Elisabeth. 2021. 'Building peace in the shadow of war: women-to-women diplomacy as alternative peacebuilding practice in Myanmar.' *Journal of Intervention and Statebuilding*, 15(3), 347–366.

Cheesman, Nick. 2017. 'Introduction: Interpreting communal violence in Myanmar.' *Journal of Contemporary Asia* 47 (3): 335–52.

Chua, Lynette J. 2019. *The Politics of Love in Myanmar: LGBT Mobilization and Human Rights as a Way of Life*. Stanford: Stanford University Press.

Chua, Lynette J. and David Gilbert. 2015. 'Sexual orientation and gender identity minorities in transition: LGBT rights and activism in Myanmar.' *Human Rights Quarterly* 37 (1): 1–28.

Cockburn, Cynthia. 2010. 'Gender relations as causal in militarization and war: A feminist standpoint.' *International Feminist Journal of Politics*, 12(2), 139–157.

Coleman, Eli, Mariette Pathy Allen, and Jessie Ford. 2018. 'Gender variance and sexual orientation among male spirit mediums in Myanmar.' *Archives of Sexual Behavior*. 47 (2–3).

Colors Rainbow. 2013. *Facing 377: Discrimination and Human Rights Abuses Against Transgender, Gay and Bisexual Men in Myanmar*. Yangon: Colors Rainbow.

———. 2016. *From Victims to Agents of Change: Lives and Voices of LGBT Individuals*. Yangon: Colors Rainbow.

———. 2017. *Strategies and Guidelines to Promote the Rights of LGBTs in Myanmar*. Yangon: Colors Rainbow.

———. 2019. *In the Shadows – Systemic Injustice based on Sexual Orientation and Gender Identity/Expression in Myanmar*. Yangon: Colors Rainbow.

Das, Veena. 2007. *Life and Words: Violence and the Descent into the Ordinary*. Berkley and Los Angeles: University of California Press.

Diamond, Larry. 2012. 'The need for a political pact.' *Journal of Democracy* 23 (4): 138–49.

Doi Ra and Khu Khu Ju. 2021. '"Nothing about us, without us": Reflections on the challenges of building land in our hands, a national land network in Myanmar/Burma.' *Journal of Peasant Studies* 48 (3): 497–516.

Egreteau, Renaud. 2016. *Caretaking Democratization: The Military and Political Change in Myanmar*. Oxford: Oxford University Press.

Elias, Juanita and Shirin Rai. 2015. 'The everyday gendered political economy of violence.' *Politics & Gender* 11 (02): 424–29.

———. 2018. 'Feminist everyday political economy: Space, time and violence.' *Review of International Studies* 45 (2): 201–20.

Enloe, Cynthia. 1990. *Bananas, Beaches and Bases: Making Feminist Sense of International Politics*. Berkeley and Los Angeles: University of California Press.

Faxon, Hilary Oliva, Roisin Furlong and May Sabe Phyu. 2015. 'Reinvigorating resilience: Violence against women, land rights, and the women's peace movement in Myanmar.' *Gender & Development* 23 (3): 463–79.

Ferguson, Jane M. 2014. 'Sexual systems of Highland Burma/Thailand: Sex and gender perceptions of and from Shan male sex workers in northern Thailand.' *South East Asia Research* 22 (1): 23–38.

Gender Equality Network. 2015. *Raising the Curtain: Cultural Norms, Social Practices and Gender Equality in Myanmar*. Yangon: Gender Equality Network. Available at: www.burmalibrary.org/docs22/GEN-2015-11-Raising%20the%20curtain-en.pdf.

Gilbert, David. 2013. 'Categorizing gender in Queer Yangon stable.' *Soujourn: Journal of Social Issues in Southeast Asia* 28 (2): 241–71.

Gusic, Ivan. 2019. 'The relational spatiality of the postwar condition: A study of the city of Mitrovica.' *Political Geography* 71 (February): 47–55.

Hansen, Lene. 2001. 'Gender, nation, rape: Bosnia and the construction of security.' *International Feminist Journal of Politics* 3 (1): 55–75.

Hedström, Jenny. 2021. 'On violence, the everyday and social reproduction : Agnes and Myanmar's transition peacebuilding.' *Peacebuilding* 9 (4): 371–386.

Hedström, Jenny and Elisabeth Olivius. 2020. 'Insecurity, dispossession, depletion: Women's experiences of post-war development in Myanmar.' *European Journal of Development Research*, 32 (2): 379–403.

Hedström, Jenny, Elisabeth Olivius and Kay Soe. 2020. 'Women's rights: Change and continuity.' In Adam Simpson and Nicholas Farrelly (eds), In *Myanmar: Politics, Economy and Society*, pp: 186–203. London: Routledge.

Ho, Tamara. C. 2009. 'Transgender, transgression, and translation: A cartography of *nat kadaws*. Notes on gender and sexuality within the spirit cult of Burma.' *Discourse: Journal for Theoretical Studies in Media and Culture* 31(3): 273–317.

Ikeya, Chie. 2011. *Refiguring Women, Colonialism, and Modernity in Burma*. Honolulu: University of Hawai'i Press.

Jackson, Peter A. and Baumann, Benjamin (eds). 2022. *Deities and Divas: Queer Ritual Specialists in Myanmar, Thailand and Beyond*. Copenhagen: NIAS Press.

Jordt, Ingrid, Tharaphi Than and Sue Ye Lin. 2021. *How Generation Z Galvanized a Revolutionary Movement against Myanmar's 2021 Military Coup*. Trends in Southeast Asia, Issue 7. Singapore: ISEAS -Yusof Ishak Institute. Available at: www.iseas.edu.sg/articles-commentaries/trends-in-southeast-asia/how-generation-z-galvanized-a-revolutionary-movement-against-myanmars-2021-military-coup-by-ingrid-jordt-tharaphi-than-and-sue-ye-lin/.

Karen Women's Organization. 2010. 'Walking amongst Sharp Knives. The Unsung Courage of Karen Women Village Chiefs in Conflict Areas of Eastern Burma.' Available at: karenwomen.org/wp-content/uploads/2011/11/walkingamongstsharpknives.pdf

Keeler, Ward. 2015. 'Shifting transversals: Trans women's move from spirit mediumship to beauty work in Mandalay.' *Ethnos: Journal of Anthropology* 81(5): 792–820.

Klem, Bart. 2018. 'The problem of peace and the meaning of "post-war".' *Conflict, Security and Development* 18 (3): 233–55.

Khan, Umayma. 2021. *The Women of Myanmar: 'Our Place is in the Revolution'*. 25 April 2021. Available at: www.aljazeera.com/features/2021/4/25/women-of-myanmar-stand-resilient-against-the-military-coup

Khin Chan Myae Maung. 2018. *Citizenship and Transgender Rights: A Matter of Dignity and Recognition*. 31 May 2018. Available at: teacircleoxford.com/essay/citizenship-and-transgender-rights-a-matter-of-dignity-and-recognition/

Khin Khin Mra. 2021. 'Women fight the dual evils of dictatorship and patriarchy in Myanmar.' *New Mandala*. Available at: www.newmandala.org/women-in-the-fight-against-the-dual-evils-of-dictatorship-and-patriarchal-norms-in-myanmar/

Krause, Jana, Werner Krause and Piia Bränfors. 2018. 'Women's participation in peace negotiations and the durability of peace.' *International Interactions* 44 (6): 985–1016.

Kyaw Yin Hlaing. 2012. 'Understanding recent political changes in Myanmar.' *Contemporary Southeast Asia* 34 (2): 197–216.

Linz, Juan. and Alfred Stepan. 1996. 'Toward consolidated democracies.' *Journal of Democracy* 7(2):14–33

Ma Khin Mar Mar Kyi. 2019. 'Book review: *Keeler, Ward: The Traffic in Hierarchy. Masculinity and Its Others in Buddhist Burma.*' *Teacircle: Book Reviews*, 27 November 2019. Available at: teacircleoxford.com/post/the-traffic-in-hierarchy-masculinity-and-its-others-in-buddhist-burma-by-ward-keeler-honolulu-university-of-hawaii-press-2017-331-pages/

Marchand, Marianne H. and Runyan, Anne S. 2010. *Gender and global restructuring: Sightings, sites and resistances.* London and New York: Routledge.

Marijan, Branka. 2017. 'The politics of everyday peace in Bosnia and Herzegovina and Northern Ireland.' *Peacebuilding* 5 (1): 67–81.

Martin De Almagro, Maria and Caitlin Ryan. 2019. 'Subverting economic empowerment: Towards securities in post-war settings.' *European Journal of International Relations* 25 (4): 1059–1079.

Meehan, Patrick and Mandy Sadan. 2017. 'Borderlands.' In Simpson, Adam, Farrelly, Nicholas and Holliday, Ian, (eds.) *Routledge Handbook of Contemporary Myanmar.* pp. 83–91. Abingdon: Routledge.

Mimi Aye, 2021. 'Myanmar's women are fighting for a new future after a long history of military oppression.' *Time Magazine*, 31 May 2021. Available at: time.com/6052954/myanmar-women-military/

Naujoks, Jana and Myat Thandar Ko. 2018a. *Behind the Masks: Masculinities, Gender, Peace and Security in Myanmar.* Yangon: International Alert, Phan Tee Eain and Thingaha Gender Organization. Available at: www.international-alert.org/publications/behind-the-masks-masculinities-gender-peace-security-myanmar/.

———. 2018b. *Mandating men: Understanding Masculinities and Engaging Men for Gender Equality and Peacebuilding in Myanmar.* Yangon: International Alert, Phan Tee Eain and Thingaha Gender Organization. Available at: www.international-alert.org/publications/mandating-men-masculinities-peacebuilding-gender-equality-myanmar/.

———. 2018c. *Pulling the strings: Masculinities, Gender and Social Conflict in Myanmar.* Yangon: International Alert, Phan Tee Eain and Thingaha Gender

Organization. Available at: www.international-alert.org/publications/pulling-the-strings-masculinities-gender-social-conflict-myanmar/.

Nyi Nyi Kyaw. 2019. 'Adulteration of pure native blood by aliens? Mixed race Kapya in colonial and post-colonial Myanmar.' *Social Identities* 25 (3): 345–59. Available at: doi.org/10.1080/13504630.2018.1499223.

Ohnmar Nyunt. 2020. *Being LGBTI* in Myanmar's Transition to Democracy*. Heinrich Böll Stiftung Myanmar. Available at: www.gwi-boell.de/en/2020/10/05/being-lgbti-myanmars-transition-democracy

Ohnmar Nyunt and Muthoni Murage. 2017. *LGBTI people in Myanmar: Second-class citizens*. Heinrich Böll Stiftung Myanmar. Accessed at: th.boell.org/en/2017/06/02/lgbti-people-myanmar-second-class-citizens

Olivius, Elisabeth. 2019. 'Time to go home? The conflictual politics of diaspora return in the Burmese women's movement.' *Asian Ethnicity* 20 (2): 148–167.

Olivius, Elisabeth and Jenny Hedström. 2019. 'Militarized nationalism as a platform for feminist mobilization? The case of the exiled Burmese women's movement. In *Women's Studies International Forum*, 76: 102263).

———. 2020. 'Young women's leadership in conflict: Crossing borders in Myanmar.' In Katrina Lee-Koo and Lesley Pruitt (eds), *Young Women and Leadership,* pp: 45–62. Abingdon and New York: Routledge.

———. 2021. 'Spatial struggles and the politics of peace: The Aung San statue as a site for post-war conflict in Myanmar's Kayah state.' *Journal of Peacebuilding and Development* 16 (3): 275–288.

Peterson, V. Spike. 1998. 'Gendered nationalism.' In Lois Ann Lorentzen and Jennifer Turpin (eds), *The Women and War Reader*, pp. 41–49. New York and London: New York University Press.

Phyu Phyu Oo and Sara E Davies. 2021. 'Access to whose justice? Survivor-centered justice for sexual and gender-based violence in Northern Shan State.' *Global Studies Quarterly* 1 (3): 1–10.

Pratt, Nicola and Yasmin Chilmeran. 2019. 'The geopolitics of social reproduction and depletion: The case of Iraq and Palestine.' *Social Politics* 26 (4): 586–607.

Quadrini, Maggi. 2021. 'Women are key to the humanitarian response in Myanmar.' *The Diplomat*, 2021. Available at: thediplomat.com/2021/06/women-are-key-to-the-humanitarian-response-in-myanmar/.

Rahman, Farhana. 2019. '"I find comfort here": Rohingya women and Taleems in Bangladesh's refugee camps.' *Journal of Refugee Studies,* 34(1): 874–889.

Rehmonnya.org. 2013. *Beyond the Male: The Case for a Gender Analysis of Illicit Drugs in Burma*. Rehmonnya.Org. 2013. Available at: rehmonnya.org/archives/2809#more-2809.

Ruddick, Sara. 1995 *Maternal thinking: Toward a politics of peace*. Boston: Beacon Press.

Sadan, Mandy (ed.) 2016. *War and Peace in the Borderlands of Myanmar: The Kachin Ceasefire, 1994–2011*. Copenhagen: NIAS Press.

Sai Lone and Renaud Cachia. 2021. 'The political economy of opium reduction in Myanmar: The case for a new "alternative development" paradigm led by and for opium poppy farmers.' *The Journal of Peasant Studies* 48 (3): 586–606,

Schissler, Matt, Matthew J. Walton and Phyu Phyu Thi. 2017. 'Reconciling contradictions: Buddhist-Muslim violence, narrative making and memory in Myanmar.' *Journal of Contemporary Asia* 47 (3): 376–95.

Shepherd, Laura J. 2018. 'Victims of violence or agents of change? Representations of women in UN peacebuilding discourse.' *Building Peace* 7259: 1–15.

Shwe Shwe Sein Latt, Kim N B Ninh, Mi Ki Kyaw Myint and Susan Lee. 2017. *Women's Political Participation in Myanmar: Experiences of Women Parliamentarians.* Yangon: Asia Foundation.

Sithu Aung Myint. 2021. 'Could Min Aung Hlaing's retirement break the political deadlock?' *Frontier*, 12 January 2021. Available at: www.frontiermyanmar.net/en/could-min-aung-hlaings-retirement-break-the-political-deadlock/

Smith, Martin. 2007. *State of strife: The dynamics of ethnic conflict in Burma.* Policy Studies 36 (Southeast Asia). Washington and Singapore: East-West Center Washington and Institute of Southeast Asian Studies.

Stokke, Kristian and Soe Myint Aung. 2020. 'Transition to democracy or hybrid regime? The dynamics and outcome of democratization in Myanmar.' *European Journal of Development Research* 32(2): 274–293.

Sylvester, Christine. 2012. 'War experiences/war practices/war theory.' *Millennium: Journal of International Studies* 40 (3): 483–503. Available at: doi.org/10.1177/0305829812442211.

———. 2013. 'War, sense and security.' In Laura Sjoberg (ed.), *Gender and International Security: Feminist Perspectives*, pp: 24-36, London and New York: Routledge.

Tanabe, Mihoko, Alison Greer, Jennifer Leigh, Payal Modi, William W. Davis, Pue Pue Mhote, Eh May Htoo, Conrad M. Otterness and Parveen Parmar. 2019. 'An exploration of gender-based violence in Eastern Myanmar in the context of political transition: Findings from a qualitative sexual and reproductive health assessment.' *Sexual and Reproductive Health Matters* 27 (2): 112–125

Thant Myint-U. 2019. *The Hidden History of Burma – Race, Capitalism, and the Crisis of Democracy in the 21st Century.* New York: WW Norton.

Tharaphi Than. 2014. *Women in Modern Burma.* London and New York: Routledge.

Tharaphi Than, Pyo Let Han and Shunn Lei. 2018. 'Lost in translation: Feminism in Myanmar.' *Independent Journal of Burmese Scholarship*, December: 1–12.

Thin Thin Aye. 2015. 'The role of civil society in Myanmar's democratization.' In *Burma/Myanmar in Transition: Connectivity, Changes and Challenges*, pp. 1–13. Available at: www.burmalibrary.org/docs21/Society and Culture/Thin-Thin-Aye-2015-The_Role_of_Civil_Society_in_Myanmar's_Democratization-en.pdf.

Tin Maung Maun Than. 2014. 'Introductory overview: Myanmar's economic reforms.' *Southeast Asian Economies* 31 (2): 165.

Tripp, Aili, Isabel Casimiro, Joy Kwesiga and Alice Mungwa. 2009. *African Women's Movements: Transforming Political Landscapes*. New York: Cambridge University Press.

True, Jacqui and Yolanda Riveros-Morales. 2019. 'Towards inclusive peace: Analysing gender-sensitive peace agreements 2000–2016.' *International Political Science Review* 40 (1): 23–40.

Väyrynen, Tarja. 2019. 'Mundane peace and the politics of vulnerability: A nonsolid feminist research agenda.' *Peacebuilding* 7 (2): 146–59.

Wibben, Annick T. R. 2010. 'Feminist security studies.' *The Routledge Handbook of Security Studies*, August 2015: 84–94.

World Bank Group. 2013. *Myanmar Economic Monitor*. Yangon: World Bank Group.

———. 2015. *Myanmar Economic Monitor*. Yangon: World Bank Group.

Women's League of Burma 2014. *'If they Had Hope, They Would Speak': The Ongoing Use of State-Sponsored Sexual Violence in Burma's Ethnic Communities*. Chiang Mai: Women's League of Burma.

Zin Mar Aung. 2015. 'From military patriarchy to gender equity: Including women in the democratic transition in Burma.' *Social Research: An International Quarterly* 82 (2): 531–51.

Zin Mar Oo and Kyoko Kusakabe. 2010. 'Motherhood and social network: Response strategies of internally displaced Karen women in Taungoo district.' *Women's Studies International Forum* 33 (5): 482–91.

Transitional Politics, Institutions and Policymaking

CHAPTER 1

When Heads of the Household become Heads of the Village

Gender and Institutional Change in Local Governance Settings in Myanmar

Khin Khin Mra and Deborah Livingstone

T ransitions can be moments of positive transformation for gender equality. Myanmar's democratization process, following decades of military rule, initially resulted in encouraging, though short-lived, changes in political structures, institutions and space for civic engagement. Many new and revised institutions, or sets of rules, emerged during the transition to semi-civilian governance between 2011 and 2020, before the military coup in 2021. These included the earlier Constitution of the Republic of Myanmar (Government of Myanmar 2008) and the Ward or Village Tract Administration Law (Government of Myanmar 2012). The latter saw Ward and Village Tract Administrators (W/VTAs) elected at the local level as opposed to being appointed by the military government. This appeared to offer women a more equal opportunity to become W/VTAs. However, at the latest election, which took place in 2015, only 0.5 per cent of the elected W/VTAs were women (UNDP 2017).

Using a Feminist Institutionalism (FI) lens, we argue that the impact of gendered social norms, such as *hpoun, yin kyae hmu,* and *karma,* on formal institutions such as the Constitution and the W/VTA Law, created unequal power dynamics that influenced the extent to which women could take up leadership or decision-making roles within the household and in local governance. Existing gender dynamics emanating from Myanmar's history, British colonialism, and the legacy of decades of military rule were sustained during the transition and continued to define new institutions. While transitions offer the possibility of change, they can also create resistance to change and perpetuate existing gender inequalities. Mackay refers to *nested newness,* where new institutions are 'profoundly shaped by [their] institutional environment no matter how seemingly dramatic the rupture with the past' (Mackay 2014: 552). Democratization processes offer opportunities for change, or for entrenching existing institutions, at a time when political institutions and cultures are created or changed (Waylen 2014). This tension between possibility and resistance makes a FI lens particularly useful in understanding the importance of institutions in relation to the possibilities for improving gender equality during periods of political transition.

This chapter draws on evidence and analysis from existing literature on gender and institutions in Myanmar, and a case study building on data that was collected and analysed as part of a wider research project on women's experiences, roles and influence in community-based dispute resolution and mediation (CBDRM) processes (Khin Khin Mra and Livingstone 2019). CBDRM mechanisms are generally led by W/VTAs, of whom few are women, which makes them a useful process within which to explore gendered rules, the gendered effects of these rules, how actors are gendered, and the gendered outcomes of CBDRM. Through exploring the impact of gendered institutions on women's roles and experiences, this chapter contributes to a better understanding of the gendered dynamics of a period of political transition in Myanmar. Analysis of how pre-existing gendered institutions shaped transitional efforts to create policy change reveals how these rules, norms and power dynamics could also influence what is possible for gender equality in the current political context.

The chapter begins by defining Feminist Institutionalism (FI) and the concepts used to analyse institutions in Myanmar. We then explore the *gendered legacy* of Myanmar's colonial history and decades of military rule. We examine how formal and informal institutions are *gendered rules*, how they are nested within the institutions that precede them, and how this shapes *who holds power*, the *gendered effects of the rules* and how these perpetuate *power dynamics* and *actors' gendered roles*. Finally, a case study explores how these formal and informal gendered institutions shape *gendered outcomes* in terms of women's roles and experiences in Myanmar's community-based dispute resolution and mediation processes.

Exploring Gender and Institutional Change using a Feminist Institutionalism Lens

FI expands on governance theory to provide an approach to analysing institutions. FI suggests that formal institutions – parliaments, laws, policies, procedures – and informal institutions – social and cultural norms and customary practices – create gendered rules that define and limit the scope of institutional reform and the ways in which actors behave and can operate within a reform process (Gains and Lowndes 2017; Krook and Mackay [eds] 2011; Mackay, Kenny and Chappell 2010; Ní Aoláin 2018; Waylen 2014). Both formal and informal institutions are gendered, meaning that they emerge from ideas around femininity or masculinity in a particular context. Moreover, masculinity tends to be 'naturalized' as the norm (Waylen 2014; Mackay, Kenny and Chappell 2010). Critically, FI adds analysis of power dynamics and asymmetries to governance theories around how institutions work, and centres women as actors in political processes (ibid.). FI helps us understand how social norms and customary practices can undermine new institutions even when these include new rules in support of gender equality or are seemingly gender neutral. This is a result of the 'practice and interplay' between institutions and actors, which creates gendered dynamics and legacies that can limit the potential of gender equality reforms (Kenny and Mackay 2011: 284).

We use Lowndes' (2020) model to help understand *how institutions or rules are gendered* in Myanmar's political transition; the *gendered effects* of these rules; how this affects the behaviour of *gendered actors who work within these rules*; and the *gendered outcomes* of these rules. This framework brings into focus how power asymmetries are created by formal and informal institutions, and how these shape and define the possibilities for change. Our analysis builds on data from 142 semi-structured interviews and 51 focus group discussions, involving a total of 339 women and 245 men (Khin Khin Mra and Livingstone 2019). Respondents included women leaders, mediators and disputants, W/VTAs, community leaders, customary leaders at the community level, and leaders of women's organizations, civil society organizations and legal aid groups in southern Shan, Mon and Kayin States and in Mandalay Region. The data were collected in September and October 2019 using in-depth semi-structured interviews, snowball sampling and case tracing methodologies.

The Legacy of Myanmar's Colonial History and Decades of Military Rule

The legacy of pre-colonial Burmese dynasties, British colonial rule and decades of conflict and military rule means that assumptions and myths about women and men's roles have been normalized in Myanmar's political and administrative systems and institutions. This influences women's roles and experience, for example as heads of households or W/VTAs in local governance settings. The idea that women had traditionally high social and economic status in Myanmar was used by male-dominated political powers to justify exclusion and discrimination against women (Ikeya 2005). At the same time, men's perceived inherent spiritual superiority led to men attaining positions of power and influence in political and religious institutions (Harriden 2012; Tharaphi Than 2013). Since the colonial era, these myths of women's traditional high status and men's innate superiority have created power dynamics that have meant that few women are now in positions of authority (Khin Mar Mar Kyi 2014).

Throughout Myanmar, women continue to face structural gender-based discrimination as a result of the prolonged period of military rule, the impact of conflict and the associated militarization of culture and politics (Khin Mar Mar Kyi 2018). During decades of military rule, successive all-male military regimes (1962–2000) did little to promote women's participation in national, state and regional level politics and instead reinforced domestic and supportive roles for women (Minoletti 2019). Myanmar has been more deeply affected by internal conflict than any other country in Southeast Asia, with some subnational conflicts being active for over 70 years (Burke 2017). Decades of armed conflict in ethnic areas created a 'masculinization' of decision-making (Hedström 2016; MSWRR et al. 2016; Cárdenas 2019). While some ethnic armed organizations have women's branches attached to their armed wings, these have predominantly focused on supportive roles, and women's leadership has also been discouraged in ethnic armed administrations (Hedström 2013).

The legacy of colonial administration and decades of military rule and armed conflict have meant that new rules and power dynamics remained nested within those that preceded them. For example, despite some progress, women remained notably under-represented in all aspects of public and political life in Myanmar's democratizing state. In the 2020 elections, women representatives were elected to all state/region parliaments for the first time, with 18 per cent of elected state/region *hluttaw* representatives being women, compared with 13 per cent in 2015, and 4 per cent in 2010 (Htin Aung Ling and Batchelor 2020). While Aung San Suu Kyi was the de facto leader, the rest of the post-2015 cabinet were all male at the national level after the second election in 2015 (the cabinet had not yet been announced after the 2020 elections, before the coup took place). Only two women were appointed as chief ministers at the sub-national level, and one woman was appointed as Speaker of the House in a State Parliament, the first in Myanmar's history (Minoletti 2019). Transitional policy priorities continued to be defined by male-dominated actors and institutions, and women's voices remained largely unheard in institutional reform and policymaking processes (Khin Khin Mra and Livingstone 2020).

Institutional Change and Political Reform in Myanmar: How the Heads of Households become the Heads of Villages

Gendered Rules and Power Dynamics

In this context, the 2008 Constitution was the key legal framework and reference point in Myanmar's democratization, providing several important principles and provisions such as general elections and the formation of a semi-civilian government. Democratic reform, initiated by the military government in 2010, offered an opportunity to transform women's participation in public life. Despite these new institutional arrangements, the military was able to maintain its power by carefully orchestrating a transition to 'disciplined democracy' (Bünte 2014:754). By allowing the military to appoint 25 per cent of seats in both national and sub-national parliaments and ministers to three key ministries – Home Affairs, Defence, and Border Affairs – the Constitution ensured the military's stranglehold on parliament and safeguarded the military's dominance in the context of political power. The Constitution, written by a group of men familiar with an extreme concentration of power resting in very few hands (Williams 2014), effectively embodied the masculine rules designed by male leadership; the old was nested within the new.

The new Constitution was a set of gendered rules, as it entrenched gender stereotypes and allowed the tradition of male dominance to continue in the democratizing state. While the Constitution guarantees all persons equal rights to vote and run for public office (Article 9) and no discrimination on the basis of sex (Article 348), the mandated 25 per cent of seats for appointed military officers (Articles 109 and 141) limited women's opportunities for participation in parliament and key ministerial positions. Gendered social norms and stereotypes that discriminate against women and restrict women's roles in public and political life were embedded in the Constitution through statements like 'nothing in this section shall prevent the appointment of men to positions that are naturally suitable for men only [...] in appointing or assigning duties to civil service personnel' (Article 352); the use of 'he' in reference to the president and vice-president; the requirement for them to be experienced in military affairs (Article 59-d); and references to women principally as mothers (Article 32-a) (Gender Equality Network 2013; Khin Khin Mra 2015). As the 2008 Constitution was pivotal in shaping and structuring political reforms, traditional norms around men's innate leadership were institutionalized. The gendered outcomes, as informal norms became formal, had explicit impacts on women's representation in public life (Khin Khin Mra and Livingstone 2020) and legalized structural discrimination (Khin Mar Mar Kyi 2018).

The 2008 Constitution provided the basic framework for restructuring local governance during the transition, whereby a highly centralized military regime was transformed through the establishment of elected legislatures and governments at sub-national level. At this level, the lowest official administrative unit is the Village Tract Administration in rural areas, and the Ward Administration in urban areas (Kempel and Myanmar Development Research 2012). A village tract is usually constituted of four to six villages and administrated by a Village Tract Administrator (VTA), a clerk and a number of 100-household leaders/Village Administrators (ibid.). W/VTAs are the primary conduit between their communities and the Township Administrators, who are appointed by the General Administration Department (GAD). Given that the Constitution, the foundation of the country's laws, is a gendered set of rules, this influenced the W/VTA Law (Government of Myanmar 2012) that guided the election process and the roles and responsibilities of W/VTAs.

The establishment of the W/VTA Law saw W/VTAs elected at the local level as opposed to being appointed employees of the GAD, as they were during the military regime. While this initially appeared to mark a dramatic change from the past, the W/VTA law remains nested within old practices and rules. The W/VTA selection process, for example, is seemingly gender-neutral; and yet it remains male-dominated. The election process starts with the appointment by the GAD's Township Administrator, who is usually male, of a supervisory board of five elders (customary leaders), who are again generally (though not always) male, to oversee the process. Secret ballots then elect 10-household leaders, 100-household leaders and, if there is more than one 100-household leader, the W/VTAs (Kyed et al 2016). Only 88 women (0.5 per cent) were elected in the 2015 election (UNDP 2017). Despite constitutional guarantees to gender equality and commitments to women's equal rights to vote and run for public office, the W/VTA law did not transform women's representation in Myanmar's new semi-civilian governance structures.

The W/VTA Law is not applied in the same way throughout Myanmar, and women's experiences of the impact of institutions such as the W/VTA law vary in different states and regions. Complex and varying governance arrangements exist in many areas as a consequence of decades of conflict over territory and authority over populations (Saferworld 2019). Contested or 'hybrid' authority areas see customary leaders, non-state political actors, and non-state armed groups play core roles in local governance (Nixon et al. 2013) often relying on customary laws rather than national legislation (Kempel and Aung Thu Nyein 2014) and with plural rather than either customary or legal systems implemented in practice (Kyed [ed.] 2020). Conflict-affected areas tend to have more women village leaders, though this is likely a result of the absence of men, who may be away fighting, or a way to protect male village leaders from violence, arrest or forced labour (Karen Women's Organization 2010; Kempel and Aung Tun 2016). In these areas, women's leadership does not appear to be sustained post-conflict (Kempel and Aung Thu Nyein 2014).

Nested Newness: How Existing Gendered Social Norms Influence Formal Institutions and Perpetuate Gendered Roles

These formal institutions, the Constitution and the W/VTA Law, emerged from and are supported by informal institutions in the shape of gendered social norms and traditional practices. The Myanmar notion of *hpoun* emphasizes male superiority and supports a situation in which men are generally considered the natural heads of households, leaders and public figures, while women are perceived to be wives and mothers. Harriden (2012) explores further the complexities involved in *hpoun* and its relation to *awza* (influential power/influence) and *ana* (political power/authority) in Myanmar. Men are seen as spiritually superior, strong, brave and productive while women are weak, less productive, fickle and impure during menstruation (Harriden 2012; MSWRR et al. 2016). Women are taught early on to 'respect their sons as masters and their husbands as gods' (*Thaa goh thakin; liin goh phaya*), which reinforces gendered roles, with women as subservient wives and mothers (Harriden 2012: 34). Other concepts, such as that women are bearers of culture and *yin kyae hmu* (politeness and deference), *arh nah deh* (the feeling that it is impolite to express one's true feelings as this might embarrass another person) and women's internalization of discriminatory social norms as their *karma* all impact on the roles that they can take on and their experiences of policy outcomes (Khin Khin Mra and Livingstone 2020). Some of these concepts, such as *hpoun* and *karma,* have more of an impact in Buddhist communities; others are more fluid and have different levels of influence in different parts of the country (Gender Equality Network 2015).

These same gendered rules create and maintain the notion of 'heads of households', *ein htaung oo si,* as the decision-makers in families and communities. The majority of *ein htaung oo si* are men, with only 23 per cent of households headed by women (Ministry of Health and Sports and ICF 2017). Women are only considered to be *ein htaung oo si* if they are divorced, separated, or widowed, or their husbands are no longer present (Khin Khin Mra and Livingstone 2019). While social norms determine the status of *ein htaung oo si,* the role is also recognized officially, for example in household registration lists and censuses. The husband or father is usually called *ain oo nat,* which means the 'spirit' or 'lord of the house'. While women from different ethnicities, ages, classes, and religions have different experiences of being heads of households, there are some common social norms that affect how women can engage in decision-making processes at home or in local governance processes (Khin Khin Mra and Livingstone 2020).

Village administration has been male-dominated throughout Myanmar history. During the pre-colonial period each village had a headman or *thugyi,* who was an appointed official under the control of the Burmese king, responsible for civil, criminal and fiscal administration (Daw Kyan 1969). As the *thugyi* position was traditionally hereditary (Badgley 1965), the transfer of the power and leadership position between the generations was typically between men, and the old power structures continued. While there were some female *thugyi* in local administration in pre-colonial Burma, they often administered villages jointly with their husbands. Occasionally a female *thugyi* who was a widow and therefore a household head administered a village on her own (Harriden 2012). British colonial powers retained the headman system, transforming it into a bureaucratic system of enforcing government regulations and reporting upwards to the Crown (Kempel and Aung Tun 2016). Villages also have village elders, or *yat mi yat pha,* who are respected customary leaders such as ex-village heads, religious leaders, and active and respected members of the community. They play a key role in in steering and providing guidance and advice to the village headman and W/ VTAs. The term *yat mi yat pha* literally means 'a village's elder mothers and fathers'; however, women are generally absent from this structure (Khin Khin Mra and Livingstone 2019).

The absence of women in the roles of *ein htaung oo si, thugyi* and *yat mi yat pha* was influenced by entrenched gendered rules around male superiority. The deeply held belief that men hold the natural authority to take on leadership roles continues to influence the rules around how someone is elected or chosen for a role and makes women feel like they do not have the authority to take on these roles (Zin Mar Aung 2015; Htun and Jensenius 2020; Khin Mar Mar Kyi 2012). While the W/VTA law apparently provides women with opportunities to be elected, in reality gendered actors – *ein htaung oo si, yat mi yat pha* and GAD officials – dominate W/VTA selection processes, with women having little or no influence over the selection of candidates. The gendered outcome of this was, and continues to be, to make it harder for women outside the structures of power to reach influential positions in local politics. As such, women's voices, agency and their participation have been constrained within their households and in local governance structures such as ward and village tract administrations. This demonstrates how the reform of an existing formal institutions can be undermined by gendered legacies, the perseverance of informal norms and rules (Mackay 2014; Chappell 2014; Waylen 2014).

The military coup has undermined any limited advances and further entrenched gender norms. Immediately after the military coup on 1st February 2021, the Village Ward and Tract Administration (W/VTA) Law was amended, the General Administration Department was reintegrated into the military apparatus by transferring it to the Ministry of Home Affairs, and democratically elected W/VTA were replaced by men loyal to the military, who are now directly appointed by the township administrative councils formed by the military regime (Annawitt 2021). However, people in several places have rejected these W/VTA and others have resigned or avoided taking on the role (Irrawaddy 2021). Gendered rules such as women being perceived to be unsuitable to perform the duties of W/VTAs (which are overtly expressed in the W/VTA Law) have been reinforced in the context of post-coup security challenges, and again prevent women from becoming W/VTAs. On the other hand, members of women's rights organizations have observed that there has been a break in the culture of relying on W/VTAs in identifying the recipients of development and/or humanitarian support. With many men being arrested or avoiding public engagement due to fear of arrest, forced recruitment and intimidation by the armed groups, the participation of heads of household, who are usually males, is becoming atypical as the model of local governance. While the impact of this is yet to be seen, this could have an impact on prevailing gender rules around men as heads of the household and leaders of communities, as more women are taking on these roles.

Case Study: How Gendered Institutions Shape Women's Roles and Experiences in Community-Based Dispute Resolution and Mediation

We have seen how, in general, gendered formal and informal institutions affect women's leadership and participation in local governance. This case study illustrates the gendered outcomes of formal institutions, such as the W/VTA Law, and informal institutions, such as *hpoun*, *arh nah deh* and *karma*, specifically on women's roles in and experiences of community-based dispute resolution and mediation (CBDRM) processes (Khin Khin Mra and Livingstone 2019). In Myanmar the formal justice system, including courts, police stations, and ethnic administrations, is complemented by a community-based justice system used to mediate a negotiated resolution to intra- or inter-community disputes, which is based partly on legal institutions and partly on tradition or custom. Here we show how, despite reforms, male authority has been retained in key roles and barriers to women's participation in local governance of community justice remain.

Formal institutions such as the W/VTA Law tend to guide who can mediate disputes in CBDRM processes. Most community level disputes are mediated by W/VTAs, as they are perceived to have been given the mandate to do this by the W/VTA Law (Government of Myanmar 2012). As W/VTA elections are organized in a way that prevents women from being elected, women's opportunities to become mediators in community level disputes are restricted. A male community leader in Shan State described this:

Only men attend the village meetings. The village heads, 10- and 100-household leaders, men, make decisions in the community. Women take responsibility for traditional dancing, greeting and treating the people with food, but the rest is managed by the male leaders.[1]

While the majority of village leaders interviewed said that there were no barriers for women to become mediators, male and female community members shared long lists of barriers or of the gendered effects of the formal and informal institutions. In Southern Shan State, for example, respondents told us that women rarely make decisions at family or community level, as only the head of the household, village heads, 10- and 100-household leaders and W/VTAs can make decisions and they are mostly male. A woman leader in Kalaw Township, Shan State told us that:

It seems that people find it very difficult to accept a decision made by a woman. Women are seen as incapable and can get things wrong. So I really have to try hard to influence and make decisions. Traditional leaders are still in powerful positions and there is no woman among the religious leaders whose words are seriously listened to. It is difficult to compete with them and to have the same influence as them.[2]

There are limited exceptions, for example a woman leader from Yay Phyu Kan village in Kalaw Township started getting involved in village activities as leader of a young women's group, which was formed primarily to support religious activities in the village and to cook for village events. She is now seen as an influential leader in the village, and she is involved in resolving local disputes and advising village leaders. However, she had to find a different route to enable her to take on a dispute resolution role. Her involvement in other local committees, her work with a youth group and young women, and her involvement with NGOs and CSOs have provided her with leadership skills and the confidence to take on a leadership role. A woman leader from Taunggyi in Shan State explained that 'if she has a strong background and people who can support her, if she is brave enough, confident, and educated, a woman can influence the decision-making process to some extent.'[3]

The ways in which formal institutions or rules impact on women's leadership vary depending on the context in Myanmar; the W/VTA Law

---

1   Male community leader, Shan State, 2 October 2019.
2   Female community leader, Shan State, 3 October 2019.
3   Female community leader, Shan State, 3 October 2019.

influences women's roles in CBDRM in different ways in different parts of the country. In conflict-affected or mixed-control areas, different gendered rules influence the possibilities for women. W/VTAs are less influential in mixed-control areas, where village leaders and community committees take on more of a role in community justice mechanisms. In Mon State, for example, the influence of the W/VTA law on CBDRM processes varies between government and mixed-control areas. In Mawlamyine, one respondent said that '100-household leaders are appointed by GAD, so they have power in disputes',[4] while a woman CSO leader in Mon State told us that: 'In the village, people regard their VTA as their parents'.[5] Unlike the W/VTA Law, the regulations of ethnic armed organizations legitimise women's engagement in CBDRM processes. New Mon State Party and Karen National Union regulations stipulate specific roles for women's representatives in the dispute resolution process. The Karen Women's Organization, for example, plays a role in justice committees at the village, village tract, township and district levels that has been shown to have positive gendered outcomes, improving gender equality and women's access to justice (Saferworld 2019). In Hlaing Bwe Township in Kayin State, respondents told us that if a dispute needs to be taken to the township level, people prefer to resolve their dispute through ethnic armed organizations such as the Karen National Union, the Border Guard Force or the Democratic Karen Benevolent Army, because using their justice mechanisms as a decision-making process is faster than the Myanmar legal system and courts (see also Kyed [ed.] 2020).

Women's legitimacy as leaders can, however, be dependent on their association with ethnic armed groups and male leaders. A woman leader from a women's community group in Khun Be explained that: 'Men usually don't dare to challenge me as my husband is ex-commander of the DKBA; if I were someone else then I'd be told that this role [dispute resolution] is not for women and women can't do it'.[6] Understanding how the formal rules are gendered, the effects of the gendered rules and how actors operating within these rules are gendered *in a specific context* could help design different ways of supporting women to take on public roles that address the specific institutional barriers and opportunities in that area.

---

4   Female 10-household head, Mon State, 12 September 2019.
5   Female CSO leader, Mon State, 18 September 2019.
6   Female community leader, Kayin State, 20 September 2019.

Informal institutions such as social norms play as significant a role as formal institutions in the roles women and men can have in CBDRM. The formal rules described in the W/VTA Law contain a long list of duties, including 'security, prevalence of law and order, community peace and tranquillity, and carrying out the benefit of the public'. Social norms dictate that women are perceived to be unsuitable to perform these types of duties, creating a barrier to their election as W/VTAs. Social norms such as *hpoun, yin kyae hmu* and *arh nah deh* affect who has power and can make decisions and mediate disputes at both household and community level. Starting at the household level, women's roles and influence are restricted, as decisions are made by the head of the household, the *ein htaung oo si*. As *ein htaung oo si* are rarely women, this affects what issues are considered serious enough to be taken to a mediation process and affects women's aspirations and their confidence that they can become mediators, due to the perceived moral authority and legitimacy of the decisions of men at the household level (Khin Khin Mra and Livingstone 2019). One woman focus group participant told us that 'the custom we follow here is that both men and women in the village have to follow the village leaders, not speak up or against them. We're afraid of the village leaders.'[7]

The ability to make or influence decisions begins at the household level and extends to the community level. In villages in southern Shan State, respondents were of the view that women should not have opinions, as this is rude or their views are irrelevant, and that decision-making is the responsibility of men only (Khin Khin Mra and Livingstone 2019). In Kayin State a male VTA said that 'while there are some women 100-household or 10- household leaders here, they are just selected for the position in name only; the real work is done by their husbands'.[8] A woman community leader in Kayin suggested that 'men don't like women who try to solve problems, as their positions can be threatened'.[9] One of the few women W/VTAs in Kayin State said that 'when the woman is the final decision-maker in the village, there are so many men who want and try to influence her decision-making',[10] demonstrating that even when women reach leadership positions, they continue to face challenges to their legitimacy.

---

7   Female focus group participant, Shan State, 3 October 2019.
8   Male village tract administrator, Kayin State, 25 September 2019.
9   Female community leader, Kayin State, 21 September 2019.
10 Female village tract administrator, Kayin State, 23 September 2019.

Concepts like *hpoun, arh nah deh, yin kyae hmu* and *karma* influence women's choices about options for obtaining justice, how they engage with village leaders and mediators and how they internalise their situation and accept outcomes as their fate. A male community leader in Mon State said that 'women are taught to be tolerant, especially if they are a wife and a mother, so they don't become involved in disputes. Even if their husband has beaten them, they are afraid he will go to jail, so they keep silent.'[11] In some areas women are not supposed to travel alone, or alone with men, especially at night which limits their ability to find a resolution outside of their community. In Thitahl Thit village in Kalaw township, it was regarded as shameful for a women to have a dispute. 'For a woman and a young girl, it is assumed that it's shameful and harmful to her dignity to have disputes so they are prohibited from going to the village leader and making a case.' (woman focus group participant, Shan State). Women usually do not want to speak up in village meetings or to inform the village leader of a dispute as they are afraid of other people knowing their business.

Customary practices also influence decisions and outcomes, though to a different extent in different parts of Myanmar. While a local MP stated that decisions are made according to Myanmar law, respondents in one village in Southern Shan State told us that people, including village leaders, do not have knowledge of laws and mostly use village customs to resolve disputes (Khin Khin Mra and Livingstone 2019). Punishments assigned after dispute resolution are often according to a village's rules, rather than the law, and include the payment of fines or contributing labour to village development activities (ibid.). A woman disputant in Kayin State told us that:

> Keeping a family together is the first priority for the village leaders; they usually ask women who want to divorce to reconsider their decision and ask them to wait, sometimes up to six months. So women have to suffer beatings for six months; only then can they get a divorce.[12]

In Mon State, community leaders told us that decisions are influenced by a combination of social norms/customary practices and Myanmar laws. Norms include the norm that it is acceptable to beat your wife and that a

---

11   Male community leader, Mon State, 7th September 2019. Cited in Khin Khin Mra and Livingstone 2019.

12   Female disputant seeking community-based dispute resolution and mediation, Kayin State, 19 October 2019. Cited in Khin Khin Mra and Livingstone 2019.

woman who is raped should marry her rapist. This influences decisions on domestic violence and rape cases (ibid.). A woman focus group participant in Kayin State explained that:

> There is nothing protecting women's interests. Decisions are made mostly by men and they don't understand women. Customs are not fair for women but are followed by both. For men, this is okay to follow as nothing is harmful for them.[13]

In southern Shan State a 100-household leader told us that 'customary practices are barriers for women in CBDRM, as no one wants to go against them because this is believed to be a big crime'.[14] Women also believed that customary practices are not the same for everyone and are unfair for women.[15]

The effect of these gendered formal and informal institutions and of these norms is to create asymmetric power dynamics that make it difficult for women to take on roles as mediators in community-based disputes and that affect the outcomes of dispute resolution processes. Power comes from personal status, such as being *ein htaung oo si* or being a religious leader, or is provided by government and ethnic armed organizations to W/VTAs and village leaders (ibid.). Respondents repeatedly referred to the power W/VTAs have, which has been legitimized by the W/VTA law; 'the VTA makes the final decision because he has administrative power'.[16] Unless women are W/VTAs or 100-household heads, women's involvement in dispute resolution is not mandatory and is upon request by women disputants, their family, or the W/VTAs and the *yat mi yat pha*. A male community leader in Kayin State said that 'the VTA is the most powerful in the village. If he makes a decision, this is final, and everyone has to follow his decision.'[17] In conflict-affected areas, while women have more of an institutionalized role in community affairs, the power lies with village leaders and EAO leaders, both of whom are also mostly male.

Women who do become W/VTAs and mediate disputes are only able to do so when they have access to power. Women W/VTAs have in common

---

13 Female focus group participant, Kayin State, 19th September 2019. Cited in Khin Khin Mra and Livingstone 2019.
14 Male 100-household leader, Shan State, 4 October 2019.
15 Female CSO leader, Mon State, 5 September 2019. Cited in Khin Khin Mra and Livingstone 2019.
16 Female mediator, Kayin State, 21 September 2019.
17 Male community leader, Kayin State, 25 September 2019.

that they are educated, have exposure to township administration, are well-connected and many have male relatives in power (e.g. ex-ethnic armed organization leaders, ex-village heads and ex-VTAs) (Khin Khin Mra and Livingstone 2019). For example, a woman mediator from Shan State's father was an ex-village leader. She was educated and gained skills and confidence as a result of her training with NGOs and CSOs and from the support of the youth and women she worked with. For many this is not perceived to be attainable: a woman mediator from Kayin State told us, for example, that 'women cannot make any decision even at the family level, forget about the community level'.[18] Women saw power asymmetries as a barrier to accessing justice or taking on roles as mediators, especially for young women, poor women, and women with less education or connections (ibid.).

Women mediators are highly motivated and described a desire to work for their village's needs and wanting their village to be a good example to be followed by others. They spoke of not being afraid and of proving that they could do what men can do.

Conclusion

In this chapter we have used FI to explore how formal and informal institutions are gendered rules and how this creates power dynamics that have perpetuated gender inequalities during Myanmar's transition from military rule to semi-civilian governance. Male heads of the household have continued to become heads of the village. We have argued that the impact of social norms and customary practices on formal institutions, such as the Constitution and the W/VTA Law, have created unequal power dynamics that have influenced the extent to which women have been able to take up leadership or decision-making roles. While transitions offer opportunities to renegotiate existing institutions or reimagine new ones, gendered rules like the Constitution and W/VTA Law, and social norms such as *hpoun, arh nah deh, yin kyae hmu* and *karma* have, in Myanmar, reinforced the power of *ein htaung oo si, thugyi* and *yat mi yat pha* (gendered actors) and have prevented women from taking on leadership roles (the effects of gendered rules). This also affects the outcomes of policies and processes, to the detriment of women (and indeed other marginalized groups) (gendered outcomes).

---

18   Female mediator, Kayin State, 22 September, 2019.

The extent to which formal and informal institutions impact on gender inequalities varies between states and regions, between urban and rural areas and according to a woman's age, education, ethnicity, religion and economic status. The case study gives examples of the impact of the combined effects of the W/VTA Law and social norms on women's roles in and experiences of community-based dispute resolution and mediation, demonstrating the institutional barriers to women becoming mediators and the unfair outcomes for women in negotiated disputes. The democratic transition process did not in this case provide an opportunity for reimagining women's roles or challenging gendered institutions that block gender equality; it served, rather, to entrench existing patriarchal formal and informal institutions around community-based justice.

This analysis illustrates what has been described as 'nested newness' – how older gender dynamics and the patriarchal power structures emanating from Myanmar's history, British colonialism and the legacy of decades of military rule were sustained during the transition and have continued to define new institutions. This means that changes in formal institutions, such as the W/VTA law, brought by democratic reform cannot transform structural inequalities on their own. Understanding how institutions are gendered and exploring women's experiences of gendered institutions during the transition can help us to understand how transitions can avoid reinstating patriarchal institutions. Existing gendered rules and power dynamics could also influence what is possible in terms of transforming gender equality in the current political context. Challenging the harmful aspects of *hpoun, arh nah deh, yin kyae hmu* and *karma* must go alongside building on positive aspects informal rules; and alongside changing formal rules such as laws. Changes for gendered actors operating under gendered rules during the military occupation could be short-lived; or, in any new transition, could lead to new gendered institutions that create spaces in which women can participate – as, for example, community leaders such as *yat mi yat pha* or W/VTA. Creating new rules that are not nested within the old rules, and transforming existing institutions in ways that separate them from existing norms and practices, can contribute to building women's confidence and a sense of legitimacy, and to developing policies, strategies and ways of working that help achieve gender equality in the future.

References

Annawitt P. 2021. 'Myanmar's junta failing despite rampant militarization; despite the military's multiple offensives of recent weeks, the opposition National Unity Government is making progress.' *Asia Times*: December 3, 2021. Available at: asiatimes.com/2021/12/myanmars-junta-failing-despite-rampant-militarization/

Badgley, J. H. 1965. 'The Theravada polity of Burma.' *Japanese Journal of Southeast Asian Studies* 2 (4): 52–75.

Bünte, M. 2014. 'Burma's transition to quasi-military rule: From rulers to guardians?' *Armed Forces and Society* 40 (4): 742–764.

Burke, A. 2017. *The Contested Areas of Myanmar: Subnational Conflict, Aid and Development.* The Asia Foundation, Yangon.

Cárdenas, M. L. 2019. 'Women-to-women diplomacy and the Women's League of Burma.' In Kolås, Åshild (ed.), *Women, Peace and Security in Myanmar: Between Feminism and Ethnopolitics*, pp. 44–57. London: Routledge.

Chappell, L. 2014. 'Conflicting institutions and the search for gender justice at the International Criminal Court.' *Political Research Quarterly* 67 (1): 183–196.

Daw Kyan. 1969. 'Village administration in Upper Burma during 1886–87.' *Journal of the Burma Research Society* 52 (2): 67.

Gains, F. and V. Lowndes. 2017. 'Gender, actors, and institutions at the local level: Explaining variation in policies to address violence against women and girls.' *Governance* 31 (4): 683–699.

Gender Equality Network. 2013. *Myanmar Laws and CEDAW.* Gender Equality Network: Yangon.

———. 2015. *Raising the Curtain Cultural Norms, Social Practices and Gender Equality in Myanmar.* Gender Equality Network: Yangon.

Government of Myanmar. 2008. *Constitution of the Republic of the Union of Myanmar (2008).* Printing and Publishing Enterprise, Ministry of Information.

———. 2012. *The Ward or Village Tract Administration Law (2012).* Printing and Publishing Enterprise, Ministry of Information, Myanmar.

Harriden, J. 2012. *The Authority of Influence: Women and Power in Burmese History.* Copenhagen: NIAS Press.

Hedström, J. 2013. *Where are the Women? Negotiation for Peace in Burma.* Stockholm: The Swedish Burma Committee.

———. 2016. 'A feminist political economy analysis of insecurity and violence.' In Nick Cheesman and Nicholas Farrelly (eds), *Conflict in Myanmar: War, Politics, Religion*, 67–90. Singapore: Institute of Southeast Asian Studies.

Htin Aung Ling and R. Batchelor. 2020. *2020 General Election: State and Region Hluttaws.* Yangon: The Asia Foundation.

Htun, M. and F. R. Jensenius. 2020. 'Political change, women's rights and public opinion on gender equality in Myanmar.' *The European Journal of Development Research* 32 (2): 457–481.

Ikeya, C. 2005. 'The "traditional" high status of women in Burma: A historical reconsideration.' *Journal of Burma Studies* 10 (1): 51–81.

Irrawaddy. 2021. 'Myanmar Regime Returns Public Administration Oversight to Home Affairs Ministry.' 6 May 2021. Available at: www.irrawaddy.com/news/burma/myanmar-regime-returns-public-administration-oversight-to-home-affairs-ministry.html

Karen Women's Organization. 2010. 'Walking amongst Sharp Knives: The Unsung Courage of Karen Women Village Chiefs in Conflict Areas of Eastern Burma.' Mae Sariang, Thailand: KWO.

Kempel, S. and Aung Thu Nyein. 2014. *Local Governance Dynamics in South East Myanmar: An Assessment for Swiss Agency for Development and Cooperation (SDC).* Swiss Agency for Development and Cooperation, Yangon.

Kempel, S. and Aung Tun. 2016. *Myanmar Ward and Village Tract Administrator Elections 2016: An Overview of the Role, the Laws, and the Procedures.* Norwegian People's Aid, Myanmar. Workshop report dated 31st January.

Kempel, S. and Myanmar Development Research. 2012. 'Village Institutions and Leadership in Myanmar: A View from Below.' Unpublished report for UNDP.

Kenny, M. and F. Mackay. 2011. 'Gender and devolution in Spain and the United Kingdom.' *Politics & Gender* 7 (2): 280–286.

Khin Khin Mra. 2015. 'A masculine Myanmar and the vote.' *New Mandala.* Available at: www.newmandala.org/a-masculine-myanmar-and-the-vote/ (accessed 20 August 2020).

Khin Khin Mra and D. Livingstone. 2019. *In their Own Voices: Women's Experiences, Roles and Influence in Community Based Dispute Resolution and Mediation in Myanmar.* Yangon: Mercy Corps Myanmar.

———. 2020. 'The winding path to gender equality in Myanmar.' In J. Chambers, C. Galloway and J. Liljeblad (eds), *Living with Myanmar,* pp. 243–264. Singapore: ISEAS Publishing.

Khin Mar Mar Kyi. 2012. 'In Pursuit of Power: Politics, Patriarchy, Poverty and Gender Relations in New Order Myanmar/Burma.' PhD thesis. Canberra: The Australian National University.

———. 2014. 'Engendering development in Myanmar: Women's struggle for *san, si, sa.*' In Nick Cheesman, Nicholas Farrelly and Trevor Wilson (eds), *Debating Democratization in Myanmar,* 305–30. Singapore: ISEAS Publishing.

————. 2018. 'Gender.' In A. Simpson, N. Farrelly and I. Holliday (eds), *Routledge Handbook of Contemporary Myanmar*, 380–392. Routledge, New York.

Krook, M. L. and F. Mackay (eds). 2011. *Gender, Politics, and Institutions: Towards a Feminist Institutionalism*. Basingstoke: Palgrave Macmillan

Kyed, H. M. (ed.). 2020. *Everyday Justice in Myanmar: Informal Resolutions and State Evasion in a Time of Contested Transition*. Copenhagen: NIAS Press.

Kyed, H. M., A. Pohl Harrisson and G. McCarthy. 2016. *Local Democracy in Myanmar: Reflections on Ward and Village Tract Elections in 2016*. Copenhagen: Danish Institute for International Studies.

Lowndes V., 2020. 'How are political institutions gendered?' *Political Studies* 68 (3): 543–564.

Mackay, F. 2014. 'Nested newness, institutional innovation, and the gendered limits of change.' *Politics & Gender* 10 (4): 549.

Mackay, F., M. Kenny and L. Chappell. 2010. 'New institutionalism through a gender lens: Towards a feminist institutionalism?' *International Political Science Review* 31 (5): 573–588.

Ministry of Health and Sports and ICF. 2017. *Myanmar Demographic and Health Survey 2015–16*. Nay Pyi Taw, Myanmar: Ministry of Health and Sports, and Rockville, Maryland: ICF.

Ministry of Social Welfare, Relief and Resettlement, Asia Development Bank, UNFPA, UNDP and UN Women (2016). *Gender Equality and Women's Rights in Myanmar: A Situation Analysis*. Manila: ADB

Minoletti, P. 2019 'Myanmar: Women's political life.' In S. Franceschet, M. Krook and N. Tan (eds), *The Palgrave Handbook of Women's Political Rights. Gender and Politics*: 657–672. London: Palgrave Macmillan.

Ní Aoláin, F., 2018. 'The feminist institutional dimensions of power-sharing and political settlements.' *Nationalism and Ethnic Politics* 24 (1): 116–132.

Nixon, H., C. Jolene, K. P. C. Saw, T. A. Lynn and M. Arnold. 2013. *State and Region Governments in Myanmar*. Yangon: The Asia Foundation and Centre for Economic and Social Development.

Saferworld. 2019. *Justice Provision in South East Myanmar: Experiences from Conflict-Affected Areas with Multiple Governing Authorities*. Yangon: Saferworld.

Tharaphi Than. 2013. *Women in Modern Burma*. London, New York: Routledge.

Waylen, G. 2014. 'Informal institutions, institutional change and gender equality.' *Political Research Quarterly* 67 (1): 212–223.

Williams, D. C. 2014. 'What's so bad about Burma's 2008 constitution? A guide for the perplexed.' In M. Crouch., and T. Lindsey (eds), *Law, Society and Transition in Myanmar*: 117–140. London: Hart Publishing.

UNDP. 2017. 'Meet Village Tract Administrator: Daw Naw June Ae Nar.' www.
mm.undp.org/content/myanmar/en/home/presscenter/articles/2017/06/
09/meet-village-tract-administrator-daw-naw-ta-bi-thar.html

Zin Mar Aung. 2015. 'From military patriarchy to gender equity: Including women
in the democratic transition in Burma'. *Social Research: An International Quarterly*
82 (2): 531–551.

CHAPTER 2

Women's Mobilization, Activism and Policy-Making in Myanmar's Transition

Aye Thiri Kyaw

*I*n January 2020, the government of Myanmar published the long-anticipated bill on Prevention of Violence against Women (PoVAW) on state-run media. This was an important move for a country with no existing comprehensive law to penalize violence against women (VAW), in particular in relation to Intimate Partner Violence (IPV). Myanmar remains one of only two countries in Southeast Asia region without specific laws on domestic violence (UN WOMEN 2013). Since 2014, activists in Myanmar had been advocating that the government should pass this law, given its urgency and in recognition of VAW as a public health and human rights concern (Faxon, Furlong and Sabe Phyu 2015; Miedema, San Shwe and Aye Thiri Kyaw 2016b). Women's rights activism around PoVAW is significant both because it has worked to counter a dangerous form of gender discrimination, and because it has represented engagement with the transitional government. Thus, the law's publication was a noteworthy milestone for the women's rights activists who actively participated in the drafting process. However, the military coup on 1 February 2021 ended the decade of policy advocacy in which women's rights activists had engaged since the transition. Shortly after the coup, women's groups announced their withdrawal from the government-led technical working groups, including the VAW technical task force that was responsible for the VAW thematic area, stating their firm stance against the coup.

After the democratic transition took off in 2011, Myanmar saw the rise of a growing independent women's movement that was active inside the country. During the previous period of military rule, the government's approach, in the name of protecting women, was to promote traditional customs and cultural norms. This makes it important to explore the ways in which women's groups seized opportunities to engage in policy advocacy within Myanmar. The opportunities that presented themselves for the expansion of women's political participation during the ten years after 2011 were vital and helped to bring about a more gender-equal environment. There were increasing prospects for political participation, which enabled women's groups to amplify their voices as a means of influencing institutions and policy making (Viterna and Fallon 2008). The changes led to women's activism being focused towards the state and to the use of laws as tools for change (which ultimately led to the formulation of the draft PoVAW law). Even after the coup, the story of the PoVAW law demonstrates the potential – as well as the limits – of policy advocacy for gender equality during transitional times.

In this chapter, I first examine changes in women's activism and in their strategies to end gender-based violence in relation to changes in the broader political context. Secondly, I present an assessment of the role of the women's movement during the transition and discuss how women's groups seized the policy space and window of opportunity presented by the ten years of democratic transition to advocate for the PoVAW law. Finally, I discuss the challenges that women's groups faced collectively throughout their policy advocacy. This analysis is partly informed by key informant interviews conducted for an MSc dissertation, supervised by Associate Professor Tania Burchardt, at the London School of Economics and Political Science (Aye Thiri Kyaw 2020). More importantly, this analysis has benefitted from the author's nearly ten years of experience of working with preventing violence against women and being involved with the Gender Equality Network's two major policy research projects, which contributed to the drafting of the Prevention of Violence against Women's law in 2013 and 2014.

Women's Mobilization and Activism in Myanmar

Myanmar women's movements have shifted and expanded during the different periods of the country's recent history, both within and beyond national borders. Nationalism and feminism were intertwined in the early days of women's mobilizations during the colonial period. These mobilizations, such as the nationalist Burmese women's association led by elite women, were established to strengthen the nationalist agenda of the General Council of Burmese Associations. However, the nationalist Burmese women's association only played a supportive role in relation to the nationalist movement, reinforcing its activities and objectives (Ikeya 2013). Throughout the socialist and authoritarian periods, many women's movements were led by elite Bamar and Buddhist women who were detached from grassroot and ethnic minority concerns (Tharaphi Than 2015).

The government's brutal crackdown on the political uprising in 1988 marked a watershed moment for contemporary women's rights activism in Myanmar. The founding of the Women's League of Burma in 1999, which incorporated 11 exiled ethnic minority women's groups, was a significant milestone in the women's rights movement in Myanmar (Women's League of Burma 1999). Informed by the global women's rights movement, exiled activist groups strategically challenged the military government's authority and brought attention to human rights violations in ethnic minority areas (Cárdenas this volume; Pepper this volume)

Advocacy efforts were not just limited to the military government's (in)actions regarding women; concerns were also raised about women's subordination in the opposing armed groups, male dominance, and domestic violence (Hedström 2016). This is historically relevant because it was a notable precursor wherein the women's groups aimed for liberation through a mass movement within their own society.

After Cyclone Nargis devastated large swathes of the country in 2008, the space for activism changed in important ways. The post-Nargis period in Myanmar saw major growth in women's rights activism inside the country. A new UN/INGO and civil society taskforce was set up to assist in the response to humanitarian needs, and recovery effort identified gaps in the post-Nargis era. This taskforce would later expand to become a leading women's rights network in the country. The network, which had more than 100 international and national organizations and individual experts as members, came to be known as the Gender Equality Network (GEN) (Faxon, Furlong and Sabe Phyu 2015; Gender Equality Network 2018). Playing a contributory role in the democratic transition since it took off in 2011, women's groups over the years evolved to form the building blocks for feminist civil society comprising both local and international non-governmental organizations and individual experts in Myanmar.

Different women's movements and activists responded to the changing political context and to opportunities using different strategies. For example, the exiled women groups led by the WLB focused their policy and advocacy efforts on eliminating VAW, in particular sexual violence, in the conflict-affected areas. Although starting off with direct relief efforts, women's groups inside Myanmar interpreted the changes as an opportunity to engage in policy efforts to change the state and its laws. The ten years of democratic transition from 2010–2020 saw both of these strands of the broader women's movement drastically changing their strategies, while keeping their focus on women's rights and the eradication of VAW. In a changing political context, women's organizations and activists had to consider how they wanted to go about influencing societal change, choosing between maintaining an independent position in relation to the state, outside of the policy-making architecture, and serving in available policy-making roles once the transition had begun. Exiled women groups continued international advocacy to hold the military accountable for their perpetration of sexual violence, while women's groups inside the country sought the opportunity to expand greater gender equality through the law and policy reforms. This presented a dilemma, as both maintaining a level of independence and playing a political role within state structures entails both opportunities and risks for feminist advocacy (Waylen 1994). For example, maintaining independence means that women's groups may sometimes be seen as dissenting voices; on the other hand, the direct involvement in government of women may be tokenistic rather than truly being based on a gender-sensitive approach. In the case of Myanmar, the exiled groups were vocal in relation to their overt critique of gender inequality (Hedström 2016, Olivius 2019) while women's groups inside the country were more limited by the traditional views predominant in policy institutions (Maber 2016; Khin Khin Mra and Livingstone, this volume). Below, I focus on policy advocacy for women's rights conducted from inside the country, and aimed especially at eliminating violence against women.

Women's Policy Advocacy during the Transition: Opportunities and Spaces

Women's groups, spearheaded by GEN, seized opportunities to leverage the space for civil society and its potential to promote gender equality that emerged after the transition took effect in 2011. As part of their efforts since the start of the transition, GEN, along with other new women's networks, such as the Women's Organizations Network Myanmar (WON), began celebrating International Women's Day with campaigns to promote awareness around violence against women.

Although social movements do not directly make or change policy, those movements can position themselves as the initial drivers of changes in social values within the society. Through these mechanisms, there is a range of possibilities that helps in rethinking the most pressing social problems and how best to tackle them (Rochon and Mazmanian 1993). Women's groups may, for instance, indirectly influence policy making by questioning long-held views that reflect public opinion and by helping to raise awareness about these social issues. Helping to replace old norms is one of the ways through which the feminist agenda is advanced (Weldon and Bahu 2011). This applies in Myanmar just as it does elsewhere. In the process of developing their advocacy messages, Myanmar feminists were informed by the voices of grassroots civil society in pushing for gender-responsive, fit-for-purpose policies to be implemented by the national government.

However, like other countries experiencing a democratic transition, Myanmar faced a huge challenge in terms of the scarcity of reliable data on gender based-violence and rights. Indeed, Myanmar did not have national prevalence data on violence against women. Therefore, the causes and pathways of VAW were yet to be comprehensively measured, and therefore largely unknown. One consequence of this is that it is not possible to effectively design policies to remedy violence if neither the extent of violence nor the root causes of it are well known. GEN saw this as an opportunity to collaborate with the Department of Social Welfare, the governmental department responsible for women's and children's affairs. In 2013, GEN carried out the first qualitative research study on VAW, which revealed different types of partner violence including economic, emotional, physical and sexual intimate partner violence or marital rape. Most women experience violence not as a one-off incident, but as a continuous feature of intimate relationships. In addition to partner violence, women described rape by other perpetrators than their partners; sexual assault; and harassment. The key findings of the study resulted in targeted policy advocacy and to recommendations that led to the PoVAW bill (Gender Equality Network 2015).

The year 2015 saw a change in the government's perspective; it recognized that violence against women is a serious social problem, and committed to preventing all forms of violence and to eliminating harmful social and cultural norms. Collaboration between women's groups and the Union Solidarity and Development Party (USDP)-led government were established even before the NLD government took office. This led, for example, to the ten-year National Action Plan for the Advancement of Women, which listed VAW as one out of ten priority areas for the government in 2013 (Ministry of Social Wefare, Relief and Resettlement 2013). Five years after the democratic transition took off, the government's Convention on the Elimination of All Forms of Discrimination Against Women (CEDAW) report recognized the role of women's organizations and their continued collaboration in addressing all forms of violence against women (Government of Myanmar 2015). This was a major shift, since previous official government reports to the CEDAW committee had claimed that discrimination, including violence against women, was non-existent in Myanmar, and had denied that there was gender inequality (Government of Myanmar 2007; Government of Myanmar 1999). This new recognition was the result of advocacy, which led to a change in the perception of VAW among policy makers.

Consistent advocacy pushed the policy makers to shift their perspective and to recognize the lack of protection for women. Commissioning qualitative research to show systematically that VAW is a problem is an example of a strategy that was adopted by women's organizations (Gender Equality Network 2015). A key women's rights activist explained that the plans for a long-anticipated national prevalence survey should open new doors for prevention programmes:

> The Department of Social Welfare has the administrative record on the incidence of violence reported from different states and regions. They also have a commitment at the ASEAN and global level to collect the VAW survey. The department will collaborate with women's groups, which will be responsible for the qualitative part of national prevalence research.[1]

This work would culminate with the publication of the draft Prevention of Violence Against Women (PoVAW) bill on state-run media in 2020. The year 2020 even witnessed an appearance on the part of the Minister of Department of Social Welfare and Relief and Resettlement department, alongside his wife, a senior government official, in an awareness campaign video by the UNFPA encouraged non-violent behaviour and positive relationships between couples, to highlight the devastating impacts of violence

---

1   Leading women's rights activist, Yangon, 30 July 2020.

against women in the context of Covid-19 pandemic. This was the result of years of unwavering advocacy by women's organizations, which culminated in the official public announcement of the PoVAW bill.

Women's Policy Advocacy during the Transition: Challenges and Obstacles

Gender-related scholarship reflects, to some degree, an optimist attitude towards the changes brought by the democratic transition, since this provided new spaces in which to advance pertinent discussions on women's rights and women's political participation (Jaquette 1994). These new-found opportunities have the potential to strengthen the ability of women's rights activists to influence the restructuring of institutions and policy changes. The changes in the perspective towards VAW and the recent call for public consultation regarding the draft PoVAW bill were quite significant feminist wins, which stand in sharp contrast to pre-transition politics. New spaces became available in which opposition groups could expand their activism in relation to gender equality and women's rights (Khin Khin Mra and Livingstone 2020). However, these changes were not without challenges. Despite the progress in women's rights activism brought about by the transition, I present below certain specific bottlenecks and obstacles that have accompanied the PoVAW law drafting.

Women's Groups are not Homogenous

Although women's groups tend to be pluralistic in nature, what seems to be a general agreement among the different groups is that addressing women's subordination is a major priority (Phillips 2002). Thus, one women's rights activist to whom I spoke said that women's groups are driven by the same goals of achieving gender equality despite their differences.[2] However, differences and the unequal status of women have often been the sources of conflict within the women's movement. Divisive tendencies such as power differences, cultural differences and socio-economic differences are often overlooked in the context of women's rights movements working on policy advocacy (Richards 2006).

---

2   Leading gender and peace advocate, Yangon, 28 October 2020.

In relation to Myanmar, there was a lack of a consensus among the women's groups in exile and those groups based centrally inside Myanmar on how to engage constructively with the military-backed government. One respondent, a long-time leading women's rights activist on VAW policy advocacy, told me that the main source of the difference between the women's groups derives from each group's stance in relation to the 2008 constitution (Cardènas, this volume; Naw K'nyaw Paw and Quadrini, this volume)

Exiled women groups opposed the 2008 constitution and advocated that it should be abolished, whereas groups inside the country sought a way to collaborate with the government policy makers and pushed for law reforms through research and advocacy. It could also be that government officials were careful when it came to deciding whom to engage with, due to the plural nature of the movement. Exiled women's groups were seen as relatively radical compared with the groups inside the country (Barrow 2015). For instance, the concerns of WLB revolve, quite justifiably, around sexual violence committed by the military in the ethnic minority areas (Women's League of Burma 2020). Inside Myanmar, GEN and WON, along with other leading networks, focused on issues such as domestic violence as a starting point, but also addressed sexual violence by non-partners. There was no easy solution to this. The decision to stay outside of governmental policy-making as opposition groups or to work together to influence policy processes through the government is multi-faceted. In general, exiled women's groups continued to promote international advocacy, while the women's groups inside Myanmar focused on internal advocacy aimed at changing policy and governance. Instead of approaching sexual violence in conflict as a standalone topic of advocacy, women's groups working with the government focused on different types of VAW. In their view, domestic violence was the most pervasive form of VAW and should be the focus of advocacy. Therefore, sexual violence in conflict areas was treated as one form of violence under the umbrella term of VAW.

It should be noted here, in relation to sexual violence in conflict-affected areas, that there was a question around the inclusion of the most marginalized populations, such as Hindu and Rohingya women, in the PoVAW bill. The Myanmar military is listed in the 2018 United Nations Secretary General list of parties involved in conflict-related sexual violence, because it is clear that it used sexual violence, including rape, as a weapon of war against Rohingya women and girls, as well as in other ethnic areas such as Kachin and Shan state (Frydenlund and Wai Wai Nu, this volume). As rightly pointed out by WLB in its analysis, there was nothing in the PoVAW bill stating how military perpetrators of sexual violence in conflict-affected areas would be held accountable. However, it would have been challenging for groups like GEN and WON to be too outspoken about these issues because they worked through the government, and the government remained under (some) military influence. Although GEN and other women's advocacy groups inside the country did not publicly speak out about the plight of Rohingya women, they felt that their informal working relationships with exiled women groups made clear what their stand was. As a result, the government began to view both exiled groups and groups inside the country in a similar way. The NLD government rejected outright the use of the term 'Rohingya', which affected women's advocacy, whether they were focusing on sexual violence in conflict or marital violence, and this in turn exposed the intertwined oppressiveness of the military and of patriarchy in Myanmar. As a result, the government began to distance themselves from the women's groups in the final round of the consultations. Finally, the PoVAW bill became a secretive document, as the government scaled back their engagement with women's civil society groups.

Rising Nationalism and Protection of 'Race and Religion'

Democratic transitions can be accompanied by a resurfacing of traditional gender expectations (Jaquette 1994). In Myanmar in the 2010s, there were competing interests at play, as there was in the country both an embracing of women's rights and at the same time a desire to preserve religious and traditional values. On the one hand, women's rights groups made considerable progress in influencing the government's policymaking and obtaining official commitments at the regional and global level (Htun and Jensenius 2020). On the other hand, conservative groups also had legislative wins (ibid.). The nationalist groups enjoyed a strong voice, which enabled them to push against liberal ideologies. The 969 movement and Ma Ba Tha (the 'Organization for the Protection of Race and Religion') sought general public support in suppressing minority Muslim groups. This led to the drafting of the so-called four laws: the religious conversion law, the Buddhist women's special marriage law, the population control healthcare law, and the monogamy law. These are collectively known as the Race and Religion Protection Laws. The proponents of these laws justified them as necessary in order to protect young, impoverished Buddhist women from exploitation by men from other religious backgrounds. The four laws met with strong opposition on the part of both civil society and the international community, due to the potential discrimination against women and religious minorities that was implied by the laws. However, they were passed, and this gives an indication of the ideology of the Union Solidarity and Development Party (USDP)-led government, juxtaposed as it was between nationalism and religion on the one hand and women's rights on the other. Although the USDP-led government embraced liberal concepts such as gender equality, the adoption of the four laws seemed to conflict with the cause being championed by women's groups (Barrow 2015).

The passing of the package of the so-called Four Race and Religion Protection Laws was opposed by international human rights groups and women's groups. However, attitudes to the laws were complex, and not all women in Myanmar were opposed to the laws. Some Myanmar women voiced their support of the four laws (Walton, Mckay and Khin Mar Mar Kyi 2014). For instance, some women saw the laws as protection for women whose husbands marry more than one wife, but who are afraid to tell their husbands about their feelings. One leading women's rights peace advocate, who was extensively involved in earlier PoVAW discussions, pointed out that women who supported the four laws did not see the associated long-term risks. For instance, they are attracted to the polygamy law because the law criminalizes men's polygamy; however, as she pointed out: 'The proposed four laws trick women who are not in favour of men's practice of polygamy.'[3]

In 2015, the National League for Democracy (NLD) assumed office following a landslide victory in the general polls conducted the same year. However, the 2008 constitution provided the military with significant privileges, including dedicated seats in the parliament. Although Daw Aung San Suu Kyi was the de facto leader of the country, she was not widely seen as the personification of gender equality in Myanmar (Minoletti 2014). It was observed that her position was not a representation of freedom for women in Myanmar. A notable women's rights activist described how their hopes were shattered, since the NLD-led government showed no sign of withdrawing the four laws, especially as there had been high hopes in terms of women's rights in the early days of NLD-led government. What had disappointed

---

3   Leading women's rights and peace advocate, Yangon, 28 October, 2020.

them even more was seeing the NLD-led government prioritizing building a relationship with the Union Solidarity and Development Party, the political party backed by the Myanmar military:

> In my opinion, the Suu Kyi government prioritised national reconcil-
> iation with the military backed USDP who had passed the four Race
> and Religion protection laws and abandoned women's rights. This is
> heart-breaking for us. We understand that a five-year term will not bring
> many changes, but the government's unwillingness to remove the four
> laws is too much to bear.[4]

The nationalist promotion of illiberal ideologies and conservative views on gender inequality hampered the progress made by the women's rights groups. Democratic transition in Myanmar provided space for women's groups to influence and get involved in policy making processes, but it also saw a resurfacing of traditional beliefs around womanhood. The opening of Myanmar to the world has led to an identity crisis, creating a desire to protect its race and religion during the democratic transition (Walton, Mckay and Khin Mar Mar Kyi 2015). This might explain why some women are in support of these laws. Strong sentiments relating to the protection of religious values, and the fear that Buddhist values might disappear due to outside influence, were widespread among the nationalists who promoted illiberal ideologies (Walton and Hayward 2014). Yet, as pointed out by rights groups, the laws do not respect to freedom of choice for women in relation to whom they marry. In the view of women's rights groups, women's support for these laws was due to this nationalist agenda. This might explain why some women were misled to support these laws. These laws are discriminatory towards religious minorities.

Lack of Evidence-Based Policy-Making in Relation to Violence against Women

The prevention of violence against women was also challenged by the lack of evidence-based VAW policymaking, as Myanmar does not have national prevalence data on VAW. The military coup halted the first national prevalence VAW survey, which was underway, commissioned by UNFPA and Gender Equality Network under the leadership of the Department of Social

---

4   Leading women's rights and peace advocate, Yangon, 28 October, 2020.

Welfare. A respondent who is involved with PoVAW draft committee as a UN representative told me that there has not been any cooperation regarding the VAW survey since the coup occurred.[5]

That said, the Demographic and Health Survey in Myanmar in 2015 did include a section on domestic violence and provided some data about the breadth of the phenomenon. One in five women in Myanmar reported having experience of violence in their responses to the Demographic and Health Survey (DHS). Experts point out that the real number of incidents may be under-reported due to social norms that prevent women from sharing their experience of violence (Miedema and Tharaphi Than 2018). Multi-purpose studies such as the DHS are not a substitute for VAW specialized surveys, as the DHS may not be best-suited to present detailed questions that are intended to collect women's experiences of violence (Ellsberg et al 2001). Myanmar women's rights experts unanimously expressed the view that the actual number of women survivors of violence may be higher than the prevalence figures from the DHS data. Based on their experiences working in this area, they said that survivors do not normally speak of their experience of violence due to social norms and stigma:

> Domestic violence was not the focus of the DHS. But their findings are useful. I think it has had some impact. We just don't have the evidence – that is why it may be under-reported. However, based on cultural norms, I can say that [as an insider]. Since people do not see the violence [psychological violence], they do not make a drama out of it. Therefore, I think it is not reflected in the DHS findings.[6]

More importantly, evidence is political in Myanmar – as it is everywhere – since different actors frame the evidence differently and use it politically (Cairney 2016). Although there is general acceptance of the use of evidence relating to violence against women in Myanmar, different actors do not always have the right technical capacities and seldom apply good international practice in using objective and ethical methodologies to collect this type of sensitive information in Myanmar (Schomerus and Seckinelgin 2015). During the military regime, VAW was not seen as a serious social or public health issue in Myanmar. As a result, there was little evidence to support its significance of the problem in the past.

---

5   UN representative on Prevention of Violence Against Women draft committee, Yangon, 15 June 2021.

6   Leading women's rights activist, Yangon, 30 July 2020.

When I started working, we didn't use the term violence for this issue. We understood it as the family problem. It was until not many years later that I realized that the issues we dealt with in the past were violence-related issues. Nowadays, women's organizations and the government is dealing with these issues. The cases are now more visible. We were not equipped with this type of knowledge before.[7]

In 2014, the first qualitative research using a rigorous methodological approach provided an initial understanding of patterns of violence, including both marital rape by women's intimate partners and rape by strangers (Miedema, San Shwe and Aye Thiri Kyaw 2016a; San Shwe, Miedema and Aye Thiri Kyaw 2015). The author of this chapter was part of the first qualitative research approved by the government team that employed rigorous methodological and ethical research practices. It is important to note that there was a distrust of foreign ideas and influence during the research period. The research team members were often informally reminded by government officials not to interpret the research findings in a way that would be critical of the government. This sentiment was echoed by our respondent's reflection that the government wanted to suppress the number of cases visible on paper – but was not committed to reducing the actual number of cases.

> Our situation is desperate. Even [in relation to] obvious cases like rape, advocacy groups have to justify a comprehensive definition of rape. As we can see, the data for sexual violence is low because the definition is very narrow. Officials are afraid that if the definition of rape is revised, the rate of sexual violence will rise dramatically. They are only interested in suppressing the numbers, not in the main causes of rape.[8]

In interviews we carried out, it was pointed out that the delay in the passing of the Prevention of Violence Against Women law (PoVAW) was partly because some policy makers were not in favour of the PoVAW bill (Metro this volume). Through the interviews, respondents told us about their experiences of working with different actors in the law-drafting process. The draft law was first proposed by the Ministry of Social Welfare with technical support from civil society actors and the international community. As a follow-up, different ministries and departments in the government that had conservative tendencies also contributed to the reviews of the proposed draft

---

7   Psychological support counsellor, Yangon, 12 June 2020.
8   Leading women's rights activist, Yangon, 30 July 2020.

law. Respondents who were involved in this lengthy law-drafting process told us that working with different stakeholders meant that they had to strike a balance: 'There were two competing versions of the PoVAW bill: one that was favoured by the government and one that was favoured by the [women's] rights groups. Which of the two versions would come out at the end was unknown.'[9] They explained that the inputs from multiple departments watered down the contents of the original proposal, but said that they had stood firm about maintaining the key protection (of rights) elements in the draft bill.

It has been noted that male reception to the VAW also needs to be considered since men are hesitant to cooperate in such arrangements. Rather than seeing the law as being about protecting women, it is seen as a potential threat to men's existing authority and to the traditional family structure. A respondent with extensive VAW policy advocacy told me that 'even senior government officials – who are mostly men – see the bill as something privileging women. They fear that their male authority could be challenged by the proposed bill.'[10]

Many officials are conservative, and they expressed long-held conservative views around IPV, in particular marital rape, portraying these issues as too 'foreign'. The text in the bill states that 'marital rape means when a husband rapes his wife'. However, there is a deep-rooted belief in Myanmar that the husband is the lawful 'owner' of the wife, and that this gives a man the power to punish his wife if she refuses to have sex with him when he wants. Therefore, the text in PoVAW bill challenges the husband's entitlement to sex, which has not been questioned before in Myanmar culture. According to the respondents, what was even more troubling was that this view was held even among some rights activists, whose job is to promote the women's freedom and gender equality. The most pervasive belief, which came up frequently during discussions in meetings about the prevention and protection of violence against women, related to attitudes towards wife-beating:

> We have the term *karma paing lin*, which means that the husband has ownership of his wife's body and sex. If a woman is not well-behaved, her husband can punish her by beating her, according to wide-spread

---

9   Leading women's rights and peace advocate, Yangon, 28 October 2020.
10 Leading women's rights activist, Yangon, 30 July 2020.

social beliefs. Even among the CSO groups working on women's rights and LGBT rights, this belief is deep-rooted.[11]

Historically, elite women in Myanmar have been known to reject gender inequality in Myanmar, instead asserting that western scholars misunderstand the Burmese form of feminism (Khaing 1984). Recent research suggests that this sentiment continues to be present among elite women, who reject the notion that forms of gender-based violence are a social problem (Barrow 2015). This resulted in debate in the context of the law-drafting process. Data from my interviews confirm that while patriarchy is a system that favours men and maintains male privilege, it has the support of both men and women. One respondent, who works for a shelter service for women victims, told me that 'even women in the official meetings resist the PoVAW bill; they fear that the new bill will give power to women and that men will feel threatened by this.'[12]

The Myanmar constitution defines women based on their sex and it therefore rejects the existence of transgender women. Transgender women are often the victims of the corrupt legal system, through the so-called 'shadow laws', formally known as the Rangoon Police Act of 1899 and the Police Act of 1945. These permit the police to punish 'any person found between sunset and sunrise, within the precincts of any dwelling-house or other building whatsoever, or on board any vessel, without being able satisfactorily to account for his presence' (Chua and Gilbert 2015). In addition, Section 377 of the penal code, a British colonial legacy, still penalizes same-sex sexual relations. Furthermore, for cultural reasons conservative policymakers oppose any discussion of protection for transgender women. A longtime activist who served on the VAWG technical working group stated that:

> When we propose that transgender women be includes in the category of 'women', the policy makers are not comfortable. They comment that this is against Myanmar culture. They only abide by the Myanmar 2008's constitution definition of women based on her 'sex'. The penal code and the Myanmar constitution is the bible for them.[13]

This binary and fixed understanding of 'sex' served to discriminate against transgender women in the drafting of the bill and this shows how hard it is

---

11 Leading women's rights activist, Yangon, 30 July 2020.
12 Shelter service provider, Yangon, 1 July 2020.
13 Shelter service provider, Yangon, 1 July 2020.

to subvert dominant ideas about what is 'appropriate'. As there is no legal recognition for same-sex relationships and no mention of transgender women in the bill, any mistreatment or oppression that occurs in relation to them will go unrecognized. Transgender women's vulnerability to violence in romantic relationships is understudied in Myanmar. Existing research from other countries suggests, however, that domestic violence incidents are more common in relationships where one or both partners are transgender or gay (Greenberg 2012). As a result, a lack of legal protection can place transgender women in a vulnerable position in abusive relationships, and abusers can use these relationship to exert control over them. Not being protected by the law therefore renders them vulnerable to violence. The women (including transgender women) of Myanmar remain unprotected from the threat of violence.

Since the women's groups announced their withdrawal from the VAW technical working groups, the passage of the PoVAW law has remained an unfinished business. However, in his speech on Myanmar Women's Day on 3 July 2021, Senior General Min Aung Hlaing stated that efforts were being made to enact the PoVAW law. The Ministry of Social Welfare, Relief and Resettlement (MoSWRR) has been advancing the PoVAW legislation processes through regular internal ministry meetings as well as meetings with related ministerial departments. The timing of this dramatic move is problematic, not least given that the PoVAW bill has experienced continued resistance since its drafting was initiated in 2014. An analyst interviewed after the coup offered some insights:

> The SAC [State Administrative Council] knows that the PoVAW law was backed by the international community as well as by WROs [women's rights organizations] in Myanmar. Therefore, it is likely that the SAC may use the PoVAW law as a tool to gain political credit.[14]

Thus, advocacy around women's rights is always tied up with specific power dynamics, which do not always serve the interests of women. As this example shows, it may instead further the intertwined oppressiveness of military and patriarchy in Myanmar.

---

14 Analyst working on women's rights and governance, Yangon, 16 June 2022.

Conclusion

The goal of this chapter has been to provide an account of how different women's groups used different strategies to advocate for an end to VAW during the 10 years of Myanmar's transition. It began with a brief background to women's movements and activism in Myanmar. Historically, the women's rights movement was latent until 1999. The founding of the WLB in 1999 and the emergence of the women's network GEN in the aftermath of cyclone Nargis provided platforms, once the transition began to take place, for women's rights activists to work together towards achieving a shared vision for gender equality, while focusing their policy advocacy with different strategies. The chapter went on to examine how different women's movements reacted to the changes brought by the democratic transition. While exiled women's groups focused on international advocacy on VAW, women's groups inside the country targeted the state and pushed for legal reforms.

This chapter is a case study of PoVAW specifically, using it as a way to discuss how women's activism has changed over time in relation to shifting power dynamics and in different political contexts. The draft PoVAW bill, which was introduced for public consultation in 2020, turned a new page in the advancement of women's rights in Myanmar, ending almost six years during which the law was being drafted. The democratic transition in Myanmar provided opportunities for women's rights activists to participate in discussions on government policies and reforms. These opportunities were used to translate aspirations into the development of the PoVAW draft law. That said, Myanmar's democratic transition also saw a rise in the expression of views relating to traditional expectations of women as well as increasing nationalism. During the transition, exposure to the world's liberal views revealed an emerging identity crisis. The passing of the protection of race and religion laws demonstrates, to an extent, that nationalist views are widespread in Myanmar. The rise of nationalist views delayed the process of passing of PoVAW law in Myanmar. This could be taken as a lesson for the future, both in Myanmar and elsewhere. Moreover, evidence was sometimes used to satisfy political and vested interests. The lack of national prevalence survey data on violence against women in the country also highlights the limited capacity to gather evidence to inform policies. Women's rights advocacy groups took the space of VAW policy advocacy and became a driving force of PoVAW, using this as an opportunity to systematically show the magnitude of the problem. This led to the publication of the PoVAW bill.

The coup d'état on 1 February 2021 has reversed the ten-year-long VAW policy advocacy in Myanmar. The coup has grave policy implications in relaion to women rights, in particular in relation to the issue of VAW in Myanmar. Meanwhile, the PoVAW Bill, which was not adopted, remains in limbo, as women's groups have firmly opposed providing technical support to the military regime, which is an institution known internationally for its perpetration of sexual violence. As a result, survivors and victims of domestic violence continue to remain unprotected.

References

Aye Thiri Kyaw. 2020. 'From Mothers to Daughters: Intergenerational Transmission of Father-to-Mother Violence in Myanmar.' London: London School of Economics and Political Science.

Bahu, M. 2011. 'Women's movements, representation and civil society.' In S. Laurel Weldon (ed.), *How Social Movements Represent Disadvantaged Group*, pp. 129–148. Ann Arbor, MI: University of Michigan Press.

Barrow, A. 2015. 'Contested spaces during transition: Regime change in Myanmar and its implications for women.' *Cardozo Journal of Law and Gender* 22: 75–108.

Cairney, P. 2016. *The Politics of Evidence-Based Policy-Making*. Basingstoke: Palgrave Macmillan.

Chua, L. J. and D. Gilbert. 2015. 'Sexual orientation and gender identity minorities in transition: LGBT rights and activism in myanmar.' *Human Rights Quarterly* 37 (1): 1–28. Available at: doi.org/10.1353/hrq.2015.0016

Ellsberg, M., L. Heise, R. Peña, S. Agurto and A. Winkvist. 2001. 'Researching domestic violence against women: Methodological and ethical considerations.' *Studies in Family Planning* 32 (1): 1–16.

Faxon, H., R. Furlong and M. Sabe Phyu. 2015. 'Reinvigorating resilience: violence against women, land rights and the women's peace movement in Myanmar.' *Gender & Development* 23(3): 463–479.

Gender Equality Network. 2015. "Behind the Silence: violence against women and their resilience in Myanmar. Yangon, Myanmar: Gender Equality Network.

————. 2018. " Ten years of progress towards gender equality in Myanmar, 2008–2018. Gender Equality Network, Yangon Myanmar.

Greenberg, K. 2012. 'Still hidden in the closet: Trans women and domestic violence.' *Berkeley Journal of Gender, Law and Justice* 27 (2) 196–251.

Hedström, J. 2016. 'We did not realize about the gender issues. So we thought it was a good idea: Gender roles in Burmese oppositional struggles.' *International Feminist Journal of Politics* 18: 61–79. Available at: doi.org/10.1080/14616742. 2015.1005516

Htun, M. and F. R. Jensenius. 2020. 'Political change, women's rights and public opinion on gender equality in Myanmar.' *European Journal of Development Research* 32 (2): 457–481. Available at: doi.org/10.1057/s41287-020-00266-z

Ikeya, C. 2013. 'The life and writings of a patriotic feminist: Independent Daw San of Burma.' In S. Blackburn and H. Ting (eds), *Women in Southeast Asian Nationalist Movements*. Singapore: NUS Press, 2013, 23–47.

Jaquette, J. S. 1994. 'Women's political participation and the prospects for democracy.' In *The Women's Movement in Latin America: Participation and Democracy*, pp. 223–238. Boulder: Westview Press. Second edition.

Khaing, M. M. 1984. *The World of Burmese Women*. London: Zed Books.

Khin Khin Mra and D. Livingstone. 2020. 'The winding path to gender equality in Myanmar.' In J. Chambers, C. Galloway and J. Liljeblad (eds), *Living with Myanmar*, pp. 243–264. Singapore: ISEAS Publishing.

Maber, E. J. T. 2016. 'Finding feminism, finding voice? Mobilising community education to build women's participation in Myanmar's political transition.' *Gender and Education* 28: 416–430. Available at: doi.org/10.1080/09540253. 2016.1167175

Miedema, S. S., San Shwe and Aye Thiri Kyaw. 2016a. 'Social inequalities, empowerment and women's transitions into abusive marriages: A case study from Myanmar.' *Gender and Society* 30 (4): 670–694. Available at: doi.org/10.1177/0891243216642394

Miedema, S. S. and Tharaphi Than. 2018. 'Myanmar debates women's rights amid evidence of pervasive sexual and domestic violence.' *The Conversation, Australia.* Available at: theconversation.com/myanmar-debates-womens-rights-amid-evidence-of-pervasive-sexual-and-domestic-violence-104536

Ministry of Social Wefare, Relief and Resettlement. 2013. *National Strategic Action Plan for the Advancement of Women (2013–2022)*. Naypyidaw, Myanmar: Department of Social Welfare.

Minoletti, P. 2014. *Women's Participation in the Subnational Governance of Myanmar.* In Subnational Governance in Myanmar Discussion Paper Series. Available at: doi.org/10.1017/CBO9781107415324.004

Olivius, E. 2019. 'Time to go home? The conflictual politics of diaspora return in the Burmese women's movement.' *Asian Ethnicity* 20 (2): 148–167. Available at: doi.org/10.1080/14631369.2018.1519387

Phillips, A. 2020. 'Does feminism need a conception of civil society?' In S. Chambers and W. Kymlicka (eds), *Alternative conceptions of civil society*, Princeton, NJ: Princeton University Press, 2020, pp. 71–89.

Richards, P. 2006. 'The politics of difference and women's rights: Lessons from Pobladoras and Mapuche women in Chile.' *Social Politics: International Studies in Gender, State, and Society* 13 (1): 1–29. Available at: doi.org/10.1093/sp/jxj003

Rochon, T. R. and D. A. Mazmanian. 1993. 'Social movements and the policy process.' *The Annals of the American Academy of Political and Social Science* 528 (1): 75–87. Available at: doi.org/10.1177/0002716293528001006

San Shwe, S. S. Miedema and Aye Thiri Kyaw. 2015. 'Application of international ethical and safety guidelines on conducting violence against women research within the Myanmar context: lessons learned and ways forward.' *Myanmar Health Sciences Research Journal* 27 (3) 232–238. Available at: www.myanmarhsrj.com/index.php?page=default

Schomerus, M. and H. Seckinelgin. 2015. 'Evidence-Based Policymaking in Myanmar? Considerations of a Post-Conflict Development Dilemma.' London: The London School of Economics and Political Science.

Tharaphi Than. 2015. *Women in Modern Burma*. London: Routledge.

UN WOMEN. 2013. *Domestic Violence Legislation and its Implementation: An Analysis for ASEAN Countries Based on International Standards and Good Practices*. Bangkok: UN Women.

Viterna, J. and K. M. Fallon. 2008. 'Democratization, women's movements, and gender-equitable states: A framework for comparison.' *Strategies* 73: 668–689.

Walton, M. J. and S. Hayward. 2014. 'Contesting Buddhist narratives: Democratization, nationalism and communal violence in Myanmar.' *Policy Studies* 71: 65.

Walton, M. J., M. Mckay and Khin Mar Mar Kyi. 2015. 'Women and Myanmar's "religious protection laws".' *The review of Faith & International Affairs* 13(4): 36–49. .

Waylen, G. 1994. 'Women and democratization: Conceptualizing gender relations in transition politics.' *World Politics* 46 (3): 327–354. Available at: doi.org/10.2307/2950685

Women's League of Burma. 1999. *The Founding and Development of the Women's League of Burma*. Mae Sot, Thailand: Women's League of Burma.

———. 2020. *Procedural and Substantive Suggestions*. Mae Sot, Thailand: Women's League of Burma.

CHAPTER 3

'My Father Is Strong and Smart, My Mother Is Helpful and Kind'

'Gender Harmony' and 'Gender Equality' in Myanmar's Curriculum Revision Process

Rosalie Metro

During Myanmar's quasi-democratic phase from 2010 to 2021, the education system – long neglected under the military regime – became a reform priority both for the government and for international development[1] partners. In 2016, the Myanmar Ministry of Education (MOE) began working with organizations including the Japan International Cooperation Agency (JICA) and United Nations Children's Fund (UNICEF) to revise basic education curricula, given that one goal of the National Education Strategic Plan (Myanmar MOE 2016a: 27) was that 'all school children develop knowledge, skills, attitudes and competencies that are relevant to their lives and to the socio-economic development needs of 21st century Myanmar'. In this chapter, I will examine how the kindergarten to third-grade textbooks released starting in 2016 provided a space for the contestation of ideologies around gender. Whereas international development organizations prioritized globalized ideologies they called 'social inclusion' and 'gender equality', textbooks developed by Myanmar's military regimes before 2010 (and still used in some higher grades) presented local conceptions of what I will call 'gender harmony'.

Therefore, the international and local consultants who developed the new curriculum faced the difficult task of appropriating the ideology of 'gender

---

1 I use "development" and "international development" in this chapter as a shorthand for a non-homogenous field of actors based in various locations in the Global North/West. I'll cite Gita Steiner-Khamsi (2014) to explain the power dynamic between these actors and the Global South/East societies they "develop." Suffice to say, for now, that "development" is not an entity, but a relationship that tends to homogenize the actors at the "developing" and "developed" ends of the spectrum.

equality' promoted by international development organizations in a way that accorded with ideals of 'gender harmony' and satisfied Myanmar's MOE. What has emerged from these tenuous collaborations is a hybridized representation of women and girls – a collection of texts and images that mostly reinforce traditional images of 'gender harmony'; occasionally showcase 'gender equality'; and sometimes interpret this concept in ways particular to Myanmar. I leave both 'gender equality' and 'gender harmony' in quotations throughout this chapter, to indicate that they are ideas, not realities – I am not discussing actual gender equality (e.g., educational, economic, and health outcomes), or actual gender harmony (copacetic relations between men and women), but rather rhetoric and representation. It is also important to note that the ideological goals of textbook authors are not necessarily realized in the classroom; the relationships between texts and their readers are complex. Therefore, I do not make empirical claims about how texts affect students, but speculate, rather, about the intended and unintended messages that these texts send.

In order to do this, I use Critical Discourse Analysis (Fairclough 2003) to compare the former and new textbooks' treatment of gender. To interpret this comparison, I use Gita Steiner-Khamsi's (2014) ideas about how local actors in the Global South/East receive, resist and translate educational policies and practices that derive from the Global North/West. I conclude that the hybridized representation of gender sends contradictory messages that ultimately reinforce sexist social structures of 'gender harmony' and gendered militarism. These textbooks show how gendered roles and norms were reproduced and changed during Myanmar's conflict-affected quasi-democratic phase. Given the military coup in 2021, these textbooks may become artifacts of a relatively brief period of cooperation between the Myanmar government and international development organizations. Or they may be superseded in a yet-to-be-imagined democratic school system. In either case, the textbooks have already made an impact, having been used by hundreds of thousands of children throughout the country.

Reception, Resistance and Translation of Development Ideology in Education

Myanmar's government curricula prior to 2010 have been the subject of several scholarly works, most of which examined their portrayal of history, ethnicity and national identity (Cheesman 2002; Metro 2019a; Salem-

Gervais and Metro 2012; Treadwell 2013; Zar Ni 1998).[2] These authors document how schooling in Myanmar has been used to promote the ideological goals of dominant social and political groups – specifically, those of Burman, Buddhist, male military leaders. These insights are situated in a wider field of curriculum studies, within which researchers have pointed out how education has been used as a political tool both in Asia (Cha, Ham and Lee 2018; Lall and Vickers 2009) and globally (Sleeter 2018; Ladson-Billings 2016). These studies grow out of theoretical work positing that schooling is never politically or socially neutral but is rather embedded in power structures that favour dominant groups (Apple 1979; Bourdieu and Passeron 1977).

While curriculum always contains ideology, the colonial encounter and the ongoing divide between the global North/West and the global South/East has shaped which ideologies are perpetuated in schools. During their colonial rule of Burma, the British used schools as an arm of the state in order to promote acceptance of their power, causing Burmese nationalists to refer to the British system as 'slave education' (Metro 2019a: 20). This colonial dynamic continues today, as international development agencies and intergovernmental organizations based in the global North/West *position themselves* as the bringers of 'modernity', 'critical thinking', 'human rights', and 'social inclusion' (including 'gender equality'). The implementation of each of these terms is debatable; just because the North/West lays claim to this intellectual territory does not mean that they enact these ideals in their own societies. Yet they package these concepts for export *as if* that were the case. In the context of Myanmar, I have referred to this process as 'educational missionization' because of the moral certainty and fervour characterizing the view of the 'missionaries' – that their brand of education is superior to anything anyone from Myanmar could produce (Metro 2014: 163).

Gita Steiner-Khamsi (2014), a scholar of international and comparative education, has developed a model for conceptualizing the neo-colonial dynamics at work in the international circulation of educational policies and practices. She describes how countries in the global North/West 'lend' educational policies and practices, while those in the global South/East are positioned as 'borrowing' them. She draws attention to the financial stakes

---

2   For an analysis of ethnicity and national identity in the new textbooks, please see Metro (2020).

involved in this transaction: 'As a requirement for receiving grants or loans at the programmatic level, policy borrowing in developing countries is coercive and unidirectional. Reforms are transferred from the global North/West to the global South/East.' (ibid. 2014: 156) In the case I describe here, as part of curriculum revision processes Myanmar 'borrows' ideologies such as 'social inclusion' and 'gender equality' from international actors based in the US, Japan and the EU. This is not to say that indigenous ideas of gender equality don't exist – I will argue that 'gender harmony' holds that place – just that, in transactions of educational policy and practice, Myanmar is positioned as a borrower rather than a lender.

However, this borrowing is not a straightforward, uncontested process. Steiner-Khamsi (2014) describes what makes educational practices attractive to borrowing countries like Myanmar as 'reception' (ibid. 2014); I find it useful to expand this term to include the ways in which borrowing countries adopt practices wholesale. Steiner-Khamsi (2014: 162) also notes that borrowing countries may actively or passively reject what is being offered, through 'resistance'; in these cases, there may be a 'reinforcement of existing structures'. Or borrowing countries may stake out a middle ground in which they 'translate' educational policies through indigenization of supposed international 'best practices'. These three strategies – reception, translation, and resistance – can be used to classify a spectrum of responses to intervention in education from the global North/West.

There are few analyses of Myanmar's post-2010 curriculum reform (Metro 2019b), and none that examine gender specifically. There are brief references to the portrayal of gender roles on pre-2010 citizenship textbooks in Brooke Treadwell's dissertation (2013: 157–158) and in Nick Cheesman's Master's thesis (2002), and articles on other topics point out that a limited conception of women's roles appears in textbooks (Faxon and Pyo Let Han 2018: para. 2). More recently, several edited volumes (Lopes Cardozo and Maber 2019; Chambers, Galloway and Liljeblad 2020) have included theoretical material related to gender and curriculum, but as Shah and Lopes Cardozo note, 'the current curricula, teachers' guides and resource books have not been assessed in terms of [...] gender sensitivities' (2019: 82). I fill this gap by using recent theoretical material on gender and curriculum as well as broader scholarly work on gender roles in Burma/Myanmar (Ikeya 2011; Tharaphi Than 2014), to add to a curriculum studies perspective on gender in Myanmar textbooks.

Analysing Curricula and Their Production

I conducted this investigation by performing Critical Discourse Analysis (CDA) on the kindergarten through third-grade textbooks and teachers' guides released since 2016, with comparisons to those produced earlier. CDA is a method that involves examining images and texts, including word choice, sentence structure, grammar and use of figurative language, in order to read between the lines for relationships of inclusion, exclusion, domination, and oppression (Fairclough 2003). CDA is not a search for objective truths; other analysts would likely arrive at different conclusions, depending on their prior knowledge and biases. In other words, positionality matters. I am a white woman from the US who has learned to read and write Burmese, but my first language is English, and my identity influences what I find. My conclusions are provisional – I invite readers to confirm, disagree with or elaborate on my interpretations of the texts.

In order to understand my conclusions, it is also important to consider the conditions under which these texts were produced. In 2012, the Comprehensive Education Sector Review process was launched by President Thein Sein in collaboration with the MOE. The MOE was supported by 'development partners' including the Asian Development Bank, Australian Aid, Denmark, the UK Department for International Development, the European Union, JICA, UNESCO, UNICEF and the World Bank (Comprehensive Education Sector Review 2018) – although, as Steiner-Khamsi's (2014) work reminds us, these 'partnerships' are far from equal. These agencies helped to carry out a Rapid Assessment and In-Depth Analysis, leading to a Five Year Plan – the National Education Strategic Plan (NESP), released in 2016.

Tellingly, this plan does not include the word 'gender'. It references the need for greater equity, but this term seems to be used only in connection with 'ethnic languages and cultures' (Myanmar MOE 2016a: 34). The plan includes the goal that 'all children, boys and girls, access primary, middle, and high schools' (Myanmar MOE 2016a: 35), and it notes the need to 'redesign the curriculum' with a 'focus on 21st century skills,' (Myanmar MOE 2016a: 19); however, the latter concept is undefined. Thus, the NESP does not include a specific mandate for increasing 'gender equality' in the curriculum. The NESP thus falls in line with other government documents that either neglect to mention gender equality, or, whether explicitly or implicitly, negate it.[3]

---

3   See, for instance, Khin Khin Mra and Deborah Livingstone's (2020) explanation of how the 2008 Constitution enshrines male privilege.

Yet 'gender equality' has been at the forefront of the priorities of what is usually referred to as international development. The United Nations (UN Women n.d.: para. 2) defines 'gender equality' as 'the equal rights, responsibilities and opportunities of women and men and girls and boys.' One of the UN's 17 Sustainable Development Goals is to 'achieve gender equality and empower all women and girls' (UN n.d.). The World Bank launched an initiative for 'gender equality and development' in Myanmar (World Bank 2013). UNICEF (n.d.) noted that more than 60 per cent of underage child workers were girls, and that this labour might prevent them from accessing school. JICA (n.d.) also places gender issues at the centre of the development work it pursues in Myanmar, and notes that while there is not a large discrepancy in enrolment of males and females at the primary level, and women even outnumber men in tertiary education, those relatively high participation rates have not led to the expansion of employment opportunities for women (JICA 2013: ii). Moreover, the World Bank's $100-million-dollar Inclusive Access and Quality Education project, launched in 2014, listed 'gender and human development' as its primary theme (World Bank 2021). While international development organizations differ in their structures and approaches, the top-down nature of the funding process means that terms like 'gender equality' become ubiquitous, even as their meaning is negotiated on the ground. In this chapter, I use the shorthand 'the ideology of gender equality promoted by "international development"' to convey this ubiquity, even while recognizing that development is a heterogeneous category, and that the term carries multiple meanings.

Thus the process of developing new curricula reflects an ideological back-and-forth among local and international actors. While individuals within the MOE may have a range of views on 'gender equality', this priority was not an explicit part of the MOE's vision for revising the curriculum as part of the NESP. However, 'gender equality' entered into the equation; this may have been because the MOE delegated the duty of revising the curriculum to development partners UNICEF (kindergarten curriculum), JICA (primary curriculum), and ADB (secondary curriculum). These organizations then used their own personnel as well as the services of local and international consultants, who created the new textbooks by selecting some texts and images from pre-existing textbooks, generating new texts and images, and adapting pre-existing texts or images. The MOE then either approved the curriculum or requested changes. Finally, the development partners evaluated the new curriculum to see if it matched the goals and priorities they had brought to the process (including 'gender equality').

This is, at least, what I have been able to gather about the process, which is not fully transparent. I entered this process when I took on a consultancy with the World Bank in 2018, in which I evaluated the newly-created primary curriculum for its potential to promote 'social inclusion' (including 'gender equality'), 'human rights' and 'peace'.[4] However, it is important to clarify that this is not an ethnographic study of the experiences of development workers, MOE personnel or consultants, and that I have had limited and anecdotal access to their negotiations. Such a study would be fascinating, but difficult to conduct given the delicate relationships involved. Instead, my data is what emerges from the black box of intra-and inter-organizational discussions: the textbooks themselves.

'Gender Harmony' in Myanmar's pre-2010 Curriculum

Myanmar's textbooks were not a blank slate on which development partners could inscribe their ideology of 'gender equality'. Brooke Treadwell (2013: 157–158) has pointed out that military-era textbooks under-represent women and foment sexist stereotypes. I agree, but I would argue that they do so in a particular way. Pre-revision textbooks[5] contained an ideology I will call 'gender harmony', in which men and women play parallel yet unequal roles, working together to serve society's needs. The most iconic representation of this ideology is the map of Myanmar surrounded by smiling male–female couples dressed in the costumes associated with each of the 'national races'; this

---

4   I have written elsewhere (Metro 2019b) about the ethical imperative for scholars of education to be more transparent about taking on the double role of consultant and researcher, because I think we need to examine how our 'expertise' is part of the borrowing/lending relationships that Steiner-Khamsi (2014) describes. This transparency is important in understanding the financial structures of international development, as well as the unequal exchange of ideas that takes place. Therefore, I feel it is important to acknowledge that I initially examined gender in these textbooks as part of a consultancy, and that I did so because 'gender equality' was a priority for the World Bank.

5   I examine pre-revision textbooks produced from 2007 to 2016, although there were minor changes in content during this time. From some transplanted content, it seems that, in revising curricula, not only were the most recent version of textbooks used as raw material, but also earlier editions.

Figure 3.1. Third Grade English textbook (2019) showing male pilot and female doctor.

Figure 3.2. Kindergarten Myanmar Reader (2009) showing male soldier and female civilian carrying rocks.

Figure 3.3. First Grade Myanmar Reader (2017) showing male soldier and female civilian carrying vegetables.

Figure 3.4. Second Grade English textbook (2018) showing a girl's ambition to be a nurse.

Figure 3.6. Second Grade Social Studies textbook (2018) showing Queen Shinsawpu's rule.

Figure 3.5. First Grade Social Studies textbook (2017) showing King Bayinnaung.

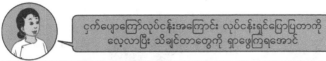

Figure 3.7. Third Grade Social Studies textbook (2019) showing female banana business owner.

Figure 3.8. Third Grade Social Studies textbook (2019) showing banana business workers.

Figure 3.9. Second Grade Myanmar Reader (2016) showing poem 'Our Mummy'.

Figure 3.10. Second Grade Myanmar Reader (2016) showing poem 'Our Daddy'.

Figure 3.11. Second Grade Life Skills textbook (2018) showing a girl objecting to unwanted touching.

ဆုံးမစာ

၁။ တန်းရည်အရက်၊
တစ်ချက်ကိုကင်း၊
ဘိန်းသင်းကစော်၊
လှေဲ့ဝါသောက်စား၊
ပြုသူများ၊
စီးပွားဖျက်မည်သိ။

၂။ လေ့ဝံမကိုင်၊
ရှိုင်ထွေခေးကာ၊
နေရာကျောခင်း၊
ဖွင်းရှိဖင့်စား၊
ပြုသူများ၊
စီးပွားဖျက်မည်သိ။

၃။ လူသွမ်းလူသောင်၊
လူသူးတောင်းဟု၊
မကောင်းမိတ်ဖက်၊
လူသူဖျက်နှင့်၊
ပေါင်းလျက်ယှဉ်သွား၊
ပြုသူများ၊
စီးပွားဖျက်မည်သိ။

Figure 3.12. Third Grade Myanmar Reader (2016) showing male figure giving moral instruction to male and female children.

ဆရာရသေ့၏ တမာရွက်ဥပမာ

Figure 3.13. Third Grade Myanmar Reader (2016) showing girl bending her body to show respect for an older male teacher.

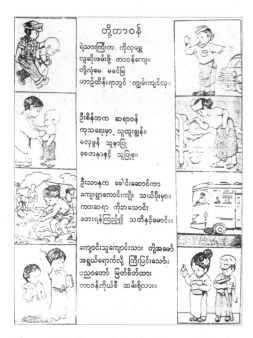

Figure 3.14. Second Grade Myanmar Reader (2007) showing poem 'Our responsibilities'.

occurs repeatedly in textbooks. This image is expanded upon in the third-grade geography and history textbook (Myanmar MOE 2007a: 4–11), where photographs of these couples appear on sequential pages alongside the characteristics of each group. In this sequence, 'gender harmony' and what could be called 'ethnic harmony' (in which ethnic groups also play parallel yet unequal roles, with Burmans leading and other ethnicities following) are fused to offer a vision of Myanmar society in which ethnic groups and genders peacefully coexist.

Another key representation of 'gender harmony' occurs in the pre-revision second-grade Myanmar Reader (Myanmar MOE 2007b: 50), which shows two columns of drawings alongside a poem called 'Our Responsibilities' (Figure 3.14). On the left, a male police officer apprehends a 'bad person'; on the right, a female officer directs traffic. On the left, a male doctor examines a patient; on the right, a female nurse takes a patient's temperature. In the bottom right, a female teacher and a male engineer provide role models for male and female students described in the poem.

Notably, this last image also conveys 'generational harmony' (in which younger and older people play parallel yet unequal roles), which is reinforced in other images. For instance, in the former third-grade Myanmar reader (Myanmar MOE 2016b: 11), a young girl bends her body to show respect to an older male teacher (Figure 3.13). We see how these 'harmonies' around age and gender reinforce each other, accumulating hegemonic power. In other images, a 'military–civilian harmony' is suggested alongside 'gender harmony.' Treadwell (2013: 158) draws attention to an illustration from the former civics textbook, of a male soldier lifting a basket of rocks and dirt onto the head of a woman who will carry it away, apparently as part of an infrastructure project (Figure 3.2). Here, the relationship between military and civilian is also parallel but unequal, suggesting a mutuality that is, at the very least, debatable.

One final example of 'gender harmony' is the parallel poems 'Our Mummy' and 'Our Daddy' (Figures 3.9 and 3.10), which are in the second-grade Myanmar reader (Myanmar MOE 2016b: 4 and 6). The mother is shown caring for children and cooking, while the father is shown working in the rice fields and earning money. These representations of gender, along with the others discussed, convey the idea that women and men play distinct roles in society. In general, men are shown in higher-status jobs (doctors, engineers, soldiers). While women are occasionally portrayed as doctors (higher status), men are never shown as nurses (lower status). And although women are sometimes represented in male-dominated fields such as policing, they are not shown doing the more confrontational work of apprehending suspects, but rather the physically demanding yet ostensibly peaceful work of directing traffic. There is an illusion of parity – the suggestion that women aren't inferior to men, just different, and due respect in their own right – but this illusion is belied by the fact that women are almost always shown in lower-status positions.

The four dimensions of harmony that I have described, related to gender, ethnicity, age and civil-military relations, work together to create a vision of a well-ordered society in which each person 'knows their place'. In contrast, the ideology of 'gender equality' promoted by development shows, as we shall see, women taking on the same roles as men; taking on high-status roles including those outside of the 'caring professions'; and disrupting a 'harmony' that depends on them accepting lower status.

Analysing Gender in Myanmar's post-2016 Curriculum

Resistance

Adherence to the 'gender harmony' model – cases in which pre-revision representations of gender roles are reproduced in new textbooks – shows resistance to the ideology of 'gender equality' promoted by development. Resistance is the overwhelming pattern that I found in the new textbooks. Women and girls are under-represented overall, and, when they are shown, they are most often portrayed in caretaking roles, rather than in positions of influence and power. For instance, when 19 occupations are described in the new third-grade English textbook, only three of the people shown (a nurse, a teacher and a policewoman) are female, whereas the farmers, doctors and members of other professions are all male (Myanmar MOE 2019a: Lesson 16). A poem in the second-grade Morality and Civics textbook describes a father working outside the home and a mother cooking (Myanmar MOE 2018c: 53). The women in the first-grade Social Studies textbook are mothers, teachers and nurses, whereas men are shown as doctors, engineers, soldiers, sailors and police officers (Myanmar MOE 2017b: 6–7; 14–15; 30). Likewise, the third-grade Social Studies textbook shows only male farmers (Myanmar MOE 2019c: 25–26), although in fact women are deeply engaged in agriculture (see Faxon's chapter in this book). Moreover, the cartoon teachers who appear on many pages of the textbooks are much more often female, especially in lower grades (which are considered less prestigious and yield lower salaries) (see Lopes Cardozo and Maber 2019 and Lall 2020 for more on the gendered nature of the teaching profession).

Interestingly, the roles of men seem to have been slightly expanded from previous textbooks (they are portrayed as artists, dancers and hairdressers), yet women's roles remain relatively confined. For instance, the second-grade English textbook shows two cartoons in which a boy and girl discuss their occupations (Figure 3.4). The boy is linked with the occupations pilot, engineer and artist, while the girl expresses the desire to be a nurse in both cartoons (Myanmar MOE 2018a: 6). This lack of parity is echoed in the third-grade English (Myanmar MOE 2019a) textbook, which includes the sentence 'My father is a pilot. He is strong and smart. My mother is a doctor. She is helpful and kind.' (ibid.: 8; see Figure 3.1) I chose these words as the title of this chapter because reversing the statement ('My mother is a pilot. She is strong and smart. My father is a doctor. He is helpful and kind') would disrupt 'gender harmony' by revealing that the women are confined in a way that men are not – men *are* portrayed as helpful, kind doctors in other parts of the curriculum, but women are *never* portrayed as smart, strong pilots. Similarly, the second-grade Science (Myanmar MOE 2018d: 6) textbook uses the example 'A boy talks loudly. A girl talks quietly.'[6] in its discussion of sound waves. Quiet, timid boys do appear in other parts of the curriculum, but a girl talking loudly would be too disruptive to 'gender harmony'. Across the curriculum, boys and men are

---

6   All translations of Burmese-language portions of textbooks are my own. I ask forgiveness for any misinterpretations.

usually shown as powerful, strong and aggressive, while girls and women are *always* portrayed as gentle, kind and quiet.

Translation

There are some cases in which the ideology of 'gender equality' promoted by development seems to have been adapted to accord with local norms. Some nearly identical images have been transplanted from the former to the new textbooks with only slight changes. The image of the woman and soldier reappears in the first-grade Myanmar Reader (Myanmar MOE 2017a: 86) (Figure 3.3), although this time the woman's basket contains vegetables. This image could be read in two ways. The soldier could be helping the woman shoulder her burden. Alternatively, he could be burdening her with what he cannot accomplish by himself. The ideologies of 'gender harmony' and 'military–civilian harmony' would encourage the first interpretation. Indeed, the replacement of rocks with vegetables seems designed to pull the reader toward the more benign interpretation; the soldier is not overseeing forced labour, he's just helping a lady get to the market. Because many images were reproduced exactly, it seems that there was a concerted effort to adapt this particular image to the ideologies of development – not just the ideology of 'gender equality' but also that of 'peace'. Neither of these condone soldiers making women carry rocks on their heads. Ironically, in changing rocks into vegetables, the curriculum tones down one of the rare occasions where a woman's physical strength is showcased.

Another example of 'translation' is the addition of Queen Shinsawpu to the third-grade Social Studies textbook. In the former third-grade Geography and History textbook (Myanmar MOE 2016c), all of the seven historical figures described (including Kings Anawrahta, Bayinnaung, and Kyansittha) were male military leaders. By comparison, of the nine leaders described across the first-, second-, and third-grade Social Studies textbooks, only one, Queen Shinsawpu, is female. Although she is included, her portrayal sets her apart from the other leaders, who are praised for their bravery and military prowess – for instance, Figure 3.5 shows King Bayinnaung on a horse, carrying a sword and leading an army. In contrast, Queen Shinsawpu (Figure 3.6) is credited with making the kingdom of Hanthawadi 'peaceful and pleasant' under her rule (Myanmar MOE 2018e: 44).

The role of the 'powerful woman' is adapted in an interesting way for modern times. The third-grade Social Studies textbook introduces the female owner of a fried banana business (Myanmar MOE 2019c: 13). This portrayal is worth attention, since it shows the intersection of ideologies around gender and class. The owner is portrayed, in a cartoon drawing, as a wealthy woman, through the fact that she wears gold earrings, a necklace, and bracelets (in contrast to the unadorned teacher who introduces her statement) (see Figure 3.7). She explains that she pays her workers ten to twelve thousand kyat per day – more than twice the current minimum wage of 4800 kyat – so that they can have a good standard of living. While she is clearly an invented character (there is no photograph of her), her workers are real people who appear in photographs of what is apparently an actual fried banana operation. In Figure 3.8, we see a male worker doing the more strenuous physical labour of stirring the bananas in the pan full of hot oil, while the two female workers then sort and pack the fried bananas for sale. The fictional female owner of the fried banana business seems to be a concession to the idea, in the context of development, that women *should* own businesses.

The overall message about gender roles is that women can occupy positions of power if they have high class status; and if, in holding positions of power, they maintain their caring personae (seen here as paying a relatively high wage, out of concern for the lives of the workers). 'Class harmony' brings together gender, age and ethnic harmony in an ideology that binds people together and fixes their roles. As one dimension of harmony (gender) is challenged, the others are reinforced. For instance, we do not see here a young, poor, non-Burman woman exerting power over an old, rich, Burman man. Yet showing this mature, potentially Burman, wealthy woman exerting power over a young, potentially non-Burman, poor man is acceptable. This mixed portrayal of women's roles shows the 'translation' of ideologies of 'gender equality' by illustrating an additive approach; former roles have not been erased, but rather complicated by the addition of new material.

Reception

In some cases, the ideology of 'gender equality' promoted by development has been adopted wholesale into the curriculum. For instance, a lone female engineer appears in the third-grade English book (Myanmar MOE 2019a: 7). But it is the Life Skills textbooks, which have no antecedent in the previous curriculum, that illustrate this dynamic most clearly, because there was no existing material on which to base the lessons.

The most obvious example of this new ideology in the Life Skills text-books is the lessons on the prevention of sexual abuse. The second-grade Life Skills textbook instructs children to protest when they are the object of unwanted touching, no matter who has touched them (see Figure 3.11). A cartoon on this page shows a young girl saying 'Don't touch me, I don't like that!' to an older man who is patting her hips and behind (Myanmar MOE 2018b: 32–33). The lesson instructs children to tell a trusted adult if someone touches them in an inappropriate way. The topic of sexual abuse is taken up again in a third-grade Life Skills lesson called 'You Need to Object', which includes a news story about a case of child abuse (Myanmar MOE 2019b: 18).

These lessons are striking because they represent a departure from messages in previous textbooks, which emphasized the duty of young people to follow the guidance of elders, and which portrayed girls in subservient positions to male leaders (see Figure 3.12). Thus, the new lessons on the prevention of sexual abuse of young girls disrupt both 'gender harmony' and 'generational harmony'. In this case, the priority of preventing violence against girls and women, supported by development partners, has not only been incorporated into the curriculum but has increasingly become part of local discourses outside of school. Aye Thiri Kyaw's chapter in this volume explores, for example, the efforts made to pass a Prevention of Violence Against Women bill in the transitional era. Furthermore, in 2019, the highly publicized case of the rape of a three-year-old girl pseudonymously called 'Victoria' prompted widespread outrage (BBC News 2019). From 2017 to 2019, the number of rapes reported increased by 50 per cent, and, in nearly two thirds of the 2018 cases, the victim was a child (BBC News 2019: 15). This increase in reporting of sexual violence against women and children does not necessarily indicate that such attacks are increasing, but that the stigma around reporting them has been reduced. It is notable that the most significant example of 'gender equality' in textbooks coincides with – or may have even been preceded by – a wider shift in social attitudes. This suggests that the Myanmar Ministry of Education 'received' what the Myanmar public was, in fact, ready for, while rejecting or translating 'gender equality' in other cases.

Challenging, Reproducing, and Transforming
Gender Roles: Possibilities for the Future

Overall, my examination of these new textbooks shows a slightly increased discourse of 'gender equality' alongside ongoing representations of 'gender harmony', which is in turn supported by other ideological 'harmonies' around age, class, ethnicity and military–civilian relations. Rare examples in textbooks show that women can break out of subservience or the domestic sphere, but these instances are contradicted by the much more frequent images of women shown in limited, caretaking roles, much as they were portrayed in the former textbooks. I would like to conclude by situating these findings within the literature on women in Myanmar/Burma, within scholarship on 'global development' practices, and within the current post-coup moment.

The way in which powerful women are portrayed in new textbooks accords with Tharaphi Than's (2014) challenge to the notion, popular both in Burma and internationally, that women in Burma enjoy relatively high status. She notes that 'very few powerful Burmese women exist' and that 'the few there are help to construct the notion of Burmese women's high status, thereby inevitably silencing the majority of "unequal" and disempowered women' (Tharaphi Than 2014: 1). Thus, the banana business owner in the third-grade Social Studies textbook is portrayed as having financial and social power, but her existence does not empower most women – any more than Queen Shinsawpu does (or for that matter, any more than does Aung San Suu Kyi – who does not appear in these textbooks). Moreover, the confinement of all of these women to the 'motherly' side of leadership roles places them solidly amongst most other women in the new textbooks, who are shown cooking, cleaning, caring for children, nursing or teaching.

To place these insights in the context of the '4 Rs' framework for sustainable peacebuilding in education used by Lopes Cardozo and Maber (2019: 22), the curriculum shows more recognition of women and gender issues, with limited improvements to representation, redistribution and reconciliation. Showing more women in textbooks is not necessarily a step toward gender equality if women are mostly shown in roles with limited power (e.g. as elementary school teachers) and if the few exceptions are tokens supposedly indicating parity where little exists.

This gendered division of labour cannot be understood without taking into account Myanmar's conflict-affected setting; it is enmeshed in this. Jenny Hedström (2020: 2) uses the term 'militarized social reproduction' to describe 'the everyday emotional, material and symbolic labour undertaken by women within the household and the non-state or parastate armed group in communities embroiled in civil wars'. Not only does militarized social reproduction occur in households associated with non-state or parastate armed groups such as the Kachin Independence Army, Arakan Army and other groups currently engaged in civil war against the Tatmadaw; this kind of social reproduction also benefits the Tatmadaw itself. In other words, all the cooking, cleaning, childcare, teaching and nursing that women do enables the militarized state to function as it does, and textbooks reinforce this message about women's responsibilities. This 'military–civilian harmony' is hinted at in the image of a soldier helping a woman carry vegetables (Figure 3.3); however, for many readers of these textbooks the image of the soldier 'helping' the woman perform what could be called forced labour (Figure 3.2) is likely to accord with their life experience much more closely.

The way in which these textbooks reinforce 'gender harmony' makes the reception of content geared toward preventing the sexual abuse of girls even more striking. This chapter has demonstrated how 'gender harmony' intersects with other social structures such as class, age and ethnicity. Mostly, in these new textbooks, we see 'gender equality' hesitantly embraced only when other hierarchies are reinforced. Yet in the Life Skills textbook we see a young girl exerting authority over an older man, disrupting at least two 'harmonies' at once. Even while acknowledging the coercive power of Global North/West-based development, we can see changing attitudes toward sexual abuse as a truly local phenomenon. Chie Ikeya's (2011) book on gender in colonial Burma and the emergence of the 'modern' or *khit kala* woman points out that people in colonial Burma did not simply react to British ideas and practices; rather, they 'actively engaged with new and foreign identities, ideas, practices and institutions' (Ikeya 2011: 2). Likewise, MOE officials and local consultants did not randomly accept this representation of a young girl telling an older man to stop touching her. This example of *selective* reception of 'gender equality' suggests to me that this girl represents a *khit kala* woman for the 21st century – and that the students who read this textbook may take the example she provides even further, in ways that none of us can yet imagine. The different dimensions of social harmony are designed to reinforce each other, but when one is weakened, others may also lose their hegemonic power.[7]

---

7   I have devoted little attention in this chapter to ethnicity, which I examine in other analyses of the new curriculum (Metro 2019a). It would also be fascinating to

Even while acknowledging the agency of Myanmar people in prefiguring and responding to the priorities presented to them by international development, the question of whether development organizations should play such a large role in reshaping social structures in Myanmar is, for me, fraught with ambivalence. By using Steiner-Khamsi's (2014) ideas of borrowing and lending of educational policies and practices as a theoretical framework, I have tried to take a critical stance, questioning the idea that the ideologies of development are inherently superior to local ones. At the same time, as is probably clear from my analysis, I do wish to see an expanded role for girls and women in textbooks and in society as a whole (both in Myanmar and in my own country, the US, which has certainly not attained gender equality). As a consultant for the World Bank, I was part of the apparatus that delivered the ideologies of development, and I cannot separate myself from the structures I describe. I do want to be clear that it is not my intention to demonize development, just as it is not my intention to denigrate Myanmar's traditional ideal of 'gender harmony'. Instead, my aim has been to unpack the process of textbook creation during Myanmar's quasi-democratic phase, and to examine its ideologically complex products. I find that these textbooks illustrate what Marie Lall (2020) calls the 'policy practice gap', which she explains in this way:

> Caught between the policy texts written by the government and the priorities of development partners, it feels like ministry-based stakeholders as well as those further below do not own the change process; some claim they do not even understand it.　　　　　(Lall 2020: 274)

These new textbooks, although stamped with the Ministry of Education's logo, actually reflect a complex interplay of ideologies coming from multiple actors, rather than a univocal endorsement either of 'gender harmony' or 'gender equality'.

Myanmar is not alone in its uneasy relationship with 'lenders' of educational policies and practices. In some cases, this subject position of being a 'borrowing country' has led to fascinating 'translations' of the terminology of development. For instance, Iveta Silova (2006) has shown how Latvian politicians

---

see how the treatment of gender in these textbooks compares to that in non-state curricula (e.g. those produced by the Karen National Union, the National Mon State Party and the Kachin Independence Organization). I lack the language skills to do this research, but I hope others will.

borrowed the Council of Europe ideologies of 'multiculturalism' and 'human rights' ,which they needed to reference in order to receive aid, to justify the continuation of Soviet-era ethnically-segregated schooling. The lesson, both there and in Myanmar, seems to be that development cannot treat 'borrowing' societies as blank slates. When new terms are introduced, pre-existing ideas do not disappear. Moreover, as terms circulate through these borrowing/lending relationships, we cannot assume that their meaning remains stable. 'Gender equality' might mean, to some, the inclusion of one female historical figure or high-status female business owner. For others, 'gender equality' would entail a radical transformation of all aspects of society. And some people might interpret 'gender equality' and 'gender harmony' as synonymous. Whichever definition one adopts, one would be able to find examples to appreciate and instances to decry in the new textbooks – which illustrates their polysemic nature, as products of Myanmar's quasi-democratic phase.

In this uncertain post-coup phase, the Civil Disobedience Movement has shaken up every supposed 'harmony'. Generation Z protesters have challenged gender roles and heteronormativity, Burman ethnocentrism, and hierarchies that kept them subordinated to their elders (The Guardian 2021). Education could become even more of a contested territory, as the opposition National Unity Government rejects what it calls the military's 'slave education' and plans a parallel school system (Myanmar Now 2021). It seems that all the ideological 'harmonies' that school textbooks have stubbornly presented in the face of increasing discord may finally give way to many new voices. I am sure that I am not alone in hoping that this may, indeed, come about.

References

Apple, M. 1979. *Ideology and Curriculum*. London: Routledge.

BBC News. 2019. '"Justice for Victoria": Toddler testifies in Myanmar "nursery rape" case.' 11 September. Available at: www.bbc.com/news/world-asia-49660087

Bourdieu, P. and J. Passeron. 1977. *Reproduction in Education, Society and Culture*. Translated by R. Nice. Thousand Oaks: Sage Publications.

Cha, Y. K., S. H. Ham and M. S. Lee. 2018. *Routledge International Handbook of Multicultural Education in Asia Pacific*. New York: Routledge.

Chambers, J., C. Galloway and M. Liljeblad. 2020. *Living with Myanmar*. Singapore: ISEAS.

Cheesman, Nick. 2002. 'Legitimising the Union of Myanmar through Primary School Textbooks.' Master's thesis, University of Western Australia.

Comprehensive Education Sector Review. 2018. *Myanmar Comprehensive Education Sector Review*. Available at: www.cesrmm.org/

Fairclough, N. 2003. *Analysing Discourse: Textual Analysis for Social Research*. London: Routledge.

Faxon, H. and Pyo Let Han. 2018. 'Learning feminism from Myanmar's women farmers.' *Tea Circle*, 19 September. Available at: teacircleoxford.com/2018/09/19/learning-feminism-from-myanmars-women-farmers/.

Hedström, J. 2020. 'Militarized social reproduction: Women's labour and parastate armed conflict.' *Critical Military Studies* 8 (1): 58–76.

Ikeya, C. 2011. *Refiguring Women, Colonialism and Modernity in Burma*. Honolulu: University of Hawai'i Press.

JICA. n.d. *Gender and development: JICA activities*. Available at: www.jica.go.jp/english/our_work/thematic_issues/gender/activity.html

———. 2013. *Country Gender Profile: Republic of the Union of Myanmar Final Report*. Available at: openjicareport.jica.go.jp/pdf/12153441.pdf

Khin Khin Mra and D. Livingstone. 2020. 'The winding path to gender equality in Myanmar.' In J. Chambers, C. Galloway and M. Liljeblad (eds), *Living with Myanmar*, pp. 243–264. Singapore: ISEAS.

Ladson-Billings, G. 2016. 'And then there is this thing called the curriculum: Organization, imagination, and mind.' *Educational Researcher* 45 (2): 100–104.

Lall, M. 2020. *Myanmar's Education Reforms: A Pathway to Social Justice?* London: UCL Press.

Lall, M. and E. Vickers. 2009. *Education as a Political Tool in Asia*. Routledge.

Lopes Cardozo, M. T. A. and E. J. T. Maber. 2019. *Sustainable Peacebuilding and Social Justice in Times of Transition: Findings on Education in Myanmar*. New York: Springer.

Metro, R. 2014. 'Post-colonial subjectivities in the post-conflict aid triangle: The drama of educational missionization in the Thai-Burma borderlands.' In C. Gagnon (ed.), *Post-Conflict Studies: An Interdisciplinary Approach*, pp. 161–181. New York: Routledge.

———. 2019a. 'Myanmar identity and the shifting value of the classical past: A case study of King Kyansittha in Burmese history textbooks, 1829–2016.' In P. Joliffe and T. Bruce (eds), *Southeast Asian Schools in Modern History: Education, Manipulation and Contest*, pp.12–29. New York: Routledge.

———. 2019b. 'We need to talk about the consulting industry in educational development.' *CIES Perspectives* Summer 2019: 39–40.

————. 2019c. 'A missed opportunity for schoolroom reform.' *Frontier Myanmar,* 12 November. Available at: frontiermyanmar.net/en/a-missed-opportunity-for-schoolroom-reform

Metro, R. (2020). 'Center, periphery, and boundary in the new Myanmar curriculum.' In *Myanmar Studies from the Center, Periphery, and Boundary. 2019 Conference Proceedings.* Yangon: Myanmar Department of Historical Research.

Myanmar MOE. 2007a. *Third Grade Geography and History.* Naypyidaw: Myanmar MOE.

————. 2007b. *Second Grade Myanmar Reader.* Naypyidaw: Myanmar MOE.

————. 2016a. *National Education Strategic Plan 2016–2021* Naypyidaw: Myanmar MOE.

————. 2016b. *Third Grade Myanmar Reader.* Naypyidaw: Myanmar MOE.

————. 2016c. *Third Grade Geography and History.* Naypyidaw: Myanmar MOE.

————. 2017a. *First Grade Myanmar Reader.* Naypyidaw: Myanmar MOE.

————. 2017b. *First Grade Social Studies.* Naypyidaw: Myanmar MOE.

————. 2018a. *Second Grade English.* Naypyidaw: Myanmar MOE.

————. 2018b. *Second Grade Life Skills.* Naypyidaw: Myanmar MOE.

————. 2018c. *Second Grade Morality and Civics.* Naypyidaw: Myanmar MOE.

————. 2018d. *Second Grade Science.* Naypyidaw: Myanmar MOE.

————. 2018e. *Second Grade Social Studies.* Naypyidaw: Myanmar MOE.

————. 2019a. *Third Grade English.* Naypyidaw: Myanmar MOE.

————. 2019b. *Third Grade Life Skills.* Naypyidaw: Myanmar MOE.

————. 2019c. *Third Grade Social Studies.* Naypyidaw: Myanmar MOE.

Myanmar Now. 2021. 'National Unity Government fights junta's "slave education" with plan for parallel education system.' *Myanmar Now,* 10 May. Available at: www.myanmar-now.org/en/news/national-unity-government-fights-juntas-slave-education-with-plan-to-build-parallel-system

Salem-Gervais, N. and R. Metro. 2012. 'A textbook case of nation-building: The discursive evolution of state and non-state history curricula under military rule in Myanmar.' *The Journal of Burma Studies* 16 (1): 27–78.

Shah, R. and M. T. A. Lopes Cardozo. 2019. 'Myanmar's education system: Historical roots, the current context, and new opportunities.' In M. T. A. Lopes Cardozo and E. J. T. Maber, *Sustainable Peacebuilding and Social Justice in Times of Transition: Findings on the Role of Education in Myanmar,* pp. 65–86. New York: Springer.

Silova, I. 2006. *From Sites of Occupation to Symbols of Multiculturalism: Transfer of Global Discourse and the Metamorphosis of Russian Schools in post-Soviet Latvia.* Charlotte, NC: Information Age Publishing.

Sleeter, C. E. 2018. 'Multicultural education past, present, and future: Struggles for dialogue and power-sharing.' *International Journal of Multicultural Education* 20 (1): 5–20.

Steiner-Khamsi, G. 2014. 'Cross-national policy borrowing: Understanding reception and translation.' *Asia Pacific Journal of Education* 2: 153–167.

Tharaphi Than. 2014. *Women in Modern Burma*. New York: Routledge.

The Guardian. 2021. '"We all know what we're facing": Divided Myanmar unites against coup.' *The Guardian*, 10 February. Available at: www.theguardian.com/world/2021/feb/10/we-all-know-what-were-facing-divided-myanmar-unites-against-coup

Treadwell, B. A. 2013. 'Teaching Citizenship under an Authoritarian Regime: A Case-Study of Burma/Myanmar.' PhD dissertation, Indiana University.

UN Women. n.d. *Concepts and Definitions*. Available at: www.un.org/womenwatch/osagi/conceptsanddefinitions.htm#:~:text=Equality%20between%20women%20and%20men,men%20and%20girls%20and%20boys.&text=Gender%20determines%20what%20is%20expected,man%20in%20a%20given%20context

UN. n.d. *Goal 5: Gender*. Available at: www.un.org/sustainabledevelopment/gender-equality/

UNICEF. n.d. *Education*. Available at: www.unicef.org/myanmar/education

World Bank. 2013. *Myanmar: Gender Equality and Development*. 19 September. Available at: www.worldbank.org/en/news/feature/2013/09/19/Myanmar-Gender-Equality-and-Development

———. 2021. *Inclusive Access and Quality Education Project*. Available at: projects.worldbank.org/en/projects-operations/project-detail/P163389

Zar Ni. 1998. 'Knowledge, Control and Power: The Politics of Education under Burma's Military Dictatorship.' PhD dissertation, University of Wisconsin-Madison.

Feminist Mobilization, Resistance and Movement Building

CHAPTER 4

Feminist Peace Building at the Grassroots

Contributions and Challenges

Mollie Pepper

*W*omen's organizing efforts at the community level have emerged in the context of protracted conflict in Myanmar and associated outmigration from Myanmar to neighbouring countries. Women's groups, on their own and in partnership with each other, have focused much of their energy around providing for the basic needs of their communities. As a result, they have worked at a grassroots level to build holistic peace and have brought these issues to discussions concerning peace in the country. Women's holistic peacebuilding efforts at the grassroots level have laid the groundwork for an effective women's movement in Myanmar that is built across ethnic lines and invested in peace and human security and which relies on gendered frames for legitimacy and acceptance. However, the necessity of focusing on immediate human security needs, in no small way a necessity created by the lack of sustainable and consistent funding, has to some degree hindered women's organizing efforts by preoccupying their energies and by resulting in activist women being underestimated as political actors. This is worsened by the legacy of the colonial idea that women in Myanmar enjoy freedoms unparalleled elsewhere in neighbouring countries, an idea that renders women's organizing for rights largely invisible (Ikeya, this volume).

Women's inclusion, if women are included at all in formal processes of building peace, is fundamentally shaped by cultural norms surrounding femininity and women's work, as is the case elsewhere (Sa'ar 2016). This framing of women's peacebuilding work is necessary because of the political priorities of men, who have a vested interest in the exclusion of women from formal peace negotiations because those negotiations constitute the arbitration of power dynamics between and within ethnic groups. Thus, by marginalizing women, they create the conditions under which women are not able to use the transition to peace to advance their own interests. In response, the discourses leveraged by women's movements in transitional periods often engage gender essentialisms and norms to appeal to supporters and to achieve acceptance. Feminist scholarship on women's activism and organizing has clearly demonstrated that women play a significant role in civic and political life, while their activism is shaped by socially-constructed gender norms (Ferree and Mueller 2004; Moghadam 2005; Ray 1999; Waylen 2007). Social movements may leverage frames, ideologies, and categories that are advantageous, but there is also a risk that the movement will lock itself into and reify categories by doing so. In particular, we have seen women in Myanmar leverage their identities as mothers and victims in order to gain traction in public life (Olivius and Hedström 2019). These identities are expressed, in part, through the grassroots work that women and women's organizations perform in an effort to build localized peace in the broader context of the previous peace process in Myanmar.

This chapter shines light on women's grassroots organizing in Myanmar and on the Thailand–Myanmar border as a form of holistic peacebuilding, albeit with consequences for women's rights organizing. The aim is to uncover the ways in which conflict has shaped the emerging women's movement in Myanmar, in order to bring attention to a facet of peacebuilding and peace activism that is often overlooked both by actors in formal peacebuilding spaces and by observers of peacebuilding. The chapter further seeks to uncover the ways in which a necessary focus on human security issues at the grassroots can hinder women's rights movement development, as women activists are constrained by the gendered social norms that shape their work and occupy their time and resources (see also Gagnon and Hsa Moo, this volume). Please note that, while I do not contextualize and historicize the activism of women from various ethnic groups and situate their activism in their unique conditions, I do not view all ethnically-identified women and groups to have the same priorities. However, an in-depth analysis that takes this diversity into account is beyond the scope of this chapter. I do not identify the ethnic group affiliation of my interlocutors. This is a conscious choice made to protect their anonymity.

The chapter begins with a discussion of existing scholarship on women's movements in transitional contexts, feminist conceptualizations of holistic peacebuilding, and women's peace activism at the grassroots. A brief context and discussion of the methods used in this research follows. Data, deriving primarily from interviews, is presented in two parts. The first examines the holistic peacebuilding efforts that are led by women at the grassroots level in the context of displacement from Myanmar. The second discusses the ways in which such peacebuilding efforts and the ways in which they are framed as 'women's work' encumber women activists and impede their progress in advocating for women's rights. The chapter concludes with a reflection on the implications of the findings.

Before proceeding, I must note that this chapter was drafted prior to the February 1, 2021 military coup in Myanmar (for further discussion, see Hedström and Olivius, this volume). At the time of data collection and analysis, the peace process was continuing to take place, though progress was slow. This chapter should be understood to have originated in that context, though I believe that the analysis and issues raised stand as valid and useful now, and are perhaps even more pertinent than they were prior to the coup. This is in part because human insecurity has increased with the instability brought on by the coup, intensifying women's grassroots efforts to alleviate the consequences of that insecurity.

Women's Political Activism and Holistic Peacebuilding at the Grassroots

Violent conflict and its aftermath are characterized by relative instability, and scholars have argued that it is this instability that creates possibilities for significant change in both social and political life (Berry 2018; Capoccia and Kelemen 2007; Collier and Collier 1991; Hedström and Olivius, this volume; Pierson 2004). Scholars of social movements have noted that political transitions and disruptions can provide an unprecedented opportunity for women's movements to engage in political life and civil society in several ways, including as citizens, nationalists and feminists (Waylen 2007). Women's movements in transition are not necessarily limited to movements that are founded on essentialisms (Viterna and Fallon 2008). However, such essentialisms do dominate and shape women's inclusion or justify their exclusion. Women's activism for peace, though it may rely on essentialisms, brings women into the public sphere, thus challenging prevailing gender norms that hold that women's sphere is that of the home and family (Aye Thiri Kyaw, this volume; Kaufman and Williams 2013). This is reinforced by policy and discourses at both the local and national level in other contexts as well as by international nongovernmental and inter-governmental organization interventions (Stienstra 1994; Hawkesworth 2018).

Entering the male-dominated public sphere by gaining access to formal political institutions and a seat at the table in political processes is not the only way in which women can have influence and exercise power (Elshtain 1981; Sharoni 1995; Yuval-Davis 1997; Gal and Kligman 2000; Berry, 2018). In fact, the power of women's informal networks has been noted by feminist scholars as being highly influential (Frydenlund and Wai Wai Nu, this volume; Purkayastha and Subramaniam 2004). Though some scholars have warned against over-estimating informal political action and organizing (Abu-Lughod 1990; Bayat 2010; Berry 2018), this research asks how women are involved in building peace and finds that recognizing women's organizing is key to understanding gender dynamics in the processes of building peace. Further, such recognition is essential to the effort to understand women's peacebuilding work in the wider context of ongoing transition.

Peace processes as conceived of by the international community and United Nations Security Council Resolution 1325 tend to assume that peacebuilding happens in formal spaces, through formal channels. What follows from this is the idea, expressed in many policy circles, that if women are brought to the negotiating table and become part of the peace process at a formal level, then the gender problem will be solved (Hunt and Posa 2001). This is inaccurate, however, as it fails to acknowledge the localized, specific and often informal ways in which women organize to influence the world around them. The weaknesses of this line of thinking have become apparent and a subject of discussion in Women, Peace and Security spaces. In response, there has been an effort to look to the local in thinking about peacebuilding and to incorporate a gender perspective in order to understand how peace processes can both empower and limit women's peace-oriented activities (George 2018).

Feminists have argued that feminist conceptualizations of peace are more holistic than prevailing masculinist understandings (Paarlberg-Kvam 2018; Reardon and Snauwaert 2015), and that women's peace activism is often built around broad visions of holistic peace (Reardon 1993). This approach to thinking about peace can be attributed to what Confortini (2006) calls feminist positive peace, which draws on Galtung's ideas. According to Galtung's work, peace is often conceptualized in terms of 'negative peace' or the absence of violent conflict (Galtung 1964: 2). However, the concept of 'positive peace' is at least as useful to thinking about peace and encourages a more holistic view of peace. Positive peace, as defined by Galtung, is a condition where people are able to realize their full potential, unimpeded by structural violence (Galtung 1969: 168). This understanding of conflict and its impacts takes into consideration the consequences of violent conflict that extend beyond direct forms of violence to include structural damage caused by that violence and conditions impeding human development resulting from conflict. Confortini's (2006) expansion of this work specified a feminist positive peace that includes consideration of gender alongside the more holistic conceptualizations of what peace could or should look like.

If we conceptualize peace as experienced by individuals at the local level holistically, then we become able to recognize grassroots-level work that strives to build peace within communities. Localized experiences are not necessarily sufficient to constitute positive peace, as positive peace also relies on institutional and systemic change, but they can demonstrate feminist holistic peacebuilding in action. In this view, the impacts of armed conflict become salient and the experiences and lived realities of non-combatants become important. This creates room for other actors in peacebuilding, including those who are not involved directly in the armed conflict but who are affected by it. Further, building holistic peace involves rebuilding a world where human potential can be realized and where health, education, food security and other aspects of human security become central. It is around these issues that some women's peace activism is expressed, as this chapter demonstrates.

This chapter uses the idea of a holistic feminist peace to frame thinking about women's contributions to the process of building peace in Myanmar. While women are included and excluded in a variety of ways in formal peace process activities, they do contribute substantially and in material ways to the development of peace within their communities, around the peace process when they are not included, and within the peace process when they are included. It is important to note that I, and other feminist scholars, do not necessarily subscribe to the idea that women are somehow naturally more peaceful than men. However, we do recognize that the ways that people of differing genders are positioned in society has a substantial effect on their engagement with peace and peace activism (El-Bushra 2007; Hedström, Olivius and Zin Mar Phyo, this volume). Further, the attention this chapter pays to grassroots women's work for human security as peacebuilding work should not be taken to suggest that this is all that women contribute to peace.

Instead, this chapter seeks to bring attention to the work that women do to build peace within their communities and beyond, which is often rendered invisible (Zin Mar Phyo and Mi Sue Pwint, this volume).

Intersectional feminism has engaged and challenged hegemonic visions of feminist power. These feminists argue that layered oppressions connected to class, race, ability, sexual orientation and a great number of other factors that are context-specific may be as important or more important than gender to some women and require intersectional analysis (Collins 2002; Crenshaw 1991; Naples 2009). Harnois (2015) argues that membership of other marginalized groups (e.g. marginalized ethnic groups) can raise levels of gendered political consciousness, which may partially explain the context in which strong ethnic women's organizations have emerged in Myanmar (Hedström 2016; Olivius and Hedström 2019). These diverse contributions have brought theoretical attention to the importance of identities and power, and provide a theoretical foundation for engaging gender, ethnic and other identities in exploring the processes of political inclusion and peacebuilding in transitioning societies. Gendered political consciousness is a key aspect of women's peace activism at the grassroots and of their localized efforts to improve human security, efforts which often engage with particular discourses.

Human Security Deficits and Collecting Data on Women's Activism

Prior to the February 2021 coup, Myanmar was in the midst of a contested peace process, through which the country's multiple ethnic groups and the Bamar majority-run centralized government sought to reach a conclusion to the civil conflicts that have raged in the ethnic areas of the country since 1949 (Fink 2009; Cheesman and Farrelly 2016; Hedström and Olivius, this volume). One impact of the decades of violent conflict has been high rates of forced outmigration to bordering countries, with Thailand receiving many refugees and migrants (Grundy-Warr 2004). Since the 1980s, refugee camps and accompanying international humanitarian aid organizations have populated the Thailand–Myanmar border. Thailand houses more than 91,000 refugees from Myanmar in nine camps along its border (The Border Consortium 2021). As a result of high levels of migration, the borderlands of Thailand and Myanmar have become a site of cross-border organization and resistance for people from multiple ethnic backgrounds (Banki 2015).

This has been the case both within and outside of refugee camps. Refugee political activism is a phenomenon that has been noted as highly influential by scholars in other locations (Malkki 1995; Holzer 2015). In this context, migrants and refugees make up the Myanmar activist population in Thailand, and while much of their work seeks to support those living in exile from Myanmar, many organizations and initiatives use the relative safety and stability of Thailand as a base of operations for human rights activist work within Myanmar as well. It is in this cross-border context that many human rights organizations, including ethnic women's organizations, have emerged as influential civil society actors (Olivius 2017).

The peace negotiations and transitional process changed the dynamics of women's activism to some extent. As Myanmar has been perceived to be increasingly open, funding has been redirected from the borderlands to efforts inside of the country. As a result, in order to keep operating effectively, many women's organizations have shifted their base of operations and many of their members of staff away from the borderlands in Thailand and into Myanmar, reducing some of the services and organizing efforts on the border (Olivius 2019).

This chapter uses data collected during 14 months of fieldwork in total conducted in the Thai cities of Mae Sot and Chiang Mai, as well as in Myanmar in Yangon and Kachin State, between 2015 and 2019. This fieldwork resulted in 65 interviews with a wide array of participants, including women's rights activists, ethnic women's group representatives, NGO representatives, and refugee and migrant women from local communities. Participants were identified based on their affiliations with or knowledge of women's organizations and women's rights activism using a snowball sampling method whereby interview participants were asked to suggest other individuals or organizations that would be able to speak on women's activism and local peacebuilding.

Interview participants had the option of speaking with me alone in English, or with an interpreter in Burmese or the ethnic language with which they were most comfortable. Interpreters were essential to this work. They served as invaluable cultural brokers and were recruited based on past work in the area and through recommendations from trusted local organizations. Interviews were recorded with permission and were later transcribed for analysis. Audio from interviews conducted through interpreters in Burmese and Karen languages were double-interpreted by a third party interpreter

103

who used the audio recordings to transcribe the entire interview in English. Verbal informed consent was obtained from all interview participants.

Data was also collected through participant observation, facilitated by volunteer positions with local grassroots organizations. This work is further informed by my time spent as a volunteer with two grassroots advocacy organizations on the Thailand–Myanmar border between 2016–2017 and as a humanitarian aid worker in the area from 2007–2008, as well as my master's thesis research conducted as a consultant to a large international nongovernmental organization in refugee camps on the Thailand–Myanmar border in 2011.

Transcripts along with detailed fieldnotes were analysed using NVivo, a qualitative data analysis software program. Data were coded following a grounded theory approach (Strauss and Corbin 1990; Charmaz 2006) to allow themes to emerge from the data through open and focused coding (Emerson, Fretz and Shaw 1995). Preliminary findings were reported back to selected interview participants and participating organizations for correction and triangulation purposes.

Women's Holistic Peacebuilding in Displacement

Women's organizations, especially ethnic women's organizations, are powerful networks that exist throughout Myanmar and on the Thailand–Myanmar border. 13 groups are united under the umbrella organization of the Women's League of Burma (Women's League of Burma 2011). Aside from these organizations, there are non-member ethnic women's organizations such as the Mon Women's Organisation and the Chin Women's Organisation, as well as many other ethnically-identified women's organizations, such as the Kachin Women's Peace Network and the Kachin State Women's Network. Further, there are organizations that are not organized around ethnic identity specifically, but rather around gender and peace, including the Gender Equality Network and the Alliance for Gender Inclusion in the Peace Process. Alliances between women's organizations that cross ethnic and other identity boundaries are not uncommon in peace activism; it is, rather, a phenomenon that has been noted in multiple contexts including the Balkans and Northern Ireland (Cockburn 1998).

The work of ethnic women's organizations includes acting as advocacy organizations for women and children, as auxiliary organizations in support of and as critics of ethnic armed organizations in some cases, and as activist organizations for human rights. These organizations can be peripheral players in state-level ethnic armed organization and nationalist politics, often receive funding from international organizations, and serve as the primary advocates for women in their communities (Salai Isaac Khen and Muk Yin Haung Nyoi 2014). Despite the wide range of their activities and the influence that results, women's organizations and representatives from those organizations, whether ethnically affiliated or not, have often been relegated to peripheral roles in the formal peacebuilding negotiations at the national level (Pepper 2018). Still, women's activism through ethnic women's organizations is influential politically, particularly in local contexts, where representatives from such organizations are often able to gain entry to decision-making spaces and have a voice in community concerns.

In the refugee camps on the Thailand–Myanmar border the activism of ethnic women's organizations extends into several arenas. Such work is directed towards immediate short-term needs and longer-term goals and engages women as symbols of cultural and national identity and tradition (Enloe 2000; Jok 1998; Giles and Hyndman 2004). Women's informal networks can emerge and develop power in contexts of insecurity to become highly influential agents for change (Purkayastha and Subramaniam 2004), and this is evident in the ways in which ethnic women's organizations have arisen in the context of conflict.

To contextualize their work, it is important to note that the Republic of the Union of Myanmar was ranked 147th out of 169 countries by the United Nations Development Program's Human Development Report in 2020 according to the Human Development Index (United Nations Development Program 2021). Decades of conflict coupled with a highly isolationist government have resulted in widespread underdevelopment in Myanmar, with the worst effects felt in the ethnic areas of the country. Violence, from the domestic to the political, is pervasive in Myanmar (Cheesman 2018; Davies and True 2017) and poverty has led to poor health outcomes (Ne Lynn Zaw and Pepper 2016) and low levels of educational attainment (Ang and Wong 2015; South and Lall 2016) throughout the country. In Thailand, the impacts of these conditions carry over with the displaced, and though health services and educational opportunities are available to refugees and migrants, access can be limited.

These conditions create women's drive to engage in political life through their work. As one prominent ethnic women's organization founding member commented during an interview, as we sat in a meeting room together drinking 3-in-1 coffees:

This is why I started [the organization]. We were without food, clothing, shelter, safety. Our children were hungry and had no school. We were not citizens in Thailand. So I decided that I must do something to change our life. Together we started [the organization] to help women and our children. This is also how we made our voices heard.[1]

As she says, it is in this context of dispossession and displacement that ethnic women's organizations arose, to meet the basic needs of their communities, and through that work they emerged as political actors. She indicates that is by virtue of engaging in community-based human security work that her organization gained legitimacy and a platform to engage in political life.

We find a similar origin story from another well-known woman activist turned political leader. In a published interview with Naw Zipporah Sein, a former leader in the Karen National Union and, before that, a key leader in the Karen Women's Organization, she noted:

When I came to live in Mae Ra Mu camp, I saw that it was necessary to reorganise the women's organization to address the needs of refugee families. We used to live in the jungle, where we had unlimited space and freedom of movement. However, the refugee camp was cramped and crowded so we need to change our living style. I set up a women's group in each section of the camp to make a list of their needs in the household and coordinated collection and distribution of essential items for pregnant women, new mothers and infants. I opened nursery schools and summer schools for children to learn basic reading and writing skills as well as to educate them with necessary health and hygiene knowledge.

(Thawnghmung 2013: 261)

Importantly, Naw Zipporah Sein's activism and leadership with the Karen Women's Organization led to her rise as a key political figure in the Karen National Union. Through the the example of her experience, we can see very clearly how human security work, as she describes it above, can translate to political influence. This resonates with the account of another member of

---

1   Ethnic women's organization representative, Chiang Mai, 15 January 2019.

an ethnic women's organization whom I met in a refugee camp office. As we spoke, with the sounds of camp life around us, she described her mobilization within the organization and explained that their work has garnered recognition and legitimacy for herself and her colleagues, as political actors within the camp community:

> When I came here, we had nothing. Even [the aid organization] couldn't help us to obtain all that we needed. So we organized ourselves to help our community and to help our people [belonging to the same ethnic group as ourselves]. Now we can join in the camp committee and in decision-making because we are so important within the community. Our work is very important for the [ethnic group]. We provide for our life, so we can be safe, and now even the men listen to us.[2]

Their social projects, aimed at addressing fundamental needs within the refugee community, include the establishment and management of orphanages, the provision of safe houses for women escaping domestic violence and training for traditional birth attendants. Thus, they contribute to building a holistic peace at the community level by addressing conditions of structural violence that emerged in the context of violent conflict and associated displacement. These efforts are in areas that are often coded as 'women's concerns', though they are fundamentally about human security needs at a basic level. This coding, unfortunately, leaves women activists and women's organizations largely at the side-lines when it comes to political power, despite the deeply political nature of their work, which is carried out on behalf of women and also addresses the security needs of their ethnic groups more broadly.

The work of women's organizations is intended to address social and structural oppressions that appear in the forms of deficits in human security as well as exclusion on the basis of gender and ethnicity. This is in contrast to the male-dominated peace process, which focuses instead on the explicitly militarized and political aspects of the idea of peace. One woman activist, a member of an ethnic women's organization, explained it to me in this way:

> For them [men], the peace process is only about discussing about political issues and things like weapons. They do not think about the social sector and they do not think about the women and children who are affected by the armed conflict.[3]

---

2   Ethnic women's organization representative, Mae La, 10 July 2015.
3   Ethnic women's organization representative, Chiang Mai, 24 November 2017.

She notes that the core of the peace process is focused primarily on masculine-coded concerns, and that more holistic conceptualizations of what peace could look like or what should be at stake in the peace dialogues are absent. This is a missed opportunity, as this work for human security is a key aspect of developing a sustainable peace that addresses structural as well as direct violence.

Through ethnic women's organizations, women prioritize serving the needs of women and children within their ethnic groups. By strategically adopting and emphasizing socially-constructed and accepted gender stereotypes in framing their key claims, identities, interests and goals, women can engage in seemingly depoliticized acts that can be conceptualized as activism, while making their activism palatable to those who might resist women's political involvement (Erickson and Faria 2014; Ray 1999). While these relationships and the opportunities they afford are based in essentialisms, they do allow for ethnic women's organizations to wield a certain amount of authority when it comes to social issues (Olivius and Hedström 2019). In turn, these essentialisms have become a way for women to assert their right to be included at the level of ethnic politics and in broader processes, such as the ongoing peace talks (Pepper 2018). The work done by ethnic women's organizations at the refugee camp level constitutes a meaningful contribution to building the conditions for a holistic peace within their communities in response to the structural and conflict-related violence they have experienced as ethnic women.

Peace Advocacy and the Future of Women's Rights

In addition to the material concerns and human security gaps that have arisen as a result of displacement and conflict, women's organizations are also concerned with structural issues that are of great importance to the future of women in Myanmar. Many of the women I spoke to emphasized the linkages between peace and rights for women and ethnic groups. A representative of an ethnic women's organization based in Thailand with operations in Myanmar noted:

> Peace, if we have a peace, that also includes women's rights, so that is what we are working for – women's rights and also peace and also justice. If we do not have justice, it will be a fake peace.[4]

---

4   Ethnic women's organization representative, Chiang Mai, 22 November 2017.

As this interviewee noted, a meaningful peace must include attention to and provisions for women's rights in the Myanmar that will hopefully emerge from the transitional period. A call for justice is also evident here, as key to building sustainable and meaningful peace. Attention to a justice mechanism is an aspect of the peace negotiations that has been lacking. However, women activists have had their lives affected tremendously by violent conflict, and they note that without justice, the peace that may be achieved will be lacking in legitimacy and will fail to address many of the concerns of women in the peace process. Despite the February 1, 2021 coup, it is possible to see how this comment still stands as significant. Women have been key players in the protest movement rejecting the coup, and have kept women's rights at the forefront of the movement.

In addition to attention to women's rights and justice, women activists from Myanmar are also concerned with ethnic rights, as many of them are members of ethnic groups that have experienced oppression and conflict at the hands of the Myanmar military. One ethnic women's organization representative put it this way:

> As ethnic women we struggle for two things. One is women's rights and the other is ethnic rights. If we have ethnic equality, we can also fight for women's rights. It's easier. That's strategic.[5]

She notes that women's rights and ethnic rights go hand in hand in their imagining of an eventual effective peace settlement and a future that moves ahead, away from violent conflict in the country (see also Cardénas, this volume). Another representative of a different ethnic women's organization operating within Myanmar noted:

> [There are] exactly 135 ethnic groups with distinct cultures and languages in their areas. The previous government, they ignored the importance of diversity. We believe that diversity is beauty, so we have to recognize it. In our vision, we also mention that we want to have a society that produces good government and a culture that rejects violence as a means of, as a method of, dealing with differences.[6]

For both of these women, ethnic issues are at the heart of what will constitute a meaningful peace resolution and forms the basis of much of

5   Ethnic women's organization representative, Chiang Mai, 17 May 2017.
6   Female activist, Myitkyina, 25 June 2019.

their activism. This demonstrates how women's activism in this context is shaped by both their identity as women and their identity as members of an ethnic group, something that was noted previously by Olivius and Hedström (2019; see also Ikeya, this volume). This is further proof of how the networks built between diverse women through their activism could be leveraged to support building sustainable peace.

Despite clear evidence that meaningful and lasting peace settlements are those that include women and minority groups in the peacemaking negotiation process, it has been a struggle to achieve the inclusion of women in peace dialogues in Myanmar at the national level (Pepper 2018; Salai Isaac Khen and Muk Yin Haung Nyoi 2014). However, women activists have continued to push for inclusion and are highly motivated by the conviction that their involvement is necessary in order to create a peace that is inclusive. The following quote is representative of what many women told me in the course of fieldwork and interviews:

> We don't want to take over, but we want to be involved. This is especially important for ethnic women because their history is different, their experience is different, their current situation is different – but we are still very much tied together by the Women's League of Burma.[7]

As this ethnic woman activist, who has worked with several different grassroots organizations, has articulated here, the idea is not that women should control the narratives that are included in the peace process, but rather that their perspectives and lived experiences offer something valuable to the process, which could contribute to greater future stability in the country.

Despite ongoing activism in the face of routine exclusion, marginalization and siloization within formal peacebuilding processes, particularly at the national level, women have persisted in calling for their voices to be heard and have worked strategically through their respective ethnic organizations to find ways to elevate their concerns and ensure that they are part of the dialogues. However, this effort has not been without detriment to women's outlook in relation to the process and to the future of Myanmar. Several interview respondents expressed frustration, pessimism and disappointment when discussing the future of women's rights and peace in Myanmar. One leader of an ethnic women's organization noted:

---

7   Ethnic women's organization representative, Chiang Mai, 15 January 2019.

Actually, I am a pessimist when I think about women's rights and the future. They keep us busy dealing with immediate problems for women so we can't work to a bigger political picture. We have to plug this hole and that hole and it's exhausting. In this way, they prevent the women's rights.[8]

This statement is important because it demonstrates one of the ways in which women's grassroots organizing and interventions lead to women's exclusion. This takes place both because their work for human security and holistic peace leaves them with less resources and energy for organizing for rights on a different level, but also because their work addressing 'women's problem' leads to their marginalization at higher levels of politics. Echoing her frustration, another activist said:

It is very difficult to think about the future of women in Burma. You ask me about our future and I want to say our future will be strong, but it is very difficult to work and work for our voices to be heard and to have no chance. Now I am not sure about our future, but I know I will keep working, and [the organization] will keep working to make a better future for women and our children.[9]

Doubt and disappointment are evident in these quotes. And these were not unique responses to the question 'what do you think will be the future for the women of Burma?' The majority of interviewees who work at the grassroots in women's organizations and women's movements expressed this type of frustration and fatigue. But, as expressed in the second quote, they were also unanimous in their conviction that the only way forward was to keep working and advocating for women in their communities at the local, regional and national levels.

What is evident from these women's comments is a commitment to addressing basic human security needs for their communities both as both a form of resistance and as an act intended to counteract the impacts of violent conflict. What is more, these activities are highly effective at working towards holistic peace in their communities and at establishing these women as leaders. However, it is also clear that, while these women also see the advancement of women's rights through the peace process and their inclusion in that process as an extension of their work at the grassroots, they often find themselves excluded and their advocacy efforts side-lined. In

8   Female activist, Mae Sot, 3 July 2015.
9   Ethnic women's organization representative, Yangon, 15 June 2019.

part, this is because they have established themselves so effectively in their communities as having legitimacy as women and mothers that they are seen by men in positions of power as irrelevant to a peace process focused on violent conflict. This is not to suggest that their peacebuilding work within their communities is not valid and essential, but rather to point out that it has not led to a corresponding level of inclusion in the formal peace process. This is a symptom of the wider problem of women's organizing in Myanmar, which is highly effective but also emphasizes their identity as women, and is thus overlooked as valid peacebuilding work. Were it recognized by those in power, it would logically lead to greater inclusion of women in formal peace processes, as they would be viewed as essential to peacebuilding efforts in the country.

Conclusion

'War, at its most fundamental level, is an accelerated period of social change' (Berry 2018: 210). I suggest further, along with other scholars, that the negotiations to conclude war and move society out of a period of war into something resembling peace is an extension of that period of social change (Klem 2018; Krause, Krause and Bränfors 2018; Shair-Rosenfield and Wood 2017). Thus, violent conflict and the processes of resolution of conflict and transition to peace contain opportunities or openings for the advancement of the interests of different groups, in this case ethnic women.

Central to understanding the changes that women's activism have undergone in the Myanmar context is paying attention to the ways in which transition has changed women's peace activism. As discussed above, this is in part a function of the transition, which leads to changes in security and to funding trends that have favoured work within the country rather than from exile, as was the case until relatively recently (Olivius 2019). Further, the transition and the associated peace process have created openings for women activists both to continue to promote peace and to use the platform they have constructed for themselves through their peacebuilding work to advocate for women's rights and advancement in the country. In the years of conflict that have plagued Myanmar, women's groups organized around ethnic identities have built connections and partnerships that have strengthened their individual groups' ability to make claims, as well as created a foundation for a unified women's movement through the peace process. However, this has not necessarily translated into gains for women's rights advocacy, in part because women leaders are viewed as performing 'women's work', which is viewed as irrelevant to masculine-coded public and political life.

The implication of this research is that attention to apparently depoliticized activities can generate knowledge concerning the political activities and impact of those who are most marginalized. Attention to the margins is indeed a feminist project that yields perspectives that are often unheard or are undervalued. It further reveals the importance of recognizing grassroots organizing as meaningful in peacebuilding. This suggests that this type of organizing leads to real consequences, both material and political, and opens up possibilities for collaboration. At a minimum, this work demonstrates that the political lives of seemingly depoliticized subjects should be taken seriously in contexts of political transition.

References

Abu-Lughod, L. 1990. 'The romance of resistance: Tracing transformations of power through Bedouin women.' *American Ethnologist* 17 (1): 41–55.

Ang, L. and L. Wong. 2015. 'Conceptualising early childhood care and development in fragile states: Understanding children and childhood in Myanmar.' *Global Studies of Childhood* 5 (4): 367–380.

Banki, S. 2015. 'Transnational activism as practiced by activists from Burma: Negotiating precarity, mobility and resistance.' In R. Egreteau and F. Robinne (eds), *Metamorphosis: Studies in Social and Political Change in Myanmar*, pp. 234–258. Singapore: NUS Press.

Bayat, A. 2010. *Life as Politics: How Ordinary People Change the Middle East.* Redwood City, CA: Stanford University Press.

Berry, M. 2018. *War, Women, and Power: From Violence to Mobilization in Rwanda and Bosnia-Herzegovina.* Cambridge: Cambridge University Press.

Capoccia, G. and R. D. Kelemen. 2007. 'The study of critical junctures: Theory, narrative, and counterfactuals in historical institutionalism.' *World Politics* 59 (3): 341–369.

Charmaz, K. 2006. *Constructing Grounded Theory.* Thousand Oaks, CA: Sage.

Cheesman, N. 2018. *Interpreting Communal Violence in Myanmar.* New York: Routledge.

Cheesman, N. and N. Farrelly. 2016. *Conflict in Myanmar: War, Politics, Religion.* Singapore: ISEAS – Yusof Ishak Institute.

Cockburn, C. 1998. *The Space Between Us: Negotiating Gender and National Identities in Conflict.* London: Zed Books.

Collier, R. and D. Collier. 1991. *Shaping the Political Arena: Critical Junctures, the Labor Movement, and Regime Dynamics in Latin America*. Princeton, NJ: Princeton University Press.

Collins, P. H. 2002. *Black Feminist Thought: Knowledge, Consciousness and the Politics of Empowerment*. New York: Routledge.

Confortini, C. 2006. 'Galtung, violence and gender: The case for a peace studies/ feminism alliance.' *Peace and Change* 31 (3): 333–367.

Crenshaw, K. 1991. 'Mapping the margins: Intersectionality, identity politics and violence against women of color.' *Stanford Law Review* 43 (6): 1241–1299.

Davies, S. and J. True. 2017. 'The politics of counting and reporting conflict-related sexual and gender-based violence: The case of Myanmar.' *International Feminist Journal of Politics* 19 (1): 4–21.

El-Bushra, J. 2007. 'Feminism, gender and women's peace activism.' *Development and Change* 38 (1): 131–147.

Elshtain, J. 1981. *Public Man, Private Woman: Women in Social and Political Thought*. Princeton, PA: Princeton University Press.

Emerson, R., R. Fretz and L. Shaw. 1995. *Writing Ethnographic Fieldnotes*. Chicago, IL: University of Chicago Press.

Enloe, C. 2000. *Bananas, Beaches and Bases: Making Feminist Sense of International Politics*. Berkeley, CA: University of California Press.

Erickson, J. and C. Faria. 2014. '"We want empowerment for our women": Transnational feminism, neoliberal citizenship and the gendering of women's political subjectivity in postconflict South Sudan.' *Signs* 40 (1): 627–652.

Ferree, M.M. and C. McClurg Mueller. 2004. 'Feminism and the women's movement.' In D. Snow, S. Soule and H. Kriesi (eds), *The Blackwell Companion to Social Movements*, pp. 576–607. Oxford: Blackwell.

Fink, C. 2009. *Living Silence in Burma*. London: Zed Books. Second edition.

Gal, S. and G. Kligman. 2000. *The Politics of Gender After Socialism: A Comparative-Historical Essay*. Princeton, PA: Princeton University Press.

Galtung, J. 1964. 'An editorial.' *Journal of Peace Research* 1 (1): 1–4.

———. 1969. 'Violence, peace and peace research.' *Journal of Peace Research* 6 (3): 167–191.

George, N. 2018. 'Liberal–local peacebuilding in the Solomon Islands and Bougainville: Advancing a gender-just peace?' *International Affairs* 94 (6): 1329–1348.

Giles, W. and J. Hyndman. 2004. 'Introduction: Gender and conflict in a global context.' In W. Giles and J. Hyndman (eds), *Sites of Violence: Gender and Conflict Zones*, pp. 3–23. Berkeley, CA: University of California Press.

Grundy-Warr, C. 2004. 'The silence and violence of forced migration: The Myanmar-Thailand border.' In A. Ananta and E. N. Arifin (eds), *International Migration in Southeast Asia*, pp. 228–272. Singapore: Institute of Southeast Asian Studies.

Harnois, C. 2015. 'Race, ethnicity, sexuality and women's political consciousness of gender.' *Social Psychology Quarterly* 78 (4): 365–386.

Hawkesworth, M. 2018. *Globalization and Feminist Activism*. New York: Rowman and Littlefield. Second edition.

Hedström, J. 2016. 'We did not realize about the gender issues. So, we thought it was a good idea: Gender roles in Burmese oppositional struggles.' *International Feminist Journal of Politics* 18(1): 61–79.

Holzer, E. 2015. *The Concerned Women of Bududruman: Refugee Activists and Humanitarian Dilemmas*. Ithaca, NY: Cornell University Press.

Hunt, S. and C. Posa. 2001. 'Women waging peace: Inclusive security.' *Foreign Policy* 124: 38–47.

Jok, J. M. 1998. 'Militarization, gender and reproductive health in South Sudan.' *Africa: Journal of the International Africa Institute* 69 (2): 194–212.

Kaufman, J. and K. Williams. 2013. *Women at War, Women Building Peace: Challenging Gender Norms*. Boulder, CO: Kumarian Press.

Klem, B. 2018. 'The problem of peace and the meaning of post-war.' *Conflict, Security and Development* 18 (3): 233–255.

Krause, J., W. Krause and P. Bränfors. 2018. 'Women's participation in peace negotiations and the durability of peace.' *International Interactions* 44 (6): 985–1016.

Malkki, L. 1995. *Purity and Exile: Violence, Memory, and National Cosmology among Hutu Refugees in Tanzania*. Chicago, IL: Chicago University Press.

Moghadam, V. 2005. *Globalizing Women: Transnational Feminist Networks*. Baltimore, ML: The Johns Hopkins University Press.

Naples, N. 2009. 'Teaching intersectionality intersectionally.' *International Feminist Journal of Politics* 11 (4): 566–77.

Ne Lynn Zaw and M. Pepper. 2016. 'Poverty and health in contemporary Myanmar.' *Independent Journal of Burmese Scholarship* 1 (1): 163–186.

Olivius, E. 2017. 'Sites of repression and resistance: Political space in refugee camps in Thailand.' *Critical Asian Studies* 49 (3): 289–307.

———. 2019. 'Time to go home? The conflictual politics of diaspora return in the Burmese women's movement.' *Asian Ethnicity* 20 (2): 148–167.

Olivius, E. and J. Hedström. 2019. 'Militarized nationalism as a platform for feminist mobilization? The case of the exiled Burmese women's movement.' *Women's Studies International Forum* 76: 1–10.

Paarlberg-Kvam, K. 2018. 'What's to come is more complicated: Feminist visions of peace in Colombia.' *International Feminist Journal of Politics* 21 (2): 194–223.

Pepper, M. 2018. '"We ethnic women are the solution for the conflict": Ethnic minority women, diversity and informal participation in Myanmar.' *Journal of Peacebuilding and Development* 13 (2): 61–75.

Pierson, Paul. 2004. *Politics in Time: History, Institutions, and Social Analysis.* Princeton, NJ: Princeton University Press.

Purkayastha, B. and M. Subramaniam. 2004. *The Power of Women's Informal Networks: Lessons in Social Change from South Asia and West Africa.* Oxford: Lexington Books.

Ray, R. 1999. *Fields of Protest: Women's Movements in India.* Minneapolis, MI: University of Minnesota Press.

Reardon, B. 1993. *Women and Peace: Feminist Visions of Global Security.* Albany, NY: SUNY Press.

Reardon, B. and D. Snauwaertt. 2015. *Betty A. Reardon: Key Texts in Gender and Peace.* Boulder, CO: Springer.

Sa'ar, A. 2016. *Economic Citizenship: Neoliberal Paradoxes of Empowerment.* New York: Bergahan Books.

Salai Isaac Khen and Muk Yin Haung Nyoi. 2014. *Looking at the Peace Process in Myanmar through a Gender Lens.* Bern: Swisspeace. Available at: www.themimu. info/sites/themimu.info/files/documents/Report_Catalyzing_Reflections_ Jan2014.pdf. Retrieved 25 June 2020.

Shair-Rosenfield, S. and R. Wood. 2017. 'Governing well after war: How improving female representation prolongs post-conflict peace.' *Journal of Politics* 79 (3): 995–1009.

Sharoni, S. 1995. *Gender and the Israel-Palestine Conflict: The Politics of Women's Resistance.* Syracuse, NY: Syracuse University Press.

South, A. and M. Lall. 2016. 'Language, education and the peace process in Myanmar.' *Contemporary Southeast Asia* 38 (1): 128–153.

Stienstra, D. 1994. *Women's Movements and International Organizations.* London: Macmillan Press.

Strauss, A. and J. Corbin. 1990. *Basics of Qualitative Research: Grounded Theory Procedures and Techniques.* London: SAGE.

Thawnghmung, A. M. 2013. 'Karen nationalism and armed struggle: From the perspective of Zipporah Sein.' In S. Blackburn and H. Ting, *Women in Southeast Asian Nationalist Movements: A Biographical Approach*, pp. 250–275. Singapore: NUS Press.

The Border Consortium. 2021. *Refugee Camp Populations April 2021.* Available at: www.theborderconsortium.org/wp-content/uploads/2021/05/2021-04-April- map-tbc-unhcr.pdf. Retrieved 12 May 2021.

United Nations Development Program. 2021. *Human Development Report 2020.* Available at: hdr.undp.org/en/2020-report. Retrieved 9 April 2020.

Viterna, J. and K. Fallon. 2008. 'Democratization, women's movements and gender-equitable States: A framework for comparison.' *American Sociological Review* 73 (4): 668–689.

Waylen, G. 2007. *Engendering Transitions: Women's Mobilization, Institutions, and Gender Outcomes.* Oxford: Oxford University Press.

Women's League of Burma. 2011. *The Founding and Development of the Women's League of Burma: A Herstory.* Chiang Mai: Women's League of Burma. Available at: www.burmalink.org/wp-content/uploads/2013/12/WLB-2011.-The-Founding-and-Development-of-the-Women%E2%80%99s-League-of-Burma_A-Herstory.pdf. Retrieved 25 June 2020.

Yuval-Davis, N. 1997. *Gender and Nation.* London: Sage.

CHAPTER 5

Navigating Contradictions

How Political Transition and the Resurgence of Conflict has Shaped the Activism of the Kachin Women's Association Thailand

Magda Lorena Cárdenas

T he political opening in Myanmar between 2011 and 2021 provided increased opportunities for civil society activism in the
country, spurring the emergence of new movements as well as
incentivizing activists to return from exile. These positive changes for civil
society actors, among them women's organizations, were, however, unevenly
distributed across the country. In Kachin areas in Northern Myanmar,
the onset of the transitional period did not bring increased freedom, but
a resurgence of armed conflict. A ceasefire between the government and
the Kachin Independence Organization (KIO) had held since 1994, but it
never resolved key political grievances, and economic marginalization and
militarization in Kachin state persisted throughout the ceasefire period.
The breakdown of this ceasefire in 2011, at the dawn of a decade of political
reforms, and the resulting intensification of armed attacks, displacement
and human rights violations throughout Myanmar's transitional period,
demonstrate that the effects of transition were never uniform, or entirely
progressive, across Myanmar (Sadan [ed.] 2016; Nilsen 2019).

This chapter explores how women activists in and from Kachin state
have navigated this paradoxical situation. It focuses on the Kachin Women's
Association Thailand (KWAT), an organization founded by Kachin refugees
and exiles in Thailand in 1999 (KWAT 2018b). After 2011, the increased space
that became available for civil society in many parts of Myanmar reshaped
the political landscape of Myanmar women's activism, as new organizations
and networks emerged within Myanmar, and many ethnic minority women's
organizations founded in exile relocated to Myanmar (Olivius 2019; Aye Thiri
Kyaw, this volume; Pepper, this volume). KWAT, however, decided to keep

their headquarters in Thailand, considering that it was not safe to move their work to Kachin state. Against the backdrop of ongoing war, KWAT activists prioritized continued documentation of state-sponsored abuses over accommodation with the Myanmar government. The resurgence of Tatmadaw aggressions against Kachin communities 'rapidly led to the displacement of over 100,000 people' (Kachin Baptist Convention et al 2018: 6) and reinforced KWAT's conviction that ethnic self-determination is a precondition for the realization of ethnic minority women's rights, thus reinforcing their support for the KIO armed struggle. This illustrates the historically close relationships that many of Myanmar's ethnic minority women's organizations have had with armed groups (Olivius and Hedström 2019). Thus the transitional period forced KWAT to reappraise its strategies and its partnerships, both with allies in the women's movement and within the ethnic Kachin struggle.

In this chapter, I draw on interviews, participant observation, reports, papers and statements produced by KWAT and other women's organizations as well as women's activism literature to trace the ways in which KWAT has navigated the dilemmas of the transitional period, which created both opportunities and constraints in relation to their work, and the ways in which this led them to change their agenda and strategies. By doing this, I hope to generate broader insights into how women's mobilization responds to changing political contexts. The chapter also adds to the literature exploring how feminist activism relates to militarism and armed movements.

The chapter is structured as follows. Firstly, I will situate KWAT and their agenda and strategies in the context of the history of conflict in Kachin state and at the intersection between the struggle for women's rights and the Kachin ethnic struggle. This is followed by an overview of the methods and data upon which this chapter is based. In the analysis that follows, I go on to discuss how KWAT has navigated substantial, but contradictory, political changes during the period of transition, and how this has challenged and reshaped their strategies and alliances. In conclusion, I reflect on how the 2021 military coup might again reshape the landscape of Myanmar women's activism.

A Twofold Activism: Ethnic Rights and Women's Rights in a Changing Political Landscape

In feminist scholarship, women's empowerment and the pursuit of women's rights has often been considered at odds with ethno-nationalist projects. As

119

Pinkaew Leungaramsri (2006) argues, ethnicity as a main identity marker overlooks the multiple narratives and experiences of marginalization. Projects that are ethno-political offer limited possibilities for addressing other experiences of discrimination and other expressions of unbalanced power relations within society. Feminist scholars have analyzed how ethno-nationalism often reinforces male-dominated power structures and dichotomized gender roles, which limit women's enjoyment of rights and their participation in formal decision making (Yuval-Davis 1997; Banerjee 2006).

However, a growing body of research has demonstrated that despite this, women sometimes do identify strongly with ethno-nationalist agendas, and use them as platforms to mobilize in pursuit of women's rights, particularly in contexts of ongoing or recent armed conflict. For instance, Ashe (2007) analyses the case of Northern Ireland and argues that women's identification with ethno-nationalist political goals and culture does not necessarily imply that they reproduce traditional gendered roles. Instead, they can find opportunities for agency and change within these contexts. Similarly, in their analysis of Kurdish women's activism Al-Ali and Tas (2018) show how this consists of a dual struggle – for the recognition of Kurds, and against male-dominated societal structures. With regard to Myanmar, Olivius and Hedström (2019) explore the ways in which women's involvement in the military structures of ethnic armed organizations has built a platform from which to expand women's participation and foster an agenda for gender equality (see also Pepper, this volume). This chapter engages with this theoretical discussion on the spaces and limitations for women's activism within ethno-nationalist movements in conflict contexts. KWAT provides an excellent case study for exploring these broader questions.

For decades, the space for Kachin women's activism has been shaped by the dynamics of armed conflict in Northern Myanmar. In order to analyze the emergence of KWAT as an organization in exile and to make sense of the evolution of its agenda, it is therefore necessary to understand the evolution of the Kachin conflict with the Myanmar government. The fighting between the KIO and the Myanmar military began in 1961 and intensified in the 1980s. The effect of the conflict on civilians became more pronounced in the early 1990s, when entire villages were forced to flee from government offensives, first to rebel-controlled areas and then to Thailand (Lintner 1994; South 2009; Sadan 2013). Despite the ceasefire agreed in 1994, conditions in Kachin state did not support refugee return, as social and economic needs were not effectively addressed by the government. As Smith argues, the ceasefire period is seen as a 'time of lost opportunities, economic marginalization and, ultimately broken political promises' (2016: 83).

In response to this situation, KIO authorities, together with Kachin community-based organizations and diaspora groups, mobilized to provide for the humanitarian needs of the IDP population (Ho 2021). In this context, KWAT was founded in Chiang Mai, Thailand, in 1999, with the primary objective of improving living conditions for Kachin women, both in Kachin state and as migrants in Thailand, particularly through providing emergency aid to Kachin internally displaced persons (IDPs). However, KWAT soon developed a more comprehensive agenda, encompassing 'women's rights, children's rights and gender equality; promoting women's participation in politics and in peace and reconciliation processes; opposing all forms of violence against women including human trafficking; providing health education and health services; and promoting women's awareness of how to manage and protect the environment' (KWAT 2021a).

The goal of promoting and facilitating women's involvement in decision-making is not just a priority; it is acknowledged by KWAT to be an integral part of the Kachin ethno-political project. While not organizationally part of KIO structures, KWAT has, since its inception, supported KIO's agenda for Kachin self-determination. The resurgence of armed conflict in Kachin state has reinforced this commitment, underlining the urgency of freedom from Tatmadaw aggression and central state domination for Kachin communities in general, and Kachin women in particular. At the same time, KWAT is a founding member of the multi-ethnic umbrella organization Women's League of Burma (WLB), and has throughout its existence also been a key driving force behind broader efforts to mobilize a national movement of Myanmar women. These alliances have, however, been challenged by the transition; after 2011, many women's organizations turned their attention to engagement with the state in order to influence transitional policymaking and governance (Aye Thiri Kyaw, this volume). For KWAT, this reorientation was not an option, given ongoing war and displacement in their areas of origin.

Thus, as an organization representing ethnic minority women and as a member of an inter-ethnic women's movement, KWAT has, since its founding, navigated two fields of political mobilization, seeking to combine the promotion of ethnic rights and support for the cause of Kachin self-determination with the promotion of gender equality and women's participation in all spheres of society. Both gender equality and ethnic minority rights are at the core of the political and societal project that KWAT envisions. However, the means and arenas through which these aims are pursued have been shaped by the political changes during the transitional period and have pushed KWAT to reappraise its relationship with the broader women's movement as well as with the Kachin struggle.

Methods and Material

The empirical material on which I draw in this chapter was collected through semi-structured interviews conducted in Chiang Mai and Yangon from October to December 2018 and through participant observation with KWAT. The interviewees included members of KWAT, both based in its Chiang Mai headquarters and in its office in Myitkyina in Myanmar. I also interviewed women activists from other organizations, including representatives of the multi-ethnic alliances Women's League of Burma, Women's Organizations Network (WON) and the Alliance for Gender Inclusion in the Peace Process (AGIPP). Among the interviewees there were also representatives of international organizations and research centres. The interviews lasted between 45 minutes and two hours, and were mainly conducted in English.

The process of participant observation was aimed at experiencing the organizational dynamics within KWAT. I enrolled as a volunteer for two months at the KWAT office in Chiang Mai. In that capacity, I was able to support the formulation of project proposals and the drafting of evaluation reports. I also participated in planning and conducting trainings. My observations and reflections on my work as a volunteer were recorded in the form of field notes. It is worth noting that the field notes express personal reflections on KWAT's agenda and ongoing initiatives. I also reflect on my personal experience of working with the organization and on my exposure to Kachin culture. The content of the evaluations and internal discussions on specific projects in which I participated remain confidential. KWAT, as my host organization, was informed of the aims of my research and verbally offered its consent, as did all of my interviewees.

KWAT in the Transitional Political Landscape

During the transitional period, KWAT found itself in the midst of intense, but contradictory, processes of change. The political opening in Myanmar generally shifted the priorities of international donors and partners, who became more focused on supporting peace and democracy efforts in collaboration with the state rather than on supporting exiled opposition groups. Many women's organizations attempted to exploit the increased political space in Yangon and Naypyidaw and to have an impact on transitional politics and policymaking; thus, they targeted their advocacy increasingly towards the state rather than international audiences (Olivius 2019). At the same time, renewed armed conflict in Kachin state gave the Kachin struggle for self-determination and freedom from majority dominance renewed urgency as a precondition to realizing Kachin women's rights. Below, I describe how KWAT negotiated this position in Myanmar's transitional political landscape in relation to three different audiences and allies: the international community; the broader Myanmar women's movement; and the Kachin ethno-nationalist struggle.

We are Still at War: Human Rights Documentation and International Advocacy

Human rights documentation and international advocacy constituted a key feature of the activism of ethnic minority women's organizations that emerged in exile from the 1990s and onwards (Olivius and Hedström 2019; Cárdenas and Olivius 2021). This was the case for KWAT (Hedström and Olivius 2021). This type of activism often involved a confrontational style focused on drawing on the power of international norms to condemn the Myanmar military and government. After the transition, this form of activism decreased in importance for many organizations, as other arenas of influence opened up in Myanmar (Olivius 2019). However, for KWAT the urgency of letting the world know about events in Kachin state was heightened, as, in their view, the world seemed to have forgotten that armed conflict and political repression was still a reality in some parts of the country. This point was made with significant frustration by a KWAT activist, in an interview with Elisabeth Olivius, explaining why KWAT needed to continue their human rights documentation activities, and why this work needed to be conducted from exile in Thailand:

Most of the big donors, international donors, are just seeing like 'Oh Burma is totally changing to democracy'. Actually, it is not. And they think we all can move into the country and then work freely, actually we … for example for social work it is okay, but political activities we cannot do freely in the country. Most of the people do not understand that.[1]

This meant that the transition made it more difficult for KWAT to capture international attention with their reporting on the situation of Kachin women. Nevertheless, KWAT continued to produce reports during the transitional period, grounded in their desire to let the world know about the ongoing suffering of Kachin people and the disproportionately gendered effects of the conflict. For example, one of the themes consistently prioritized in KWAT's advocacy work is conflict-related sexual violence. This is the topic of reports such as *Ongoing Impunity: Continued Burma Army Atrocities Against the Kachin People* (KWAT 2012) and *Justice Delayed, Justice Denied* (KWAT and Legal Aid Network 2016). Reports such as these highlight the fact that state-sponsored sexual violence continued, in conflict areas, throughout the transitional period. Research conducted by KWAT and Asia Justice and Rights (2019) also delved deeper into the challenges experienced by civil society in trying to bring perpetrators to justice, given the constant interference of the military and the structure of the military and police courts.[2] Particularly in relation to cases of sexual violence, the report reveals that 'prosecutions and convictions in military and police courts are extremely rare, and punishment is often weak and not adequate in comparison to the seriousness of the crimes' (KWAT and Asia Justice and Rights 2019: 22). Emphasizing the limits of on-the-ground improvements in political freedom and human rights in Kachin areas due to emergency rule and ongoing military operations, a recent press release states that:

> Justice is not being served under Burma's military justice system. At the same time, fear of the military is preventing the civilian legal system from functioning. Lawyers are afraid to take up cases against the military, and in the rare instances they do, the cases are dismissed: such as the case of 28-year-old Sumlut Roi Ja – abducted, sexually assaulted and killed by

1   Interview with activist, Chiang Mai, 8 November 2017. Cited in Olivius 2019: 159.
2   In accordance with the 2008 Constitution, the military and the police have complete control of the investigation and prosecution of their own members.

the Burma Army in October 2011 – which was dismissed by the Supreme Court for 'lack of evidence'. (KWAT 2020: 2)

In recent years, KWAT's work on documentation of cases and advocacy has provided an important counter-narrative to widespread international perceptions of Myanmar as a democratizing state.

Moreover, KWAT has investigated the ways in which the post-2011 context has given rise to new forms of insecurity, for example through a spiralling drug crisis in Kachin State. In the report *Silent Offensive: How Burma Army strategies are fuelling the Kachin drug crisis* (2014), KWAT analyses how production and trafficking of drugs has been used as a counter-insurgency strategy to combat the KIO. Building on surveys and interviews in Kachin areas, it states that:

> [M]embers of the military including Border Guard Forces and proxy militia are leading armed players in the drug business [...] They are either involved directly in growing, producing and trafficking drugs, or else tax and provide security to others carrying out this trade.
>
> (KWAT 2014: 12)

KWAT has also analysed the gender dimension of this problem, manifested in women's vulnerability to abuse and the increased financial burden they have had to take on. The testimonies collected in the report mentioned above also reveal the difficult situation of 'mothers, wives or sisters, who not only have to become the main family breadwinners, but also have to deal with the debts and sometimes criminal charges incurred by the addicts. At the same time, they have to continue taking responsibility for all household tasks' (KWAT 2014: 26).

After the resumption of war, resulting in large-scale displacement in Kachin state, the issue of human trafficking became a new central issue for KWAT, again reflecting a changing conflict landscape. High levels of displacement and poverty, along with a demand for 'brides' across the border in China, created a market for the trafficking of Kachin women (Kamler 2015). In response, the issue of human trafficking received increased attention in KWAT human rights documentation work, resulting in reports such as *Pushed to the Brink – Conflict and human trafficking on the Kachin–China border* (KWAT 2013). A recent study conducted by Johns Hopkins University in partnership with KWAT explores the conflict-related determinants of forced marriage and trafficking of women to China. This study reveals that 'a total of 157 (39.8%) out of 394 Kachin women in interviewed by KWAT in Kachin state, Northern Shan state and Yunnan province in China, have experienced forced marriage and among them, 103 (65.6%) were trafficked' (Johns Hopkins and KWAT 2018: viii).

Thus, by drawing attention to the persistence of armed conflict and human rights abuses in conflict-affected areas of Myanmar, KWAT has attempted to counter a simplified perception of Myanmar as a democratizing state among international audiences, which, particularly in the early years of the transition, tended towards optimistic accounts of Myanmar as a 'development partner' and a new market for investment (Bächtold 2015). While human rights documentation and international advocacy was not a new form of work for KWAT, the transition increased the urgency of this work, while also posing new challenges.

Expanding Women's Alliances: Bridging Differences in the Pursuit of Gender Equality

As noted above, the initiation of political reforms after 2011, such as steps towards democracy, increased media freedom and the release of political prisoners, signaled a new era with regard to political space for civil society in Myanmar. In response, the transitional period saw a rapid expansion and growing role of new women's networks such as the Gender Equality Network (GEN), WON and AGIPP (Aye Thiri Kyaw, this volume). Ethnic minority women's organizations, organized under the umbrella of the WLB, had dominated the pre-transition landscape of women's activism in terms of visibility and international support. This quickly changed as Myanmar women's mobilization expanded in numbers and diversity. In response both to shifting donor priorities and to new opportunities to impact processes of change in Myanmar, many organizations founded in exile began to relocate their offices and activities into Myanmar, and in 2017 the WLB congress voted to move the WLB secretariat to Yangon (Cárdenas and Olivius 2021). For organizations within the WLB alliance, the question of return to Myanmar gave rise to significant tensions and difficult choices; exile had provided a conducive political environment for feminist mobilization, and public work within Myanmar demanded that they reinvent themselves and their ways of working in the hope of furthering feminist goals through a new, broader national women's movement (Olivius 2019). One activist in exile contended that this geographical shift jeopardized the cohesion of the movement. In her words, 'the movement won't be broken but it will be weaker'.[3]

This argument is echoed by another activist, who expresses her concern about the future of the women's movement as an actor that can openly address politically sensitive issues and express criticism in national and international forums:

> Before, their [women's organizations which relocated to Myanmar] statements were stronger. Now they have to be more careful. Many organizations increase their self-censorship because of the pressure from the authorities. There is a close monitoring [...] At the end of the day you have to remember why you are doing what you do. Organizations based in the borderlands and in the conflict zones are reminded of the threats.[4]

For KWAT, it was not an option to relocate completely to Myanmar. As noted in an interview excerpt above, KWAT activists did not feel that their human rights documentation work could be safely and freely carried out in Myanmar; indeed, as noted by the activist just cited, organizations that did relocate experienced significant surveillance. However, KWAT was present in Kachin areas of Myanmar through offices in KIO-controlled areas and in the Kachin capital of Myitkyina. From these locations, they have developed practices in response to everyday needs, such as health care provision and humanitarian aid. KWAT was one of a handful of WLB members that kept their main office in exile throughout the transitional period.

The growth and increased diversity of Myanmar women's activism also meant that differences among women activists and organizations became more significant. While women from different ethnic minority organizations could find common ground in their experiences of armed conflict and displacement at the hands of the Tatmadaw and in their aspirations to a federal democratic state, the urban, middle-class activists of many new organizations in Myanmar did not share these experiences and goals. From the perspective of KWAT, the transition to democracy is not the ultimate goal in itself. Their vision is federal democracy, which implies self-determination for the Kachin people. Moreover, for KWAT the goal of gender equality cannot be separated from political solutions to core conflict issues, such as addressing long-standing dynamics of injustice for the ethnic minority

3   Interview with activist, Chiang Mai, 13 December 2018.
4   Interview with activist, Yangon, 16 November 2018.

populations. This, as argued by the activist quoted below, sets KWAT apart from women's activists and organizations that lack experience of armed conflict and ethnic persecution:

> They only think on the democracy, like if we have a democracy in Burma, the mission will be fulfilled. But for us, democracy is not enough, right? [...] So, they are just focused on gender equality, only work for women's rights, you know, in general. It is fine and may be easier and they are very free to work on that issue, but who are working for more focus on conflict area?[5]

Another tension within the women's movement emerged in relation to women's participation in the peace process. While women's organizations and activists, particularly in the urban areas of Myanmar, advocated for women's participation in the official peace process, other organizations, including KWAT, did not recognize the Nationwide Ceasefire Agreement as a legitimate framework. Therefore, the debate about women's participation 'is not about having women sitting at the table'[6] but about making sure that women's voices from conflict areas are also recognized and incorporated in peace talks. An activist, in an interview with Elisabeth Olivius, echoes this argument:

> The women from conflict area should participate in [the peace process]. So that is why we are worried that some are thinking only about women's participation. Our meaning of women's participation is not like that. So not only women, but women who can really, you know, represent women's voices from the ground.[7]

During the transition, differences between women from conflict-affected areas and organizations based in Yangon became more salient. Moreover, different positions in relation to the ongoing peace process under the National Ceasefire Agreement (NCA) framework created tensions within the WLB alliance, as described by a KWAT representative:

> There is ongoing offensive and ongoing war crime and crime against humanity happen in the Kachin area. So, how can we feel the same with the other organizations who are just based in the urban area and also

5   Interview with activist, Chiang Mai, 15 December 2018.
6   Interview with activist, Chiang Mai, 15 December 2018.
7   Interview with activist, Chiang Mai, 1 December 2016.

non-conflict area? So this kind of, you know, position is now is little bit different with the WLB and other member organization. [...] especially for the position on ICC[8] or something for finding justice. We strongly, strongly call for ICC, you know, but as the other members, not all members, but other member who are signing the NCA, they don't want to speak out on this kind of risky issue [...] So that's why this signatory NCA women's leaders have a different feeling and different position with us.[9]

In sum, the transition has expanded and reshaped the political landscape of Myanmar women's activism, giving feminist agendas and goals far more visibility in Myanmar public life. At the same time, for KWAT the strain of bridging growing differences, and the frustration of seeing movement allies ignorant of the conditions in conflict-affected Kachin state, has been deeply felt. During the transition, strategies aiming at promoting gender equality and women's empowerment in transitional politics were prioritized among women's organizations that relocated to Myanmar, while KWAT continued to emphasize the protection of women in conflict-affected areas and the need to link women's rights and ethnic rights.

The Kachin Struggle: Opportunities and Challenges to Change from Within

Historically, there were important linkages between KWAT and the leadership of the KIO. While KWAT was founded as an independent organization, there are significant personal relationships between the two organizations, and KWAT has supported the KIO armed struggle as a means to Kachin self-determination. This position derives from the conviction that ethnic equality and gender equality are interlinked political goals. The resurgence of armed conflict in Kachin state in 2011 reaffirmed KWAT's loyalty to KIO, as it underlined the importance of freedom from majority aggression and domination as a precondition for the realization of Kachin women's rights. Moreover, over time KWAT has earned the recognition of KIO leaders, not least on the basis of their work with human rights documentation and international advocacy. Through this, KWAT has improved the visibility and

---

8   As part of its international advocacy work, KWAT has constantly demanded the opening of investigations by the International Criminal Court with regard to human rights violations perpetrated by the Myanmar Armed Forces.

9   Interview with activist, Chiang Mai, 19 December 2018.

legitimacy of the Kachin struggle in relation to international audiences, and has thus proved itself instrumentally useful to KIO (Hedström and Olivius 2021). As a result, new opportunities for pursuing change from within the ethno-nationalist project have opened up. For example, KIO has been holding public consultations with civil society, including women's organizations, since 2011. These links to civil society are a source of legitimacy for KIO, as it also demonstrates commitment to staying in touch with Kachin grassroots (De la Cour Venning 2019). This is in itself a small step towards change, and has also led to further changes in KIO rules and governing practices:

> They [KIO] are aware of people caring about gender equality but I am not sure that they know what this means [...] anyway, they gradually understand a little bit more. Some rules have changed, for instance, opening possibilities for women to get married and continue working in service.[10]

Seeking to better exploit these openings for women's participation in KIO decision-making, KWAT has contributed to strengthening the leadership skills of women from the Kachin Women's Association, a women's wing that is organizationally part of KIO, through its internship programme and trainings. More than 50 women holding leadership positions within KWA have received these trainings. Through these, the aim is to create a critical mass of women who can position themselves within the structures of Kachin leadership and transcend the support roles traditionally expected from women within KIO. The content of these trainings encompasses democracy, human rights and political affairs, aiming to provide women with tools to take part in KIO decision-making and policymaking.

However, seeking to advance women's rights from within the militarized, male-dominated structures of the KIO also entails significant challenges and obstacles. There is still a long way to go before KWAT can effectively influence the agenda-setting in Kachin politics and the ethno-political project as a whole. One of the recurring demands and policy recommendations expressed by KWAT has been a guarantee of women's participation in peace efforts. As one KWAT representative argues, although the KIO has been receptive to input from KWAT, this sign of political will has not been translated into outspoken acknowledgement of the contribution that Kachin women can make to the Kachin struggle:

---

10   Online interview with representative of Kachinland Research Center, 16 June 2020.

They listen to KWAT about women's participation. They have accepted 30% quota, actually they have said 'you can come as much as you want. You should empower women, don't ask, just come'. They don't listen to women in public, only at the back. But, slowly, they are listening.[11]

Nevertheless, there is resistance to accepting and articulating the problem of gender discrimination within the KIO. This is probably informed by a desire to maintain a sense of social stability and of the status quo in a highly unstable political context. This can be clearly seen in the sensitivity around raising issues of violence against women within the Kachin community. While KWAT advocacy that draws attention to sexual violence perpetrated by Tatmadaw troops is readily taken up and publicized by KIO, violations perpetrated by KIO soldiers are raised only in closed meetings with KIO leaders (Hedström and Olivius 2021).

There is also an apparent unwillingness on the part of KIO commanders to address issues of sexual violence during ongoing conflict. Sexual violence acquires political significance when is portrayed as violence by the enemy against the ethnic minority. Although this can be an entry point for women's organizations to get access to the KIO agenda, it is still insufficient from a women's rights perspective. A KWAT representative reflects on the low priority that sexual violence more broadly holds on the KIO agenda:

They [ethnic rights and women's rights] should be combined but some men leaders don't understand that. They are just thinking 'this is an important time, we cannot talk about women now'. When we discuss that sexual violence should be brought to the table most of them don't understand that. They say 'Later, later, later ...' And later is when many women have been raped.[12]

A similar pattern can be seen in KIO attitudes to the issue of human trafficking of Kachin women. As Kamler (2015) argues, this topic is still considered by KIO leaders to be a women's issue, and despite having been in dialogue with women's groups, they have not developed effective policy responses.

Thus, during the last decade there has been improvement in KIO awareness of the importance of women's involvement, but the possibility of greater participation depends on a structural transformation of social attitudes and

11   Interview with activist, Chiang Mai, 19 December 2018.
12   Interview with activist, Chiang Mai, 15 December 2018.

narratives in the Kachin community as a whole. Not only does the political and military KIO leadership continue to be male-dominated, but so does the religious leadership in Kachin State, and this is something that constrains the possibilities for the societal change in gendered dynamics that organizations like KWAT envision. Christian Baptist networks have been crucial in shaping Kachin identity (Pelletier 2021). The Kachin Baptist Convention (KBC), in particular, played an important role after conflict resumed, as one of the most prominent civil society organizations, as providers of emergency relief and as a bastion for the nationalist project.

Recently, support for the promotion of traditional values has gradually grown among the youth. One of the interviewees described how he had witnessed 'young men complaining about women's rights' as part of 'a shift in pro-western narratives and attitudes to more traditional views'.[13] Thus, one of the main challenges for KWAT in maintaining a role of influence within the Kachin community is demonstrating how the idea of gender equality does not oppose ideas of Kachin identity; instead, it is important to convince sceptics that it is an integral part of a broader agenda for justice.

Concluding Remarks

This chapter has explored how KWAT has navigated contradictory political changes during the transition, namely the simultaneous opening of political space in many parts of Myanmar and the resurgence of war in Kachin state. This has pushed KWAT to respond by reappraising and adjusting their strategies and alliances both within the women's movement and within the ethnic Kachin struggle. These developments shed light on the potential as well as the challenges of pursuing feminist agendas from within ethno-nationalist, armed movements, and thus adds to existing scholarly debates on this theme. The work of KWAT illustrates the possibility of navigating two fields of political mobilization: the promotion of ethnic rights and support for the cause of Kachin self-determination on the one hand, and a feminist activism focusing on promoting gender equality and women's participation in all spheres of decision making on the other hand.

Since its foundation, KWAT's agenda and main political goals have been aligned with the KIO aim of securing Kachin self-determination through

13   Online interview with scholar, 12 June 2020.

adopting a model of federal democracy for Myanmar. Kachin women's activism is largely located within this ethno-nationalist struggle, and is in many cases motivated by a sense of duty towards the Kachin community as well as by the opportunity to position itself politically within that community (Hedström 2016a). However, KWAT activism has increasingly emphasized the fact that a genuine model of federal democracy requires that women be included in decision-making. These arguments have been strengthened in the post-2011 context. During KWAT's 10th Congress in February 2019, there was a reaffirmation of 'KWAT's strong commitment to work towards genuine peace and reforming federal democracy in Burma and to promote women's participating in decision making at all levels' (KWAT 2019). Thus, for KWAT gender equality and a just political settlement of the conflict are interlinked political goals. Activism deployed by KWAT since 1999 demonstrates that in its political vision, ethnic rights, self-determination and federal democracy are key aspects of a political landscape in which minority women can enjoy equal rights. Thus, it is not possible to focus on women's rights in isolation, as KWAT suggests that some other organizations within the women's movement have done in response to the dynamics of transition. However, promoting women's rights within and in close association with militarized, male-dominated KIO structures comes with significant challenges.

Even if Kachin self-determination is eventually achieved, this will not mean that the struggle for gender equality will be over, and KWAT's activism will continue promoting the agenda of women's participation within all spheres of Kachin community. The relationship with KIO remains strategic and became more reciprocal in the context of transition, but structural changes are needed in order to challenge the militarized and patriarchal structure, which constrains the advancement of the agenda for gender equality. In order to guarantee women's involvement in political affairs it is necessary to address the structural barriers obstructing women's enjoyment of rights within the Kachin community and the persistent narratives that disenfranchise women's leadership. Women activists have made efforts to transform this mindset and raise awareness about the role of women in the context of the political project of federal democracy. However, there are challenges making it difficult for them to play a more assertive and independent role within KIO structure. Questions about gender equality are still considered a domestic matter and therefore outside of political discussion. From the KIO perspective, the aims of self-determination, democracy and enjoyment of human rights are understood in relation to the struggle against the Myanmar government, and not as a process of change that also needs to take place within the Kachin leadership and community (Nilsen 2019).

The transition has made it more urgent to overcome these challenges, as the resurgence of armed conflict has, for KWAT, underlined the necessity of the KIO struggle in order to secure rights for Kachin women. The transition has also brought new challenges concerning the work of KWAT within the broader women's movement, as international donors as well as women's organizations have increasingly turned to the Myanmar state as a partner and target for advocacy. One of the implications of the relocation to Yangon by several of the organizations that are members of the multi-ethnic alliance has been a more limited space in which to make outspoken denunciations of the human rights violations perpetrated by the Myanmar Armed Forces, and limited capacity to do this. These limitations have been criticized by KWAT as a factor that jeopardizes the cohesion of the women's movement.

The military coup on 1 February 2021 can be expected to reshape the political conditions for Myanmar women's activism yet again. The coup, and the new junta's violent repression of protesters, have already reversed the shift towards the state in donor and investor strategies, and many women's activists have fled to neighbouring countries or gone into hiding. KWAT, along with other organizations, has called on the international community to prioritize 'placing at the center of its response local CBOs and CSOs that have the expertise, agency and legitimacy' (Progressive Voice 2021). KWAT statements and actions after the coup continue to draw attention to the ongoing conflict in Kachin State and to underscore the continuing need for a dual struggle – for democracy and for self-determination.

Drawing on historical experiences, the women's movement may thus resurface and reorganize in exile once more. Furthermore, it is possible to argue that the differences between women's organizations in terms of political agendas and strategies during the transition period may be reduced and that they may converge again. This might be expressed in a more vocal and articulated international advocacy. While the effects of the coup are still uncertain, recent developments emphasize how for KWAT, and for women's organizations more broadly, their work has been and continues to be constantly negotiated in response to changing political conditions.

References

Al-Ali, N. and L. Tas. 2018. 'Reconsidering nationalism and feminism: the Kurdish political movement in Turkey.' *Nations and Nationalism* 24 (2): 453–473.

Ashe, F. 2007. 'Gendering ethno-nationalist conflict in Northern Ireland: A comparative analysis of nationalist women's political protests.' *Ethnic and Racial Studies* 30 (5): 766–786.

Banerjee, S. 2006. 'Armed masculinity, Hindu nationalism and female political participation in India: Heroic mothers, chaste wives and celibate warriors.' *International Feminist Journal of Politics* 8 (1): 62–83.

Cárdenas, M. and E. Olivius. 2021. 'Building Peace in the Shadow of War: Women-to-Women Diplomacy as Alternative Peacebuilding Practice in Myanmar.' *Journal of intervention and statebuilding.* 15(3), pp.347–366.

De la Cour Venning, A. 2019. 'Revolutionary law abidance: Kachin rebel governance and the adoption of IHL in resistance to Myanmar state violence.' *International Criminal Law Review* 19 (5): 872–904.

Hedström, J. 2016a. 'Before I joined the army I was like a child!: Militarism and women's rights in Kachinland.' In Mandy Sadan (ed.), *War and Peace in the Borderlands of Myanmar: The Kachin Ceasefire, 1994–2011.* Copenhagen: NIAS Press.

Hedström, J. and Olivius, E. 2021. The politics of sexual violence in the Kachin conflict in Myanmar. International feminist journal of politics. 23(3), pp. 374–395.

Ho, E.L.-E. 2021. 'Border governance in Kachin State, Myanmar: Un/caring states and aspirant state building during humanitarian crises.' *Modern Asian Studies.* 56(2), pp. 639–660.

Johns Hopkins and KWAT. 2018. 'Estimating Trafficking of Myanmar Women for Forced Marriage and Childbearing in China.' Available at: kachinwomen.com/wp-content/uploads/2018/12/ETFM_Full-Report_07Dec2018_Final.pdf. Accessed 15 March 2021.

Kachin Baptist Convention, Metta Development Foundation, Naushawng Development Institute, Nyein Foundation, Oxfam International and Trócaire. 2018. 'Displaced and Dispossessed. Conflict-Affected Communities and their Land of Origin in Kachin State, Myanmar.' Available at: www-cdn.oxfam.org/s3fs-public/file_attachments/bp-displaced-dispossessed-land-myanmar-210518-en.pdf. Accessed 5 May 2021.

Kamler, E. M. 2015. 'Women of the Kachin conflict: Trafficking and militarized femininity on the Burma-China border.' *Journal of Human Trafficking* 1 (3): 209–234.

KWAT. 2013. 'Pushed to the Brink: Conflict and Human Trafficking on the Kachin–Burma Border.' Published in June. Available at: kachinwomen.com/pushed-to-the-brink-conflict-and-human-trafficking-on-the-kachin-china-border

————. 2014. 'Silent Offensive. How Burma Army Strategies are Fueling the Kachin Drug Crisis.' Published October. Available at: reliefweb.int/report/myanmar/silent-offensive-how-burma-army-strategies-are-fueling-kachin-drug-crisis

————. 2018b. 'Activity Report 2014–2018.' Available at: kachinwomen.com/wp-content/uploads/2019/09/Book_2014-2018-Activity-Report-KWAT-2nd-Proof.pdf. Accessed 9 May 2021.

————. 2019. 'Statement on the 10th Congress of the Kachin Women's Association Thailand' Available at: kachinwomen.com/statement-on-the-10th-congress-of-the-kachin-womens-association-thailand/

————. 2020. 'No Justice for Ongoing Burma Army Crimes in Northern Shan State. Briefing paper by the Kachin Women's Association Thailand.' Available at: kachinwomen.com/no-justice-for-ongoing-burma-army-crimes-in-northern-shan-state-briefing-paper-by-the-kachin-womens-association. Accessed 25 February 2021.

————. 2021a. 'Background.' Available at: kachinwomen.com/about-us/. Accessed 5 May 2021.

KWAT and Legal Aid Network. 2016. 'Justice Delayed, Justice Denied. Seeking Truth about Sexual Violence and War Crime Case in Burma (with a special focus on the Kawng Kha Case, in Kachin Land).' Published January. Available from: www.burmalibrary.org/sites/burmalibrary.org/files/obl/docs21/KWAT-2016-01-Justice_Delayed_Justice_Denied-en-red.pdf

KWAT and Asia Justice and Rights. 2020. 'Seeking Justice.' Available at: kachinwomen.com/wp-content/uploads/2020/07/Seeking_Justice_English_version.pdf. Accessed 4 March 2021.

Lintner, Bertil. 1994. *Burma in Revolt: Opium and Insurgency since 1948*. Boulder: Westview Press.

Nilsen, M. 2019. 'No peace in a ceasefire: Women's agency for peace in the Kachin conflict' In Å. Kolås, (ed.), *Women, Peace and Security in Myanmar: Between Feminism and Ethno-Politics*. London: Routledge. 58–72.

Olivius, E. 2019. 'Time to go home? The conflictual politics of diaspora return in the Burmese women's movement.' *Asian Ethnicity* 20 (2): 148–167.

Olivius, E. and J. Hedström. 2019. 'Militarized nationalism as a platform for feminist mobilization? The case of the exiled Burmese women's movement.' *Women's Studies International Forum* 76: 102263.

Pelletier, A. 2021. 'Identity formation, Christian networks, and the peripheries of Kachin ethnonational identity.' *Asian Politics & Policy* 13 (1): 72–89.

Pinkaew Leungaramsri. 2006. 'Women, nation and the ambivalence of subversive identification along the Thai–Burmese border.' *Sojourn: Journal of Social Issues in Southeast Asia* 21 (1): 68–89.

Progressive Voice. 2021. *Nowhere to Run: Deepening Humanitarian Crisis in Myanmar.* Available at: kachinwomen.com/wp-content/uploads/2021/09/No-Where-To-Run-Eng.pdf. Accessed 16 June 2022.

Sadan, M. 2013. *Being and Becoming Kachin: Histories Beyond the State in the Borders of Burma.* Oxford: Oxford University Press.

Sadan, M. (ed.). 2016. *War and Peace in the Borderlands of Myanmar: The Kachin Ceasefire, 1994–2011.* Copenhagen: NIAS Press.

Smith, M. 2016. 'Reflections on the Kachin ceasefire: A cycle of hope and disappointment.' In Mandy Sadan (ed.). *War and Peace in the Borderlands of Myanmar: The Kachin Ceasefire, 1994–2011.* Copenhagen: NIAS Press.

South, A. 2009. *Ethnic Politics in Burma: States in Conflict.* London: Routledge.

Yuval-Davis, N. 1997. *Gender & Nation.* London: Sage.

CHAPTER 6

'I will Fight such Dictatorship until the End'

From Student Rebel to Feminist Activist, Mother and Peace Negotiator

Zin Mar Phyo and Mi Sue Pwint

Introduction

*M*i Sue Pwint is a leading member of the All-Burma Students' Democratic Front (ABSDF), one of the founders of both the Women's League of Burma (WLB) and the Burmese Women's Union (BWU), and one of very few women included in the post-2011 nationwide ceasefire process. Mi Sue Pwint was born in Kayah State, and comes from a multiethnic background: her mother was Innthar and her father was Shan. She is the main caretaker of her daughter, who was born in a rebel student camp and has cerebral palsy. Zin Mar Phyo writes about women's rights and experiences in Myanmar for the Honest Information (HI) project, an online platform featuring women's stories, and for the Irrawaddy. She has been involved in BWU since she was a teenager.

In this conversation, Zin Mar Phyo and Mi Sue Pwint trace Mi Sue Pwint's political awakening and her journey from being a young carefree student in the city to becoming a revolutionary leader living in the jungle. Drawing on Mi Sue Pwint's experience of the struggle for democracy and rights over more than three decades, they focus on the many ways in which women's political participation is informed by their overwhelming reproductive responsibilities and care work for families and communities, as well as by dominant gender norms that frame young women as in need of protection. As discussed in other chapters in this volume, a prevailing belief that men, not women, should lead armed struggles and revolutions also limited Mi Sue Pwint's political participation, at least initially. Zin Mar Phyo and Mi Sue Pwint discuss the strategies used by Mi Sue Pwint to overcome the gendered challenges she faced as a female political leader and explore the ways in which Mi Sue Pwint has sustained her focus and determination over time. Mi Sue Pwint also reflects on how being a mother has impacted her political career, and why she decided to return to Myanmar after the transition in 2011 to partake in political dialogues with the government. In closing, Mie Sue Pwint shares her thoughts about how the 2021 military coup will affect women's rights, and her own beliefs about the future.

Becoming a Political Activist: 'I Tried to Forget about the Fact that I was Female!'

ZMP: What was your childhood like before 1988? Could you briefly share some of your experiences?

MSP: Our family life before 1988 was just like other ordinary civilians. Since we were from a middle-class family, we did not have many difficulties or concerns. My parents encouraged us to read books, and they often had political discussions that we could listen in to. After high school, I moved to Yangon, to enrol at Yangon University. There I met writers, poets and artists, most of them men, and I began to be more aware of the political situation in the country. I tried to forget about the fact that I was female! I mostly liked to sit in the tea shop with my friends and talk about literature and art and politics, rather than going to school. I learned a lot, not only about the feelings and the fights of students in politics, but also about the struggles and lives of ordinary people.

ZMP: So growing up, most of your friends and colleagues were male and that was unusual for women. For example, you sat at the tea shop together with men, which women usually didn't do. How did the society respond to you because of this?

MSP: When I went to university, I actually stayed at one of strictest boarding houses for female students. My mum found that boarding house for me. We had to be home at a certain time, and so on. But me and a close girlfriend of mine stayed out late anyway, to attend literature talks and political discussions. So we were viewed as bad girls by other people because we didn't follow the boarding house rules, we were out late, we had many male friends, and, of course, we sat in the tea shops. You know, during that time, women never went to tea shops because that was men's place. Even if they had to sit there for some reasons, they sat there really quickly and left as soon as they could. Even me, even though I sat there with my male friends and chatted with them all day, I did not like my younger sister sitting in a tea shop! I usually told her 'you eat quickly and go back', 'You do not stay here for long' and so on, since I did not like other men staring at her. I worried a lot for my sister. She wore make-up, which made me worry that people would think that she only went to the tea shop to try to get attention from men. You see, even I had those conservative ideas! I did not know about gender equality, didn't think that women, regardless of having make-up or not, have choices and rights. I did not understand about the gender stereotypes and norms which we have to fight against. To be honest, that didn't change until I came to the border, really. Even then, though, I thought that young women leaders like you shouldn't drink alcohol or behave improperly. I didn't think like that about men. I have been dealing with these types of thoughts for a long time. It is very difficult to get rid of such deep-rooted practices or thoughts. I am explaining this since I would like to highlight that even we, who are empowering women and work for women's rights, grow up with gender stereotypes. It takes time to change this, even for us.

ZMP: So what motivated you to take part in the 1988 uprising?

MSP: Before the uprising, I saw how people lived their everyday in poverty. I remember when the military demonetized the bank notes, and the economy collapsed. When this happened, an old woman who sold rice and food near our boarding house started screaming in grief and desperation. But even besides this, the students had a conflict with the military. A student called Phone Maw was shot dead by the military, but they lied about it. I demonstrated with my friends and colleagues against the military regime. We marched from Yangon's Arts and Physics University to the University of Technology. And then the military cracked down on the protests. I ran into a small street to avoid arrest. I felt so disappointed with the military's behaviours – their bullying and the crackdown on peaceful demonstrators. I could not even sleep or eat. As a young student, I could not accept such injustice. I knew that I could be beaten, arrested, and even shot or killed, if I joined the demonstrations. But I felt I did not have any other options: I had to respond to and resist this crisis. Soon, the students living in the boarding houses were broken up by the military and forced back to their home regions. When I arrived home again to Loikaw, I helped to organize the student movement in my home town. But I had to do this very secretly as the town was very small, and everyone knew each other. We started the movement in Loikaw with four to five young student leaders. And then we grew. When 8888 happened, I was one of the key leaders in Loikaw, I gave public speeches and organized the protests.

At the night of military coup, on September 18, we had to flee. We took some clothes, and hid in houses around Loikaw. But after a couple of weeks, I decided to go to the border and join the armed revolution to fight for democracy, as we didn't know how long the coup would last for. When we arrived at the border, we met with Karenni National Progressive Party (KNPP). They took us in. We didn't know how to live in the jungle. We had to build our own accommodation; carry the bamboo; lift and hold the building equipment, and so on. We also struggled with our food. We had to live on fish paste and banana plants, or fish paste and pumpkin, but we tried to get energy and strength from each other.

ZMP: At that time, how did the political participation of women look like in Myanmar, and in the movement?

MSP: Many women actively participated in the uprising. But parents worried for their daughters, more than for their sons, and wanted them to come home. For their sons, they gave them advice on how to avoid being shot and arrested, instead of calling them back to home. Even among the parents who were politically active, they encouraged their sons while they tried to stop their daughters from their political participation.

There were many active women who were always ready to take any roles and any duties for the sake of the movement, and many supported the movement in different ways from men. During 8888, whether students or housewives, they all came out to the street. Some walked in the protests, some supported protesters with food such as banana and water. But many women were pressured to stay back.

When I left for the border, we were the fifth group leaving. The students would leave in groups, you see. There were only three women in our group. Among those women, there was one I was really proud of. Her mother was seriously sick in hospital and was in a critical condition. She got the news about her mother's death while we were attending the military training together in the jungle. So, you see, there were many strong women; some, like my friend, were even stronger than men. In my experience, women are calmer than men and can solve the problems easier. Men get very emotional and aggressive. Yet most of our male colleagues looked at us women as being burdens. Some men screamed at women: 'You shits! We are tired of helping you and doing things for you!' For women, when we arrived at the border, there were two types of jobs: medical training or communication training, not front line. Fortunately, I did not have to choose between those two things since I had the same education levels with other male colleagues, and I also reminded the men that we women had helped lead the movement inside Burma. I told them: 'You cannot pressure us to choose the medical training while you are choosing to be in authority roles of the camps.' After that I became part of the camp committee; I became a leader.

ZMP: So many women left the revolution for different reasons. But you stayed there. Why? What made you strong, what made you stay with revolution?

MSP: What I always think about is shame. I feel shame if I do not accomplish what I decided I should do. I could not go back until we had achieved our goals. I tried to remain strong, although I have had many anxieties and disappointments. I have spent 20 years of my life in exile, fighting for democracy, and I have often felt like I wanted to give up. I have felt depressed. Whenever I feel lost I try to think about the good things I have done, or the success that I have had. I try to remind myself that 'at least I am still useful being here'. Maybe the reason as to why I could keep going forward with the revolution was the fact that I always tried to recognize and value every single thing that I have done. I reminded myself that younger students or soldiers were dependent on me. I always kept that in my mind, in order to go forward and to keep going. Since I have joined the armed revolution after 1988 uprising, I have decided that I will fight such dictatorship until the end and I will go back home only when such military dictatorship fall down. That's it.

Becoming a Revolutionary Woman Leader:

ZMP: When we look at old photos of ABSDF, it is rare to see women. But you are in these photos. At that time, very few women were involved in decision-making in the border areas. Why do you think you were one of those few ones? What were the challenges?

142

MSP: For me, I was used to having male friends since I attended the university. I was confident that I could protect myself well from any harassment. Also, most of the men in our camp were from the provinces, and they preferred to do practical tasks rather than political ones. For example, they were not good at public speaking, and so whenever visitors or guests came to us, me and my female comrades would greet them and talk to them. There were also many relationship problems between leaders that I had solved out. Therefore, people recognized my skills and I think this recognition gave the space for me to be included in the leadership roles. However, even though I was in the leadership role, it was obvious that women could not get the highest position such as Battalion Commander or Chairperson, even in the camp. And to get to the headquarter level, regardless of women's political knowledge or great capacity for alliance relationship, no women could reach that level.

Even though we fought for democracy, what we practiced in reality in our groups was not democratic decision-making; instead we sought people's agreement. And most people believed that even though women were active in politics and they had as much revolutionary experiences as men, women should not be leaders. They even said this in front of me. They said: 'Yeah, we know women can do it but they should not be in this position just because they are women.'

ZMP: So how did the women's movement in exile start? What was your role in that movement and what pushed you into women's activism?

MSP: In the beginning, I did not have a strong commitment for women's rights. But I noticed that women did not have space, like men, and that women had to try much more than men, and women were criticized even when they tried hard. For instance, many female soldiers came to ABSDF's Headquarter and worked in the financial department, the organizing department and research and documentation department. There were all women who were very busy with computer for all day and night. They had very strong political commitment. They had the same resistance as men; they could live in a hard situation and in hunger if needed. But they did not receive any recognition for their work or their commitment. We could count with our own fingers the number of women in political leadership roles. Some women came to our headquarter because they got married with some soldiers and they followed their husbands. Once they had arrived, they took different responsibilities, such as cooking, gardening, growing animals to sell, etc.

After Manerplaw fell, our headquarter was also affected. We had to hide, stay in small groups across the river in Thailand. Then the ABSDF top leaders began to discuss about women's political participation, since they thought that the armed revolution might take a lot longer. I think they started to get the idea of promoting women's political participation to foster the political battle. They called me in to discuss this, since they thought I could organize the younger generation. They wanted to form a women's group to promote women's political participation. At first, ABSDF wanted this group to function as a wing. But we women, we sat together after we had formed the group, and thought that we would rather be an independent group, not a women's wing. ABSDF leaders opposed this, they said we would break up the revolution, but finally they relented, although it took at least six meetings!

ZMP: You were fighting for democracy, overthrowing the dictatorship and struggling for women's rights at the same time. As a political leader and as a women's leader, what were the challenges for you? How did you overcome them?

MSP: I will give you an example. I became a member of secretariat team of NCUB. As a member of secretariat team, we regularly had to do political position papers. In the beginning, it was so difficult for me. The political analysis that most men discussed were like guessing what would happen based on the news information they had got. For instance, they would compare the latest news and the old news, they would guess what possible could happen. Clearly, there were many things which did not happen as they guessed in reality. They were just guessing the things. But people were impressed when they would talk a lot and broadly.

I tried to be confident to do the same as the men. If they spoke for five minutes for discussing their political analysis, I did the same time. If they took 10 minutes, I did the same. I tried guessing what would happen.

Another difficulty I had was about decision-making. I thought that if we discussed one thing in this meeting and we did not come to an agreement, we would have to discuss it again the next day. But for men it was not like that. They gathered at night time and decided among themselves, when they were drinking and eating. For me, I came to the next meeting, well-prepared for the things I would discuss, but the decision would already be made without my knowledge.

Another difficulty I had was that they ignored my contributions. No one responded to my political points, and they just went through the meeting the way they wanted to. It was very hard. But I kept reminding myself that if I gave up, it would be even harder for other girls and women to participate in politics in the future.

Returning Home: 'We have a Duty to do Right'

ZMP: What do you think about the peace process led by U Thein Sein after the transition in 2011? I am asking because there was a controversy between armed groups who participated in the peace process, like ABSDF, and those who did not. As one of the leaders of ABSDF, why did you decide to participate?

MSP: In the beginning, I was not sure if we should meet him or not. I had a lot of concerns. Finally, I decided to take any political opportunity that we could get from this process. You know, when we came back to Burma, we faced many challenging questions about our decision. But while we faced criticism, there were also opportunities to meet with and talk with other political groups inside Burma. I tried to hold the ABSDF's flag high among these challenges. There was a reason why I wanted to hold it. Once the national ceasefire period started, and we returned to Burma, we almost didn't have any leaders or any members left. We were broken. Some of our members had been disabled due to the fighting, some were hurt in other ways, and some lived in the jungle. They had already sacrificed their lives. Some had been arrested, and some were tortured to death. They gave their lives for the revolution, under the flag for ABSDF, maybe more than 700 people in total. We have a duty to do right for them. Seeing the grief of their parents, brothers and sisters, I decided that the sacrifices of these people could not be in vain. So, I decided to participate in the peace process only with one ambition: to hold the ABSDF flag high, to reach our goals, and walk the road we wanted to walk.

Also, no one wins through fighting. Some have had war for 20 or 30 years. Some ethnic armed groups have been at war for 70 years. Until now, we have not won and they have not won too. The civil war does not stop. We cannot defeat them and they cannot get rid of us. It feels like a situation that will last for a lifetime. So I thought it was time to try to find a solution through political dialogues. That's why I took part in the peace process. But I also had concerns. It had been almost 25 years of working for the revolution through

ABSDF when we decided to come back Burma. We have always worked in partnership with our allies. Could we still participate in the dialogues if we didn't do it in partnership with our allies? And should the ABSDF end its revolution without success?

ZMP: What do you think has changed with the peace process, since the National League for Democracy (NLD) took over from U Thein Sein?

MSP: Personally, I don't want to judge NLD's actions, or indeed Daw Aung San Suu Kyi's actions since I don't know much about her thoughts. But I can clearly say that NLD is really very weak when it comes to ethnic issues. For instance, Dr Tin Myo Win, who worked with Daw Suu with the peace process, is just her family doctor. He doesn't know about ethnic issues at all. So, when he tried to work with this he got very stressed. He was stressed when he had to meet with KNPP. He was stressed when he met with the Kachin. He eventually developed a heart disease and went to see doctor in Singapore to get treatment. And from the military side, they do not want the peace process to succeed under the NLD. The military still think that fighting against ethnic groups is the right thing to do.

ZMP: How did the peace process (in both U Thein Sein and the NLD periods) impact on women's rights, gender equality and women's participation in politics? What has been changed?

MSP: Under U Thein Sein era, the decision was made to include at least 30 per cent of women's participation in the NCA. But while the ethnic armed groups had so many women, the government side was not ready. So, instead of putting the words 'at least 30 per cent', the government representative requested that we put 'appropriate number' in NCA. Later, the government side did bring some women to the dialogues, such as the wife of U Aung Min and his wife's friends. But these women did not have any position or any decision-making power.

In terms of women's participation in the peace process, the EAO's [ethnic armed organization's] side is even more active than the other sides. Even though they do not have much willingness, they try to listen to the Women's League of Burma (WLB). In terms of women's participation, I can say that it doesn't move forward in peace process. It might look like women are in the peace process. but in essence they are not. They just add women to ceremonial roles, and to facilitator roles, not decision-making roles.

ZMP: Can you say something about your own participation in the peace process and the current political process? How has that been?

MSP: I have taken part in the peace process everywhere I have been assigned to. There are 16 members from EAO's sides (two representatives from each signatory group) in UPDJC. I set my own standard to try my best in the meetings. For instance, I set the rule that I won't talk about women's issues at every opportunity. I will only strongly say it when it is really necessary. If we try to talk about women's issues all the time in the meeting, people there will go to toilets or they do not give concentration just after we raise our hand to discuss. That is what most men are doing in reality. So, as a woman leader in such male dominated community to have recognition on our voice, I set the rule only to discuss about women when it is necessary. I work hard, but try to be strategic about when and how I bring in women's perspectives and rights.

ZMP: How does the current coup impact on women's rights and their opportunities?

MSP: There could be wars. Women will suffer. Anything could happen; women have to give birth in war, will be gang raped, will be gang tortured and there will be sexual violence against women. It will be like the hell will be alive again for women. We will have to do our best to find the pathway where we could collectively make decision and work in a united manner. We must pray that the era of war where women are violated will not return.

ZMP: What are the differences between 8888 and 2021 coups in terms of women's participation and ethnic situation?

MSP: In 2021, the women's participation in the movement has increased significantly. Women are vital in leading negotiations and guiding the crowds. Women's participation in 2021 is a lot stronger than before. Women are everywhere. Their voices are coming out. In the past, it was not that women weren't in the movement. They were involved in the movement but their roles and participation were not very visible. Right now, many women were arrested under the current coup. Many women have spoken out with great courage. Even among the celebrities, there are many female celebrities who are bravely speaking out against the military coup.

Being a Mother and a Revolutionary: 'The Work I have Done is not Easy'

ZMP: As a female revolutionary politician, how have your choices affected your family life? Has being a female political leader made it easier for your family relationships?

MSP: If women want to go through their lives as politicians, they will have to think about their private lives! If you have a strong commitment to be in politics, and stay with your duties no matter what, you need to think carefully about your private life. You should only get married if you have supporting family structure. If not, I will say that your journey will be very tough, for sure. Like me! I even have more difficulties since I have a disabled child.

You know, the work I have done is not easy. It might be even more difficult than fighting in a war. I know there will be more challenges for my political journey. However, my decision is still to continue my political life. Due to my decision to continue my political work, there will always be argument or disagreement in my family life. My partner will keep telling me: 'You are stubborn. You are trying to hit your head to the highest mountain, it is the time for you to be with the child and you should work for our child stuffs.' As I see, of course, I have a responsibility and I try my best to take such responsibility. The pathway I have walked through before is the road I want to keep walking on. Whoever tell me to stop the things that I want to do will be my enemy. Therefore, I know there will be consistent argument and disagreements in my marriage. Things will be like that.

Because of this, I did not want to encourage the young women to get married while I was in women's organization. I was not happy when I heard a woman got pregnant since I want women to be in politics very actively and freely. I want women to do politics.

ZMP: What are some of those difficulties?

MSP: My daughter has a disability. At the time of her birth, it was so difficult to give birth. And I did not have the opportunities to have regular medical check as the pregnant women needed. Some suggested that I should not give birth in the jungle due to my age. However, according to ABSDF's rules, we could only be sent to the hospital in the city when we were seriously sick and when we could not give birth. If not, everyone have to give birth in the jungle. That was our rules. I was afraid the other people would feel it was unfair that I could go to city to give birth. If they would feel it was unfair, this would affect to our organization. Also, I was healthy and I thought I would be easy to give birth. So, I gave birth in the jungle but it was difficult. And my child now lives with a disability. But I have been lucky because I have had my BWU sisters to help me take care of my child when I work. My husband only needed to sleep beside my child at night. Even at night, they would wake up to look after her when she woke up.

Now I do my work alongside taking care of my child. At first, I had so many difficulties. For instance, I had to go by flight to attend the discussion but I did not have the cost for my child. But I decided to bring my child with me no matter what; regardless of feeling hungry or thirsty, in order to keep my work.

I am the only person who is there for my daughter all the time. She is always with me. But sometimes, when I try to focus on my child my work suffers. When I focus on my work, my child suffers. It is balance.

ZMP: What would be your future dream for your family life?

MSP: I do not expect very much regarding my family. But right now the military has taken power. We have no more income, and we have to worry for money. But everyone will die one day. Rather than thinking about what kind of history I want to write or what kind of children I want to have, I just want to live in peace and accept my life. Of course, sometimes I worry for my child, how can she survive without her parents? Sometimes I think the worst things. Whenever I think about the future of my child, I feel very stressed, my heart burns, and I can't sleep for days. But as a human, we have our own fate and luck, which we cannot change. I will try my best for her. The rest will be her fate and depending on her. I try to think like that. If we can arrange something for her future where she could earn money, she could have a safe place to stay and where she could live in harmony with the community. That's all we have in our mind right now. That's the most important thing.

CHAPTER 7

Women's Leadership for Transformative, Feminist Change at the Grassroots Level in Karen State

Naw K'nyaw Paw and Maggi Quadrini

Introduction

For over 70 years, the Karen people have faced persecution by Myanmar's military regimes. Tatmadaw policies, which have aimed to defeat armed ethnic opposition groups by targeting civilian communities to eliminate sources of food, finance, recruits and intelligence, have for decades caused widespread suffering, displacement and poverty in Karen state. As a result of these counterinsurgency strategies, women and children have been raped and sexually abused, as systematic offensives by the Tatmadaw have been designed to terrorize and subjugate Karen civilians.[1] Alongside military aggression, administrative policies (only offering education to Karen children in the Burmese language, for example) have been designed to subjugate and destroy the unique culture of the Karen people.[2]

Since the 2021 military coup, the regime has broken a ceasefire in place for a decade and intensified their attacks by carrying out multiple air and ground strikes. Families have had to move and hide in the forest where they are deprived of access to food, water and shelter; at the time of writing, at least 250 000 people have been displaced.[3] The atrocities that the military junta are committing against innocent people amount to the most serious crimes under international law, including crimes against humanity and

---

1   Karen Women's Organization 2022a.
2   Ibid.
3   UCA News 2022.

war crimes. Amidst this quickly escalating humanitarian crisis, women's organizations have played a critical role in responding to urgent needs.[4]

Naw K'nyaw Paw, a Karen woman and refugee, is the General Secretary of the Karen Women's Organization (KWO), a feminist, indigenous rights community-based organization, with more than 70,000 members, which plays a leadership role in the struggle to bring democracy and human rights to Myanmar. KWO focuses[5] on capacity building, increasing and amplifying women's voices and influence, and providing[6] emergency support, including food, household items and women and children's hygiene kits. Naw K'nyaw Paw was born on the Thailand–Myanmar border, and became a refugee at the age of 11. She has been working for KWO since 1999, after completing her education in Mae Ra Moe refugee camp in Thailand, and was elected to become General Secretary in 2013.

Maggi Quadrini works on human rights with various women-led organizations on the Thailand–Myanmar border, and assists KWO by providing technical assistance. In this conversation, Maggi Quadrini discusses the origins of feminist resistance with Naw K'nyaw Paw, who speaks from lived experience on the progression of women's rights in her homeland of Karen State, Myanmar. Together, they unpack what revolution means to Naw K'nyaw Paw and how the participation of women in resistance movements is paramount for a future in Myanmar which is free, fair and feminist. They also explore the challenges women from Karen state face in terms of accessing gender justice and rights, and the impacts of the coup on women from ethnic minority communities.

Growing up in a War Zone

MQ: What was life like growing up?

KP: I grew up in the conflict areas in Karen State, Burma.[7] My parents ran from one place to another. Every summer, the Burma Army would increase its attacks on Karen people and my parents had to run. So they sent me and

---

4   Quadrini 2022.
5   Karen Women's Organization 2022b.
6   Ibid.
7   This book uses the term 'Myanmar' to describe the country otherwise known as Burma, unless used otherwise in specific quotes, such as here.

my siblings to stay with my aunt and study along the Thailand–Burma border when I was six years old. They thought I would be safer there.

MQ: Did women and men have different roles in your community?

KP: The roles for men and women were significantly different. For example, my father was always involved in the community as a village head or a committee member. He went out looking for jobs to find money to raise the family. My mother was the one doing the household work at home. She cooked snacks and sold them. Taking care of the family and the home is a lot of work in remote villages with no electricity and no appliances. Everything must be done by hand. My mother is the eldest child, so she also had to look after many of her siblings. Her mother passed away when the youngest child was not even five years old. I grew up in a big family with six brothers and sisters, plus my aunties and uncles together.

MQ: Did these gender roles impact the roles women held in the Karen revolution?

KP: Yes, the contribution of women to the revolution in the past was mainly work in the communications sector, health, education and offering support behind the scenes during the conflict. This included cooking and packing food for soldiers on the frontlines, caring for wounded soldiers and arranging funerals for dead soldiers, caring for the widows of fallen soldiers and helping look after their families. On the other hand, most of the Karen soldiers were men and were on the frontlines or fulfilling other military roles. Still now, the majority of the government administration are men.

'Women are Capable of Doing Anything': Karen Women and Revolutionary Change

MQ: Is it important that women participate in resistance and revolutions?

KP: It is very important that women participate in resistance and revolutions. For a revolution to be successful it needs the whole population taking part, not just half of the population. Women are capable of doing anything only if they are given opportunities and are treated with respect and equality. There should not be any different roles. Instead, the revolutionary organizations should have clear policies that promote women by creating working environments conducive to supporting their full participation, and where they are not afraid of being harassed or discriminated against. If this kind of working environment is created in our revolution, we will achieve our goals and have great, long-standing success.

In my community, women resist by breaking gender stereotypes, by challenging the status quo, by advocating for law changes that reflect women rights, by building women's capacity – particularly young women – so we can lead and be good examples in the community. However, women face lots of obstacles, particularly young women, who face double standards. They are not valued or respected by the male leaders in the community, and they often do not get support from their families either. Many women are restricted when there is a lack of co-operation from some male leaders and when some community members want to maintain stereotypical roles for women.

In fact, I decided to join KWO because I experienced discrimination from my male friends when I was a teenager. My male friends would often talk down to us girls and we were not allowed to play football because it was for boys only; we could not wear this and that and we had to keep our hair long, etc. There were so many restrictions on our personal choices. At that time, I was not aware of women's rights or human rights. I just felt it was not fair; I felt in my heart that it was an injustice. I joined KWO to learn about women's rights, and to understand more about women's issues. I wanted to develop skills to help girls and women who had experiences like me. I feel I made the right decision. Since joining KWO I have had a lot of opportunities to attend training in human rights, women's rights, and many rights- based workshops. I've had access to short-term training, and I have met other women's rights activists who have inspired me. I have travelled and seen the world. It has opened my eyes and my mind! KWO provides a lot of opportunities for women to develop, build their capacity so they can solve their own problems, so that women can become leaders, have more power, and can challenge the patriarchy. All of these make me feel I'm in the right place at the right time.

To me, revolution means to resist any injustice, unfairness, inequality and oppression upon us. I would like to see a future where we have self-determination in our own affairs, genuine peace, a community that respects gender equality, and where women and girls can make decisions on their own, where there is a government and laws that protect and promote women's and girls' rights and there is real respect for our ethnicity, our culture and for diversity.

MQ: What has changed since you became involved in the fight for women's rights in terms of women's rights and opportunities in your community?

KP: I have seen a lot of changes. There have been changes in perspectives from the community towards the role of men and women. Particularly in refugee camps where there is more training and more awareness raising on women's rights and human rights. There are more women working in leadership and community work in the refugee camps. We even see more girls playing football which has always been seen as a boys-only sport. Women are now wearing non-traditional clothing, like long pants, whereas before we had to wear long skirts or sarongs. Now, more girls wear skirts that are a bit shorter. In the past, all women's skirts had to cover the knees. In general, the community has moved from being very conservative to more progressive and more accepting of equal roles for men and women.

In the revolutionary areas in Karen State, the Burma Army carried out brutal operations against the Karen people, and often targeted men. They were afraid and ran away to hide. Women and family members remained in the villages and the women took up the village chief roles. They defended the people and challenged the Burmese military whenever they came to their areas.

Now there are many more women who are working as leaders and leading the services in the community by participating in decision-making, attending meetings and protecting the rights of members of the community. People can see that there are more roles for women in leadership. This is a good change. However, there are still far too few women in leadership roles. In the military, the view that the job of a soldier is only for a man has not changed.

Transitional Changes and the Military Coup: Impact on Women's Rights

MQ: Can you explain why you did not move back to Myanmar after 2011, like some other women's rights activists did?

KP: I was born on the Thai side of the border in a temporary village because my parents fled from Burma each time the Burmese Army attacked their home village. We moved back after the attacks calmed down. My family became refugees when I was 10 years old in 1991. I continued my education in the refugee camp and graduated High School there. I lived with my family in the camp until I joined KWO, when I went to live in the KWO staff house and office. All my family resettled in 2008 to Canada through the UNHCR programme. Now I have no family members left in the refugee camps or in Burma. We were forced to be separated and spread over the world because of the Burmese army. Now my family is KWO, where my work is. KWO implements its programmes and projects in all the Karen refugee camps in Thailand and in the Karen community in Burma. Even after 2011, the year that the Burmese military government started to open up a little bit, there were still many conflicts and clashes in our homeland. There was no guarantee of safety for the people or for refugees either, so we could not return to our villages. There were no livelihood opportunities and no social services available for them. Refugees still need support: the support of INGOs and the support of CBOs like KWO. They are dependent on aid. I am committed to helping them.

Even after 2011, there was still no democratic government in Burma. The Burmese military remained in power through the 2008 Constitution, which it wrote to grant special privileges and power to the military over any form of civilian government. In the ethnic areas, the Burmese army has maintained its position of ruling over us all. There was never any attempt at a democratic government for the ethnic areas. The military kept full control of those parts of the country. The ceasefires and peace-talks have failed to materialize into safe, peaceful situations on the ground. It is not safe for refugees or IDPs to return home. There is also still no respect for human rights, which is evident through the lack of recognition of the ethnic education, health and administration systems that we had to set up in our areas because the Burmese military government did nothing for us, except attack us and steal our land. There is still now militarization going on in the Karen areas by the Burmese army. They build roads so they can set up more army bases, with more soldiers in our areas. KWO can only provide aid to our community in Burma by working across the border from Thailand. We could not do the work freely based in Burma because it is never safe enough. The Burmese military government demanded, for example, that we ask their permission to go into our own communities to provide services. They follow us everywhere and refuse approval to enter conflict zones or ethnic areas where our people live. Life and work under their control is just impossible. Due to these challenges, I could not move back to Burma. I would become powerless again.

MQ: What has changed since the transition in Myanmar, in terms of women's rights and justice?

KP: I cannot deny that since 2012 more space has opened, particularly opportunities for women's rights in urban areas. That is a good thing, of course. In the communities where we work, there have been fewer military clashes and we have been able to travel around more freely than before and so we have been able to help build the capacity of women in the community much more. However, in recent years – even before the Burma Army staged the coup – in our Karen areas the Burmese army has been building roads for military purposes. They have confiscated our land amid a significant increase in the number of Burmese army posts and soldiers. Consequently, this has resulted in more offensives and human rights violations against Karen villagers.

MQ: How do you think the events since the attempted coup on 1 February 2021 will affect women's rights and opportunities in your community?

KP: It got worse after the Burma Army staged their coup. Since the coup, there have been air strikes and air bombardment of our people, and this had previously not happened for more than 30 years. This is a whole new level of terror for women and their families. They must find caves and rocks to shelter in. Their daily survival is their highest priority. Other issues fade away very quickly when you are fighting for your life.

References

Karen Women's Organization. 2022a. 'Background of the Karen People.' Available at: karenwomen.org/background-of-the-karen-people/

———. 2022b. 'About.' Available at: karenwomen.org/about/

Quadrini, M. 2022. 'Women are key to the humanitarian response in Myanmar.' *The Diplomat*, 23 June. Available at: thediplomat.com/2021/06/women-are-key-to-the-humanitarian-response-in-myanmar/

UCA News. 2022. 'Thousands of Karen Flee as Myanmar Junta Air Strikes Escalate.' 5 May. Available at: www.ucanews.com/news/thousands-of-karen-flee-as-myanmar-junta-air-strikes-escalate/97156

Labour, Land and Everyday Lives

CHAPTER 8

Mobile Bodies, Stolen Land

Visualizing Gendered Landscapes

Hilary Faxon

I n 2017 I found myself in Naypyidaw, speaking on a panel about marginalized women and digital technologies. Ours was one session in a two-day event on women and tech, which featured a story from an organizer about how her mother had become more emancipated through online shopping. In the evening, my roommate, a Myanmar woman building apps, asked me, a white American, to explain what rural Myanmar was like. Like many *yangonthu*, or people from Yangon, this young entrepreneur had rarely left the city and readily admitted to knowing little about the countryside. Her curiosity and our discussion, one of many similar exchanges I had after explaining that I conducted research in villages and on farms, highlighted the gap between urban and rural perspectives on development priorities and women's rights.

As I spent more time in rural Myanmar, the importance of moving beyond urban and elite accounts to consider rural women's embodied perspectives became increasingly clear. One theme that emerged beyond the city was the centrality of land, both to livelihoods and to larger projects of cultural reproduction, family and autonomy. Agriculture has long been the backbone of Myanmar's economy, and while its relative share of GDP has declined, in 2017 just over half of the labour force was employed in agriculture, forestry or fishing (Central Statistical Organization 2020). Even as urban occupations increased, the majority of Myanmar's population was born in, and remained tied to, rural places. In many parts of the country, these landscapes were spaces both of violence and of cultivation: battlefields and farmers' fields overlapped. Land was central to forging a just and lasting future, as seen in efforts to establish ethnic territorial autonomy, formalize farmland registration or redistribute military crony plots. But the importance of gender in these processes

159

was often obscured. Elsewhere, I have drawn on rural women's perspectives to show that gendered reproductive work produces social value on the land; at stake in Myanmar's land reform debates, I argue, is the challenge of securing meaningful life (Faxon 2020). Here, I focus in on the ways in which gender structures landscapes in the southeast of Myanmar, in the context of two major rural issues: labour migration and land grabbing.

To do so, this chapter centres images from a photovoice project, in which women took and explained photographs of their own lives on the land. These images, and the connections and conversations they spark, highlight the gendered and contested nature of land and rural places, as well as possibilities for solidarity and positive change. Using a participatory photography methodology and a feminist political ecology approach allows me to explore themes that are often obscured in accounts of rural Myanmar – namely, how changing forms of gendered work, knowledge and identities have shaped rural transformation in the face of increasing migration and struggles over land. I argue that in order to understand the meaning of gender in Myanmar, both before the coup and afterwards, feminist activists and scholars must leave the city in search of rural women's perspectives. Rural women's own visual insights ground our understanding of gender not in urban dialogues of equality and rights, but rather in lived relations of soil, struggle and care.

In what follows, I briefly outline the key role of land in Myanmar's decade of agrarian and political transition, my feminist political ecology approach, and the photovoice methodology, before turning to a selection of women's photographs of mobile bodies and stolen land. In Kawkareik, a site close to the Thai border with high mobility, plural authorities and a recent history of civil war, I focus on the ways in which women explained the impacts of labour migration on daily practices and the physical environment. In Dawei, which was the focus of high-profile and controversial foreign investments in a Special Economic Zone, oil palm plantations, offshore oil extraction and mining, I show how gendered labour and interfaith resistance shaped and took shape on layered and contested landscapes. I close each section with a reflection on the methodology in each site, highlighting the types of insights that photovoice can bring.

Transforming Gendered Landscapes

While land rights and rural development took centre stage in debates over Myanmar's transition (Hong 2017; S. McCarthy 2018; Suhardiman,

Kenney-Lazar and Meinzen-Dick 2019), relatively little attention has been paid to how women and men differently experience and participate in these processes (for a recent exception see Hedström and Olivius 2020). In the context of historic and ongoing land grabbing by the military and economic elite (Buchanan, Kramer and Woods 2013; Ferguson 2014; Woods 2011) and decades of restrictive colonial and socialist agrarian policies (Mark 2016; Thawnghmung 2003), Thein Sein's government prioritized new regulations for land and rural development. While, under the 2008 Constitution, all land and resources remained the property of the state, laws since 2012 introduced new procedures for registering different types of land, and more expansive usufruct rights. Under the NLD, drafting began of a National Land Law, and a high-level commission investigated the return of land taken under the military regime. Despite living and working on the land, rural Myanmar women were notably absent from these land reform processes (Faxon 2017). This finding aligns with a broader trend of gender inequality in political participation, in particular in rural governance (Minoletti, La Ring and Bjarnegard 2020). The result was new patterns of gendered exclusion. For example, the government promoted farmland titling, but women were unlikely to have farmland registered in their own names (Pierce and Oo 2016), even though they had been adversely affected by land confiscation (Pierce, Hurtle and Bainbridge 2018).

From the hilly agroforestry systems of the north and southeast to the dry central plains and the rice-growing delta, Myanmar's diverse agrarian landscapes form the basis of life and livelihoods for the majority of the country's population. Previous work has highlighted the diversity of gendered relations on the land, including variations in inheritance patterns across ethnic groups, as well as the ways in which gender structures daily practices of work and care that are intimately tied to particular landscapes. A gendered division of labour in rural Myanmar, which often separates men's work in the fields from women's work in home and gardens, are accompanied by dominant cultural norms that reward 'tough' male work with higher wages and social status (Gender Equality Network 2015; Metro, this volume).

At a time of momentous change in relation to the way in which land is valued, used and controlled, empirical investigation into how men and women actually use, access and own land is critical to understanding Myanmar's rural transformation. Here, I focus on two important national trends: mobile labour and stolen land. Both internal and international migration rose sharply in the 2010s, with the International Organization for Migration reporting that 20 per cent of the population were internal migrants, while over four million lived abroad, including three million in Thailand alone (IOM 2021). New patterns of mobility not only brought remittances into rural places, but also reworked relationships between husbands, wives and children. While estimates of land grabbing are difficult to come by, even existing data indicates staggering amounts of land transfers: across Myanmar, the government allocated over five million acres of land to agro-business between 1991 and 2016, much of it so-called 'vacant, fallow and virgin' (U San Thein et al. 2018).

I focus on two sites in the southeast in order to understand women's experiences of landscapes marked by conflict and change. In and around Kawkareik, ceasefires in 2011 and 2012 with the Karen National Union (KNU), the Democratic Karen Benelovent Army (DKBA) and the Karen Peace Council (KPC) gave way to mixed administration (Jolliffe 2016), even as the completion of the Asia Highway link in late 2015 accelerated travel to and from the Thai border at Myawaddy–Mae Sot. In Dawei, long histories of militarized resource extraction had produced landscapes of dispossession that were slated for billions of dollars of foreign investment for one of Southeast Asia's largest SEZs. Women's photographs of stolen land in Dawei and mobile labour in Kawkareik provide new perspectives on questions typically considered with a gender-blind, political economy perspective, allowing us to better understand and imagine equitable rural transformation.

Feminist Political Ecology

Political ecology offers a way to interrogate the shifting and multiple channels through which women and men negotiate access to land, bringing attention to the materiality of resources and to relations of power (Ribot and Peluso 2003; Rocheleau and Edmunds 1997). Here, I align my analysis with a new wave of feminist political ecologists who move beyond assumptions of women's uniform (disadvantaged) position and instead ask how gender intersects with age, race and class to mediate social status and control of resources (Elmhirst 2011; Mollett and Faria 2013; Nightingale 2011). Gender is not a static or separate category. Rather, women's relationships to land are multi-scalar and situated, conditioned not only by national policies, but also by ethnic norms and market and family structures in specific times and places (Radcliffe 2014; Razavi 2003). Bringing this feminist political ecology approach to women's images of the southeast underscores how rural women's labour and status as farmers, daughters, wives and grandmothers shape the politics and practices of mobility and dispossession on Myanmar's landscapes.

Extensive scholarship on labour migration in Southeast Asia has highlighted the gendered pathways and effects of mobile work (Bylander 2015; Mills 1999; Resurreccion and Ha Thi Van Khanh 2007). Over the last two decades, various patterns of migration have reshaped agrarian economies, identities and landscapes (Kelly 2011), even as smallholder farmers (Rigg, Salamanca and Thompson 2016) and conventional gender norms (Parrenas 2005) persist. Relationships between labour mobility and land use and control are historically conditioned and vary across sites (Kelley et al. 2020). Across Southeast Asia, migratory labour provides capital that finances houses (Rigg and Vandergeest [eds] 2012), purchases livestock and reshapes forest use (Peluso and Purwanto 2017), and remakes what Deirdre McKay (2005), writing of villages in the Philippines, calls *remittance landscapes*. In Myanmar, recent increases in both domestic and international labour migration are reshaping livelihoods and aspirations, even as grounded relations of work and care help to explain the persistence of the smallholder farmer and the social value of land (Faxon 2020).

Scholars have convincingly argued that gender and other social relations structure experiences of and responses to land grabbing in Southeast Asia (Lamb et al. 2017; Morgan 2017; Park and White 2017) and globally (Behrman, Meinzen-Dick and Quisumbing 2012; Chung 2017). Land loss can have catastrophic consequences. For example, a report by the Tavoyan Women's Union on the impact of the Dawei Special Economic Zone on rural women linked land confiscation, often without compensation, to reduced incomes, rising food insecurity and inability to afford schooling for children (Tavoyan Women's Union 2014). In his comparative historical analysis of the gendered implications of dispossession, Michael Levien (2017: 1111) writes that land loss often intensifies women's work, threatens their livelihoods and reduces their autonomy, noting that, 'while defensive struggles against land dispossession will not in themselves transform patriarchal social relations, they may be a pre-condition for more offensive struggles for gender equality'. Writing of gendered land reform and state-making in nearby Cambodia, Alice

Beban (2021) not only notes the disproportionate negative impacts of titling on women, but also women's role in mobilizing for land justice and imagining alternatives to authoritarian violence. Below, I build on what Beban calls a feminist ontology of land to centre women's images and descriptions of their embodied relations and generative connections to place.

Picturing Rural Land

While existing analyses of land in Myanmar tend to use a combination of political economy and interviews, often with male experts, to understand resource conflicts, participatory visual methodologies highlight women's own perspectives – here, on what I have called mobile bodies and stolen land. To understand gendered land issues, I worked with a talented team on a mixed-method participatory action research project from 2016–2018.[1] The project included events such as a women farmers' forum and participatory photography exhibition and produced policy briefs and a final research report (Faxon and Knapman 2019). Like other feminists working in Myanmar, we combined scholarship and activism with the goal of listening to and amplifying women's voices (Frydenlund and Wai Wai Nu this volume; Hedström and Zin Mar Phyo 2020).

The photovoice methodology was developed by feminist public health professionals seeking to understand the perspectives of women and marginalized groups and has been used widely to understand and advocate for transformative social change (Hergenrather et al. 2009; Wang and Burris 1997). Scholars have used photovoice and related methodologies to explore perspectives on environmental change, rural community life and migration globally, for example in work on women's perspectives on resource extraction and ecological destruction in Indonesia (Spiegel 2020); the value of women's unpaid care work in rural Tanzania (Chung, Young and Kerr 2018); and youth perspectives on migration and land concessions in Laos (Sentíes Portilla 2017). In our study, we recruited groups of around six rural women each through grassroots partners in three study sites, then spent approximately one week with each group working together on basic photo skills and on taking and presenting images of gendered life on the land. Here,

---

1   I gratefully acknowledge Land Core Group and my co-lead Catriona Knapman as well as collaborators including Naw Mu Paw Htoo, Pyo Let Han and Agatha Ma for their work in design, data collection and analysis for this project.

Figure 8.1. 'We will go harvest the rice and collect the hay.'

Figure 8.2. '[Threshing] rice with the machine. It is easy and we won't be tired.'

Figure 8.3. 'The new village to come.'

Figure 8.4. 'Money from nature.'

Figure 8.5. 'Because I don't want it to go extinct.'

I draw on photovoice data from two of our research sites in the southeast of Myanmar: Kawkareik in Karen State and Dawei in Tanintharyi Division. My discussion of the images is informed not only by the women's explanations of them and by our interviews and analysis for the project, but also by an additional 26 months I spent conducting ethnographic fieldwork on agrarian change and land politics in Myanmar.

Kawkareik

The history of armed conflict, the persistence of plural authorities and the pervasiveness of labour migration across the nearby Thai border have all shaped how land has been used and imagined in Kawkareik. In nearby villages, Buddhist Karen people farmed a mix of rice, durian and other fruits on paddy and orchard land. Armed conflict between the KNU, the DKBA and the Myanmar Government had given way to mixed administration, visible through overlapping land titling, taxation and policy schemes (Suhardiman, Bright and Palmano 2019, Mark 2022). When I visited in 2017, both the Myanmar Government and KNU taxed and administered land and appointed local leaders in the villages where our women photographers lived. Kawkareik is about an hour's drive from the Myawaddy–Mae Sot border on a recently-improved road, and labour migration to Thailand was common. Women's photos illustrated how mobility spurred new farming practices, reshaped family relations and patterns of care work, and remade the physical landscape.

One photo essay by a Karen woman in her early 30s illustrated the material shifts in village life. Nann Z's essay, entitled 'The Changes in the Village', featured roads, bridges, schools and solar panels that had recently appeared and proliferated around her home. Two images from her collection highlight a technological shift with widespread impacts in agrarian communities around the country. In the first (Figure 8.1), the photographer captured a traditional method used by Myanmar farmers: an ox and cart. Nann Z explained that, in the past, everyone in the village used cow carts for transportation and farming, but that now most families had replaced them with tractors. In the second image (Figure 8.2), she pictured a newer machine: a rice thresher. She explained that this machine was more and more popular. While there was currently only one machine in the village, villagers could rent it out for a modest fee. This machine was always operated by men.

Tractors, threshers and combine harvesters have changed patterns of farming by replacing or supplementing animal and human labour, for example when the harvest is performed not by the daughters and sons of the landowner or by local landless men and women but by threshing machines or combine harvesters operated by waged, male drivers, often from outside the village. While the complex gendered effects of mechanization are still playing out in rural Myanmar, these photos underscore the immediate importance of this technological change for agrarian communities. Nann Z's captions – 'We will go harvest the rice and collect the hay' and '[Threshing] rice with the machine. It is easy and we won't be tired' – hint at new questions about the shifts in farm work that go hand-in-hand with the arrival of the new machines.

In 2010s Myanmar, migration was often intimately tied to mechanization – studies in other parts of the country have shown that as young people have departed and farm labour has become more scarcer, rural wages have increased and machines have become more economical and attractive (Belton and Filipski 2019). Migration was widespread in the villages around Kawkareik, prompting changes not only on the farm but also in the family. Unlike other parts of Myanmar I worked in, where the destinations, jobs and remuneration for women and men's labour abroad was quite different, the numbers and earnings of men and women who migrated from Kawkareik to Thailand were roughly equivalent. Yet their combined absence prompted a redistribution of care work to women in their extended families. In our photovoice group, both a grandmother and a teenage girl shared photos of grandchildren, nieces and nephews whose parents worked in Bangkok, and whom they fed, washed and cooked for during the parents' absence. But our discussion also highlighted the strength of family connections grounded on specific landscapes, even in the face of mobility, for example in one returned female migrant's image of her daughter in the family fields, titled 'farmland and the new generation.' These images index broader shifts in gendered and generational roles and identities that are taking place across Karen State as increasing numbers of young women move back and forth between town and village, and migrate abroad for work (Chambers 2019; Balčaitė and Chambers in press).

Across Myanmar, reciprocal and hierarchical relations of work, care and charity have historically played an important part in funding, developing and maintaining communities (Griffiths 2018; Hedström 2022; G. McCarthy 2019; Ong and Steinmüller 2020). Over the decade between 2008 and 2018, the World Bank reported that the national volume of remittances increased 5,000 per cent, even as the legalization of some forms of migration and remittance transfer as well as the partial cessation of conflict provided new chances to invest in the landscape. While some new infrastructure around Kawkareik, such as roads, was financed by the Myanmar Government, many of the changes Nann Z documented were funded by remittances. The clearest example was her image of a new, concrete multi-storey home, a type of structure that had only appeared, she explained, in the last five years, funded by money from Bangkok. In Kawkareik, new homes, tractors and solar panels were visible evidence of this broader phenomenon.

Another Karen Buddhist woman in her late 50s, Daw SK, took a photograph (Figure 8.3) that featured a mango tree in the foreground and, in the background, two houses erected on land purchased with money earned in Bangkok. She explained that the owners were currently working abroad, but planned to return and settle. Such buildings evidence the ways in which remittances are invested to make homes in rural places, even in the midst of intermittent conflict and economic uncertainty. In the face of new livelihoods and mobilities, the connection to land persists. This insight was underscored with her caption for the image, which attests not to decline, but rather to future flourishing: 'The new village to come.'

In comparison with other sites I worked in as part of this project, the process of learning from women in Kawkareik was particularly poignant. This was, in part, because, unlike other study sites, these I did not personally visit. Our team decided that permission for foreigners to visit the villages where our photographers were living would be difficult to obtain. As a result, we had discussions about the photographs in Kawkareik town. The women's images and descriptions are therefore critical to my understanding of these particular landscapes. This experience highlights the potential for photovoice methodology to provide insights not only into marginalized perspectives, but also into inaccessible places.

Our conversations were also, at times, uncomfortable. Women in Kawkareik and other field sites shared images that they had taken of places where women were not allowed to go, including pagodas, waterfalls, boats and mines. These photos presented my colleagues and me with a question of whether to intervene, questioning the patriarchal cultural norms that constructed these as male spaces, or to simply listen. Usually we choose to do the latter, opting to validate women's knowledge, even if their views chafed with our feminist values. These uncomfortable moments highlight a tension inherent in photovoice and other forms of participatory action research, between documenting local perspectives and enacting transformative change.

Finally, my time in Kawkareik was memorable because my parents joined our trip. Despite not sharing a language, my mother and Daw SK shared a strong and immediate connection, holding hands during a get-to-know-you game and going on to ask about each other months, even years, later. Such experiences are an intimate and visceral reminder of how my own position as mobile worker and daughter shapes my research questions, connections and analyses. These images and encounters underscore the fact that changes in farm and migrant work, rural demographics and remittance landscapes are fundamentally the gendered and generational questions of family relations.

Dawei

Dawei became a national flashpoint for land conflicts and mobilization during the 2010s. Like neighbouring Karen State, Tanintharyi Division has seen its hills, plains and beaches remade by waves of conflict. As Myanmar opened up, these landscapes became targets for foreign investments in fisheries, offshore gas, oil palm and conservation, projects that often dispossessed locals even as they strengthened Myanmar government authority (Barbesgaard 2019; Woods 2019). This rich and violent history makes the area around Dawei a particularly important case for understanding and resolving land conflicts nationally, for example as seen in the internationally funded multi-stakeholder platform established to address land disputes in the region (Bächtold, Bastide and Lundsgaard-Hansen 2020). Women in our photovoice project identified as Burman, Dawei, Karen, and mixed ethnicity and lived both in coastal communities and hilly orchards further inland, all of which were fully under Myanmar Government control. Their images showed how struggles over land and environments in and around Dawei were inflected through and enacted by gendered work and identities. Together, their photos revealed the gendered nature of land grabs and pointed towards possibilities for inclusive mobilization.

In comparison to Kawkareik, the women we worked with in Dawei were more likely to be aware of and involved in land rights struggles. For example, one woman devoted her photo essay to documenting different parcels of land that had been taken by the Myanmar government, oil palm companies, or EAOs, and to discussing the effects of dispossession. Another two produced images and descriptions of places scarred and polluted by mining companies. This focus reflects not only the prevalence of land grabbing around Dawei but also the strength and reach of local organizations working on land justice. While we worked with civil society organizations to recruit participants and host trainings in both sites, most of the photographers in Dawei had worked with that organization's female director on regional land issues or led campaigns in their home communities, whereas none of the women in Kawkareik had participated in that male-led group's past activities.

If the emphasis on land grabbing set the Dawei photos apart, the theme of gendered work that appeared in the Dawei images was common across all study sites. In our wider set of images, pictures of women and their mothers repairing nets, tending home gardens, cooking and weaving contrasted with images of men fishing, harvesting hay, and tapping rubber, illustrating common gender norms and work. An image by Daw S encapsulates these themes of labour and loss. Daw S was in her mid-40s, and had lived in Yangon and Myeik before returning to her hometown on the coast, where she was involved in grassroots work on land issues. She took a photo related to one of her activism activities: writing petition letters for farmers whose land had been taken by the government as part of an urban development plan. In another of her photos (Figure 8.4), a man climbs a palm tree to extract jaggery, a dangerous job culturally understood as male. This gendered work takes place upon a landscape of layered land grabbing. Daw S explained that behind the palm tree was land that had been taken by the government; further back, land had been claimed by a company. Her description highlighted the multiple actors involved in land grabbing around Dawei, while also underscoring the continued centrality of this land for local livelihoods. While grabbed land could no longer be farmed, harvesting jaggery provided essential family income. Her caption, 'Money from nature', emphasized the value of this land both to the jaggery worker and his family and to the powerful actors who lay claim to it. Her visual account powerfully illustrated that a land grab is not a single, violent incident; rather, waves of acquisition and everyday gendered work remake living landscapes.

The centrality of land to local livelihoods and the rising number of both legal and illicit acquisitions made mobilization for secure land rights and safe environments essential. During the 2010s, a number of civil society organizations and grassroots groups emerged to protect local land, water and resource access around Dawei. Many of these groups negotiated with foreign companies and the regional government about extraction and development projects, for example in the case of the Dawei Development Association's work on the Dawei SEZ (Aung 2018). Women often played key roles in these movements, whether by leading organizations, preparing legal cases or recruiting their neighbours. One strategy to raise awareness and build solidarity in land-related struggles was the *su taun bweh*, or prayer ceremony. These events brought villagers and activists together to pray for land return or for the withdrawal of foreign companies polluting local environments. Often, the prayer ceremonies were explicitly inter-faith, bringing together different ethnic and religious groups in solidarity. NT, a Karen Christian woman in her mid-30s from a hillside village two hours inland from Dawei, took a photo that captured a *su taun bweh* that brought Muslims, Christians and Buddhists together to protest against the operations of a foreign mining company in the area and to pray for the protection of their farming practices and cultural heritage (Figure 8.5). In the photo, Karen blouses, Burmese *htamiens* and Muslim skullcaps appear together as the participants gather to share prayers, protest and encouragement. In her description of the image, she explained:

I take great satisfaction from this photo. There are a lot of problems involving Muslims in Rakhine at the moment, with a great deal of discrimination against different religious communities. By looking at this photo, I want people to know that it's possible for people [from different faiths] to congregate together like this.

The image in Figure 8.5, and the description of it by the photographer, NT, resonate with other accounts that highlight women's memories of inter-ethnic and inter-religious relations (cf Frydenlund and Wai Wai Nu, this volume) and of women's roles in forging inclusive social movements (Faxon, Furlong and May Sabe Phyu 2015; Agatha Ma, Poe Ei Phyu and Knapman 2018; Olivius and Hedström 2019). The subsequent circulation of NT's text and image point towards the possibilities of using participatory photography for broader emancipatory change. Six months after the photo was taken, I travelled to Mandalay University with my colleague to share some of the images from our project at a workshop on research approaches. During the two-day meeting, we displayed images and captions from the project in the foyer of the Department of Anthropology. At the end of our time, my colleague suggested that we let the students select one image to keep. The students, mostly Burman Buddhists from Mandalay Region, chose this image of a *su taun bweh* held over 1,000 kilometres away. They explained to us that they had never seen anything like this before. Showing these students an example of inter-faith cooperation and mobilization had opened their minds to the possibility of new types of solidarity and social change.

Conclusion

Women's photographs provide a window into local experiences of land, and the gendered nature of agrarian and political transitions. In Kawkareik, new remittance infrastructures emerge on former battlefields as men and women navigate work abroad and remake home. In Dawei, everyday gendered work and interfaith resistance take shape on layered land grabs. Viewing these images together gives us new perspectives on the ways in which labour migration and land grabbing not only impact broad trajectories of rural development and inequality, but also reshape intimate relations of work, care and struggle. In these accounts, gender is not an abstract category, but is rather a relationship that, alongside relations of age, class and ethnicity, structures resource access and everyday life. These social processes are embedded in particular, dynamic landscapes, which carry the physical imprints and collective memories of violence, whether past armed conflict or contemporary pollution by foreign corporations. And yet women's images also provide powerful possibilities for resurgence and solidarity, as encapsulated in the *su taun bweh* photo and its circulation to Mandalay University students.

My discussion here highlights not only the gendered dynamics of mobile bodies and stolen land, but also the importance of rural women's perspectives. Some of the women who participated in our project came to discuss their images at a photography exhibition we organized in Yangon in 2017. Seeing rural women speak to urban journalists and visitors about their own experiences as experts and artists inverted traditional hierarchies, sparking new conversations and demonstrating the power of participatory photography to bridge the gap between elite and grassroots perspectives. In light of the 2021 coup, building understanding and solidarity across these class and geographic divides is even more crucial for gender equality and social justice.

While rural women's voices are often excluded from discussions of land, development and equity, theirs are not the only perspectives crucial to understanding the dynamics of gendered landscapes. Photovoice provides powerful tools, for example, to explore how masculinity and youth identities are forged in relation to work, mobility and dispossession on and across particular landscapes. In using a selection of women's photographs from the southeast of Myanmar, this chapter is not an endpoint but rather an invitation to seek perspectives – outside the city and across the gender spectrum – on the material and social processes of rural and political transformation.

References

Agatha Ma, Poe Ei Phyu and C. Knapman. 2018. 'In the land of wise old men: Experiences of young women activists in Myanmar.' *Gender and Development* 26 (3): 459–476.

Aung, G. 2018. 'Postcolonial capitalism and the politics of dispossession: Political trajectories in Southern Myanmar.' *European Journal of East Asian Studies* 17 (2): 193–227.

Bächtold, S, J. Bastide and L. Lundsgaard-Hansen. 2020. 'Assembling drones, activists and oil palms: Implications of a multi-stakeholder land platform for state formation in Myanmar.' *European Journal of Development Research* 32: 359–378.

Balčaitė, I and J. Chambers. In press. 'The daughters' burden or opportunity? Negotiating gender roles in Karen women's labour mobility from Myanmar to Thailand.' In *Ceasefire Aspirations and Anxieties among the Karen in Myanmar.* Copenhagen: NIAS Press.

Barbesgaard, M. 2019. 'Ocean and land control-grabbing: The political economy of landscape transformation in Northern Tanintharyi, Myanmar.' *Journal of Rural Studies* 69: 195–203.

Beban, A. 2021. *Unwritten Rule: State-Making through Land Reform in Cambodia.* Ithaca: Cornell University Press.

Behrman J., R. Meinzen-Dick and A. Quisumbing. 2012. 'The gender implications of large-scale land deals.' *The Journal of Peasant Studies* 39 (1): 49–79.

Belton, B. and M. Filipski. 2019. 'Rural transformation in central Myanmar: By how much, and for whom?' *Journal of Rural Studies* 67: 166–176.

Buchanan, J., T. Kramer and K. Woods. 2013. *Developing Disparity: Regional Investment in Burma's Borderlands.* Amsterdam: Transnational Institute.

Bylander, M. 2015. 'Contested mobilities: Gendered migration pressures among Cambodian youth.' *Gender, Place and Culture* 22 (8): 1124–1140.

Central Statistical Organization. 2020. *Myanmar Living Conditions Survey 2017: Socio-Economic Report.* Nay Pyi Taw and Yangon, Myanmar: Ministry of Planning, Finance and Industry, United Nations Development Programme and World Bank.

Chambers, J. 2019. 'Enacting morality on shifting moral ground: Young Plong Karen women in southeastern Myanmar.' *Asia Pacific Journal of Anthropology* 20 (3): 261–277.

Chung, Y. B. 2017. 'Engendering the new enclosures: Development, involuntary resettlement and the struggles for social reproduction in coastal Tanzania.' *Development and Change* 48 (1): 98–120.

Chung, Y. B., S. L. Young and R. B. Kerr. 2018. 'Rethinking the value of unpaid care work: Lessons from participatory visual research in central Tanzania.' *Gender, Place & Culture* 9: 1237–1251.

Elmhirst, R. 2011. 'Introducing new feminist political ecologies.' *Geoforum* 42: 129–132.

Faxon, H. O. 2017. 'In the law and on the land: Finding the female farmer in Myanmar's national land use policy'. *The Journal of Peasant Studies* 44 (6): 1197–1214.

———. 2020. 'Securing meaningful life: Women's work and land rights in rural Myanmar.' *Journal of Rural Studies* 76: 76–84.

Faxon, H., O. Furlong and May Sabe Phyu. 2015. 'Reinvigorating resilience: Violence against women, land rights, and the women's peace movement in Myanmar.' *Gender and Development* 23 (3): 463–479.

Faxon, H. O. and C. Knapman. 2019. 'From the Ground Up: Land Governance through the Eyes of Women Farmers in Myanmar.' Yangon: Land Core Group.

Ferguson, J. M. 2014. 'The scramble for the waste lands: Tracking colonial legacies, counterinsurgency and international investment through the lens of land laws in Burma/Myanmar.' *Singapore Journal of Tropical Geography* 35 (3): 295–311.

Frydenlund, S. and Wai Wai Nu. 2022. 'From Mutual Aid to Charity: Violence and Women's Changing Interethnic Relationships in Rakhine State.' In J. Hedström and E. Olivius (eds), *Waves of Upheaval in Myanmar: Gendered Transformations and Political Transitions*. Copenhagen: NIAS Press.

Gender Equality Network. 2015. 'Raising the Curtain: Cultural Norms, Social Practices and Gender Equality in Myanmar.' Yangon. Available at: www.burmalibrary.org/docs22/GEN-2015-11-Raising%20the%20curtain-en.pdf. Accessed 12 October 2017.

Griffiths, M. 2018. 'Networks of reciprocity: Precarity and community social organisations in rural Myanmar.' *Journal of Contemporary Asia* 49 (4): 602–625.

Hedström, J. 2022. 'Militarized social reproduction: Women's labour and parastate armed conflict.' *Critical Military Studies* 8 (1): 58–76. Published online 12 January 2020.

Hedström, J. and E. Olivius. 2020. 'Insecurity, dispossession, depletion: Women's experiences of post-war development in Myanmar.' *The European Journal of Development Research* 32: 379–403.

Hedström, J. and Zin Mar Phyo. 2020. 'Friendship, intimacy, and power in research on conflict: Implications for feminist ethics.' *International Feminist Journal of Politics* 22 (5): 765–777

Hergenrather, K. C., S. D. Rhodes, C. A. Cowan et al. 2009. 'Photovoice as community-based participatory research: A qualitative review.' *American Journal of Health Behavior* 33 (6): 686–698.

Hong, E. 2017. 'Scaling struggles over land and law: Autonomy, investment, and interlegality in Myanmar's borderlands.' *Geoforum* 82: 225–236.

IOM. 2021. 'Myanmar.' Available at: www.iom.int/countries/myanmar. Accessed 5 May 2021.

Jolliffe, K. 2016. *Ceasefires, Governance, and Development: The Karen National Union in Times of Change*. Yangon: The Asia Foundation.

Kelley, L. C., N. L. Peluso, K. M. Carlson et al. 2020. 'Circular labor migration and land-livelihood dynamics in Southeast Asia's concession landscapes.' *Journal of Rural Studies* 73: 21–33.

Kelly, P. F. 2011. 'Migration, agrarian transition, and rural change in Southeast Asia: Introduction.' *Critical Asian Studies* 43 (4): 479–506.

Lamb, V., L. Schoenberger, C. Middleton et al. 2017. 'Gendered eviction, protest and recovery: A feminist political ecology engagement with land grabbing in rural Cambodia.' *The Journal of Peasant Studies* 44 (6):1215–1234.

Levien, M. 2017. 'Gender and land dispossession: A comparative analysis.' *The Journal of Peasant Studies* 44 (6): 1113–1136.

Mark, S. 2016. 'Are the odds of justice "stacked" against them? Challenges and opportunities for securing land claims by smallholder farmers in Myanmar.' *Critical Asian Studies* 48 (3): 443–460.

———. 2022. 'The forging of legitimate authority in the ceasefire mixed-control Karen areas of Myanmar.' *Journal of Contemporary Asia* 52 (2): 226–246. Published online 27 February 2021.

McCarthy, G. 2019. 'Democratic deservingness and self-reliance in contemporary Myanmar.' *Sojourn: Journal of Social Issues in Southeast Asia* 34 (2): 327–365.

McCarthy, S. 2018. 'Rule of law expedited: Land title reform and justice in Burma (Myanmar).' *Asian Studies Review* 42 (2): 229–246.

McKay, D. 2005. 'Reading remittance landscapes: Female migration and agricultural transition in the Philippines.' *Geografisk Tidsskrift: Danish Journal of Geography* 105 (1): 89–99.

Metro, R. 2022. '"My Father Is Strong and Smart, My Mother Is Helpful and Kind": "Gender Harmony" and "Gender Equality" in Myanmar's Curriculum Revision Process.' In J. Hedström and E. Olivius (eds), *Waves of Upheaval in Myanmar: Gendered Transformations and Political Transitions*. Copenhagen: NIAS Press.

Mills, M. B. 1999. *Thai Women in the Global Labor Force: Consuming Desires, Contested Selves*. New Brunswick: Rutgers University Press.

Minoletti, P., P. La Ring and E. Bjarnegard. 2020. 'Gender and Local Politics in Myanmar: Women's and Men's Participation in Ward, Village Tract and Village Decision Making.' Yangon: Enlightened Myanmar Research Foundation.

Mollett, S. and C. Faria. 2013. 'Messing with gender in feminist political ecology.' *Geoforum* 45: 116–125.

Morgan, M. 2017. 'Women, gender and protest: Contesting oil palm plantation expansion in Indonesia.' *The Journal of Peasant Studies* 44 (6): 1179–1198.

Nightingale, A. J. 2011. 'Bounding difference: Intersectionality and the material production of gender, caste, class and environment in Nepal.' *Geoforum* 42: 153–162.

Olivius, E. and J. Hedström. 2019. 'Militarized nationalism as a platform for feminist mobilization? The case of the exiled Burmese women's movement.' *Women's Studies International Forum* 76: 102263.

Ong, A. and H. Steinmüller. 2020. 'Communities of care: Public donations, development assistance and independent philanthropy in the Wa State of Myanmar.' *Critique of Anthropology* 41 (1) 65–87.

Park, C. M. Y. and B. White. 2017. 'Gender and generation in Southeast Asian agro-commodity booms.' *The Journal of Peasant Studies* 44 (6): 1105–1112.

Parrenas, R. S. 2005. 'The gender paradox in the transnational families of Filipino migrant women.' *Asian and Pacific Migration Journal* 14 (3): 243–268.

Peluso, N. L. and A. B. Purwanto. 2017. 'The remittance forest: Turning mobile labor into agrarian capital.' *Singapore Journal of Tropical Geography* 39: 6–36.

Pierce, C. J., L. Hurtle and J. Bainbridge. 2018. 'Gendered Experiences of Land Confiscation in Myanmar: Insights from Eastern Bago Region and Kayin State.' Yangon: Saferworld.

Pierce, C. J. and N. T. T. Oo. 2016. 'Gendered Aspects of Land Rights in Myanmar: Evidence from Paralegal Casework.' Yangon: Namati.

Radcliffe, S. A. 2014. 'Gendered frontiers of land control: Indigenous territory, women and contests over land in Ecuador.' *Gender, Place and Culture* 21 (7): 854–871.

Razavi, S. 2003. 'Introduction: Agrarian change, gender and land rights.' *Journal of Agrarian Change* 3 (1–2): 2–32.

Resurreccion, B. P. and Ha Thi Van Khanh. 2007. 'Able to come and go: Reproducing gender in female rural–urban migration in the Red River Delta.' *Population, Space and Place* 13 (3): 211–224.

Ribot, J. and N. Peluso. 2003. 'A theory of access.' *Rural Sociology* 68 (2): 153–181.

Rigg, J, A. Salamanca and E. C. Thompson. 2016. 'The puzzle of East and Southeast Asia's persistent smallholder.' *Journal of Rural Studies* 43: 118–133.

Rigg, J. and P. Vandergeest (eds). 2012. *Revisiting Rural Places: Pathways to Poverty and Prosperity in Southeast Asia.* Honolulu: University of Hawai'i Press.

Rocheleau, D. and D. Edmunds. 1997. 'Women, men and trees: Gender, power and property in forest and agrarian landscapes.' *World Development* 25 (8): 1351–1371.

Sentíes Portilla, G. 2017. 'Land concessions and rural youth in Southern Laos.' *The Journal of Peasant Studies* 44 (6): 1257–1276.

Spiegel, S. J. 2020. 'Visual storytelling and socioenvironmental change: Images, photographic encounters and knowledge construction in resource frontiers.' *Annals of the Association of American Geographers* 110 (1): 120–144.

Suhardiman, D., M. Kenney-Lazar and R. Meinzen-Dick. 2019. 'The contested terrain of land governance reform in Myanmar.' *Critical Asian Studies* 51 (3): 368–385.

Suhardiman, D., J. Bright and C. Palmano. 2019. 'The politics of legal pluralism in the shaping of spatial power in Myanmar's land governance.' *The Journal of Peasant Studies* 48 (2): 411–435.

Tavoyan Women's Union. 2014. 'Our Lives Not For Sale: Tavoyan Women Speak Out Against the Dawei Special Economic Zone Project.' Mae Sot: Tavoyan Women's Union.

Thawnghmung, A. M. 2003. 'The socio-economic impacts of rice policies implementation in rural Burma/Myanmar.' *Soujourn: Journal of Social Issues in Southeast Asia* 18 (2): 299–321.

U San Thein, J.-C. Diepart, U Hlwan Moe and C. Allaverdian. 2018. 'Large-Scale Land Acquisitions for Agricultural Development in Myanmar: A Review of Past and Current Processes.' Vientiane: Mekong Region Land Governance.

Wang, C. and M. A. Burris. 1997. 'Photovoice: Concept, methodology and use for participatory needs assessment.' *Health Education and Behavior* 24 (3): 369–387.

Woods, K. 2011. 'Ceasefire capitalism: Military–private partnerships, resource concessions and military-state building in the Burma–China borderlands.' *The Journal of Peasant Studies* 38 (4): 747–770.

———. 2019. 'Green territoriality: Conservation as state territorialization in a resource frontier.' *Human Ecology* 47: 217–232.

CHAPTER 9

Troubling the Transition

Gendered Insecurity in the Borderlands

Jenny Hedström, Elisabeth Olivius and Zin Mar Phyo

I n many of Myanmar's conflict-affected borderlands, armed violence was significantly reduced as a result of ceasefire agreements implemented largely in the 1990s. New peace negotiations began in 2011, which alongside larger processes of change set in motion by economic and political reforms, facilitated a drastic increase in foreign investment and state development initiatives in many border regions, primarily focusing on expansion of agribusiness, energy and infrastructure projects (Bjarnegård 2020; Burke et al. 2017; Décobert 2020; Tin Maung Maung Than 2014). In Mon and Kayah states, the geographical areas in focus in this chapter, these processes were accompanied by, and indeed legitimated, increased militarization and new forms of depletion and dispossession. Empirical realities in Mon and Kayah states therefore illustrate how post-war transitions often bring about intense societal changes, but may also reproduce wartime dynamics and introduce new forms of insecurity and injustice.

Based on a study undertaken in 2019, this chapter examines how these post-war changes were understood and experienced in the gendered everyday in Mon and Kayah states. Building on interviews, focus groups and observation with over a hundred farmers, politicians, civil society activists, religious leaders and higher-ranking members of armed groups, we seek to centre the experiences of women and men living in these areas and understand how their lives were affected by the end of armed violence, intensifying state-led development efforts, new versions of militarization, and other processes of change in the two decades leading up to the coup. In particular, we examine how these processes were conditioned by, and contributed to reshaping, gendered norms, divisions of labour, and relations of power. Through this analysis, we draw out and theorize the gendered connections and contradictions between macro-processes of post-war transitions and embodied everyday realities in conflict-affected areas.

Our findings trouble conventional notions of a transition in several ways. First, while a reduction in armed violence during the decade of transitional change had a positive impact on people's everyday lives, increasing security and livelihood opportunities, this period did not represent an unambiguous, unidirectional movement from worse to better. Rather, as we see in both Kayah and Mon state, wartime forms of insecurity, such as forced labour for the military, torture, and women's unrelenting burden of keeping families alive in the absence of welfare provisioning, continued across ceasefire periods and into the transitional phase. These familiar forms of insecurity were also complemented by new forms of insecurity caused by the expansion of state-led development agendas, such as land grabbing. The dynamics and effects of these processes are shaped by existing gender relations and norms. This analysis supports a more critical conceptualization of post-war transition as a period of multifaceted, messy, and contradictory processes of change (Klem 2018; Gusic 2019), and shows how the micro-dynamics of such processes are fundamentally gendered.

Second, our findings suggest that present realities cannot be disentangled from past experiences of violence, and trouble narratives that seek to posit Myanmar's transition as a linear, forward-moving process (Rhoades and Wittekind 2019; Hedström 2021; Hedström and Olivius 2022). Indeed, as we found, present life is made sense of and experienced in close proximity to trauma and insecurity suffered at both the individual and the community level. Fear, deprivation of education, and physical depletion and harm based on sometimes life-long histories of war shape experiences of the present and expectation for the future. The past 'flashes up' (Benjamin 2007 [1968]: 255) in the present, serving to restrict people's opportunities to participate in or benefit from transitional changes. In addition, from the perspective of villagers' everyday lives, time was not experienced as a progressive, linear movement towards the future but as recurring cycles or episodes of violence, displacement and dispossession (also see Wittekind 2018). While the transition changed the character of some insecurities, everyday experiences over time nonetheless conveyed an image of recurrence and continuity rather than a distinct before and after in relation to the transition (Rhoads and Wittekind 2019). Our respondents' frequently expressed expectations of recurring upheaval and violence were confirmed in February 2021, when the

Tatmadaw took power in a coup and thereafter intensified violent repression against protesters in the cities as well as against rural communities.

In the next section, we develop our theoretical points of departure, building on feminist interventions in peace and conflict studies and political economy, as well as critical scholarship on time and space, to trouble androcentric and binary interpretations of peace, violence and war. We then describe the context of Mon and Kayah states, and introduce the methods and materials of our study. In the analysis, we explore the gendered dynamics and effects of Myanmar's transition through the everyday lives and experiences of our respondents.

Situating Myanmar's Transition in the Gendered Everyday

Feminist peace research has played an important role in broadening discussions about *who* and *what* matters in research on conflict and post-war contexts, by looking beyond military and state-centric perspectives that have traditionally dominated the discipline (Lyytikäinen et al. 2020; Wibben et al. 2020). Instead, feminist peace research has drawn attention to the everyday as a key site for exploring war and peace, and to everyday experiences as important sources of knowledge (Sylvester 2012; Enloe 1990; Das 2007; Choi 2021). Crucially, the everyday is a space permeated by gendered relations of power, where people's actions and experiences are shaped by gendered norms and hierarchies. It is a site of violence and oppression as well as resistance, love and care (Berents 2015; Hedström 2021; Elias and Shirin Rai 2015, 2018; Marijan 2017; Väyrynen 2019; Agatha Ma and Kusakabe 2015; Rahman 2021). Peace can be practiced here, but it can also be a space where war, violence and trauma are felt and experienced, serving to restrict opportunities for resistance and change (Scheper-Hughes 1992; also see Ardeth Maung Thawnghmung 2011, 2019). This focus necessitates analysis of the gendered everyday as a temporal as well as a spatial site, wherein the past leaks into the future, upsetting any neat distinction between (past) war and (future) peace.

Examining the relationship between gender, violence and militarization (Cockburn 2010; Enloe 2000), feminist interventions have also destabilized fixed and binary understandings of peace and war. Instead, feminist scholars locate war and peace as a continuum, understanding violence as experienced within a context of unequal gendered relations of power shaping

182

post-war contexts (Yadav and Horn 2021). This body of research helps us foreground the ways in which present-day insecurities are embedded in, facilitated by and made sense of in relation to historical episodes of violence and oppression (Das 2007). Approaching war and peace as a continuum of gendered violence rather than a binary draws attention to changes as well as continuities over time, and allows us to better understand if, and how, overarching political shifts manifest in the everyday. Informed by these contributions, we foreground people's everyday experiences of life in Mon and Kayah states as a way to learn about the gendered dynamics and effects of Myanmar's transition.

Moving away from a binary understanding of war and peace also destabiliz-es conventional ideas about a transition *from* war *to* peace as a forward-moving, linear process that is inherently progressive (Keen 2007; Gusic 2020). This implicit assumption features strongly in literature on so-called war to peace transitions (Klem 2018), as well as in literature on democratic transitions (Linz and Stephan 1996). Indeed, prior to the 2021 military coup much of the literature analysing Myanmar's transition took linear time as a pre-given (Jones 2014; Callahan 2012), anticipating that the country is 'going *from* a highly authoritarian military regime *to* something else' (Diamond 2012: 138). Within these accounts, the notion of the transition itself is often left unexamined; instead the transition is assumed to exist in a causal relationship to progress. This obfuscates that which remains across time – such as insecurity, violence and dispossession – treating such things as exceptions rather than the rule.

Insights from literature that problematizes a linear understanding of time and history (Wittekind 2018; Hom 2010) can help us move away from expectations of improvement over time, and make sense of how our respond-ents experienced the meaning of the transition and the relationship between past, present and future. We also draw on Bart Klem's conceptualization of post-war transition as 'a process of fundamental and intense changes in society ("transition"), which take place after large-scale organized violence has ended ("post-war")' (Klem 2018: 237). Notably, this definition does not pre-suppose the direction of these changes or assume that they will always be beneficial – or for whom they might be so. Rather, it opens these questions up to empirical scrutiny. While it is important to situate post-war changes in light of the war that came before, it is equally important to avoid determinism (post-war changes are simply effects of war dynamics) and normative assumptions (post-war changes constitute a shift from war to peace, from chaos to order, etc.) (Gusic 2020; Keen 2007). This approach to understanding political transitions is a fruitful starting point for recognizing the messy, multi-directional and contradictory nature of post-war processes of change.

Thus, in summary, our analysis is informed by insights from feminist and critical peace research, enabling us to approach Myanmar's transition through the lens of the gendered everyday. This means that people's experiences constitute the site where the nature and effects of the transition are assessed. Further, as the everyday is shaped by gendered norms and hierarchies, so are experiences of war and peace. Tracing gendered experiences of violence and insecurity destabilizes binary conceptions of war and peace, as well as conventional temporal frameworks that posit the post-war transition as a progressive, linear movement towards a better future. Questioning the temporal order of things in this way opens up 'alternative conceptualizations of the relationship between past and present' (Wittekind 2018: 276) by making visible the ways in which predatory relationships experienced by members of ethnic minority communities vis-à-vis the Burman state remain, in some shape or form, across time (Wittekind 2018; Ferguson 2014; Kyed 2020; Naw Wai Hnin Kyaw and Soe Soe Nwe 2019), including across postwar and transitional reforms. These analytical points of departure allow us to trouble pre-conceived notions of what the transition was or meant, and instead examine how it was experienced in the gendered everyday realities of our respondents in Mon and Kayah states.

Context, Methods and Material

Most of independent Myanmar's history has been marked by military dictatorship, civil war and violence (Callahan 2003; South 2008; Simpson and Farrelly [eds] 2020). The country's border regions, home to ethnic minority communities, have been the focus of much of the conflicts being fought between the state military and multiple armed groups (Women's League of Burma 2011). Many of these armed groups have split off into fractions and uneasy alliances, producing highly militarized, volatile and insecure spaces (Meehan and Sadan 2017). The effects of these conflicts on local communities have been disastrous, resulting in widespread poverty, precariousness, dispossession and death. Although national-level politics in the form of ceasefires and reforms undertaken between 2011 and 2020 reduced active conflict in some areas of the country, new or continued insecurities were experienced around extractive and predatory forms of development and state building (Meehan and Sadan 2017; Hedström and Olivius 2020; L. Gum Ja Htung 2018). Thus, in conflict-affected, ethnic minority populated areas of the country, political and economic reforms during the transitional period coexisted with persistent continuities and legacies of war.

This was clear in the two areas adressed in this chapter, Mon state and Kayah state. These are both located along Myanmar's southeastern border with Thailand, and have been scenes of armed conflict, including brutal counter-insurgency campaigns waged by the state, for decades. In Kayah state, the smallest of Myanmar's ethnic minority states, the main ethnic insurgent group is the Karenni National Progressive Party (KNPP), formed in 1957. Further south, in Mon state, the main insurgent group, the New Mon State Party (NMSP), was established a year after the KNPP, although the armed struggle in Mon areas had already begun in 1948 (New Mon State Party 1985). Over time, breakaway factions and failed alliances have led to the establishment of numerous smaller armed groups, sometimes fighting each other as well as the central state, creating highly militarized and complex conflict landscapes. The 2021 military coup has exacerbated this fragmentation, with hundreds of new local and people's defence forces emerging throughout the country, upsetting old alliances and creating new ones (Hmung 2021).

In both areas, the regime's infamous 'four-cuts' counter insurgency campaign resulted in widespread human rights abuses, including forced relocation, sexual violence, arbitrary executions, forced labour, land confiscation and the destruction of villages. In June 1995, the NMSP agreed to a ceasefire with the military regime. In 2012 they signed a bilateral ceasefire agreement with the new, semi-democratic regime, and in 2018 they signed the National Ceasefire Agreement (NCA). The KNPP, however, did not successfully conclude a ceasefire deal until 2012, and, although they were a participant, never signed the NCA. After the start of the transitional period, armed violence decreased overall, but the situation on the ground continued to be fragile and tense, with occasional flare-ups in fighting. The 2021 coup exacerbated tensions and insecurity across the country, leading to arrests of political activists and deadly crackdowns against protesters in Mon and Kayah state. Beginning in late May 2021, the Tatmadaw retaliated against resistance to the coup with air strikes in Kayah state (Myanmar Now 2021).

Further, tensions around state-led initiatives for economic development and reconstruction have been prominent in both regions (Hedström and Olivius 2022), while decades of armed conflict and underdevelopment of welfare services and infrastructure have resulted in extensive poverty. This has exaggerated women's care and reproductive labour, and led to a widespread perception of state and other actors as violent and predatory. Previous research has shown how this has resulted in constraining women's access to land, justice, authority and opportunity (Agatha Ma and Kusakabe 2015; Mi Thang Sorn Poine 2018).

In order to explore how people living in these conflict-affected borderlands experienced and understood violence, peace and war, we interviewed just over a hundred women and men living in Kayah state, southern Shan state and Mon state in 2019, using a combination of focus group discussions and semi-structured interviews. To elicit interactive discussions, we employed life history diagrams (Söderström 2020; Skidmore 2009). These allowed us to identify specific events or circumstances shaping changes in how peace and war was experienced in everyday life. This methodological tool meant that the participants were themselves able to pinpoint and draw out specific events that they felt affected their day-to-day lives. This proved helpful for highlighting continuities of violence and insecurity across macro-political changes, which troubled any assumptions of change being inherently progressive or unidirectional. Through this, we were able to trace participants' experiences and perceptions of war and peace across time, and better understand the temporal frameworks through which they made sense of changes and continuities in their lives.

Gendered Insecurity: Continuity and Change

In Mon and Kayah states, ceasefire agreements generally led to reductions of armed violence and improvements in basic security and livelihoods.[1] From the mid-1990s, as described above, ceasefires were agreed between the government and various armed groups at different times, and after 2011 there has been little outright fighting in both Mon and Kayah areas. Alongside

---

1   An important exception was a 1995 ceasefire between the government and the KNPP agreement, which lasted less than three months, and was followed by an intensification of the war in areas contested by the KNPP. See Hedström and Olivius 2020.

this relative stability, the post-2011 period brought about an increase in development projects and foreign investment, accompanied by a strengthened central state presence in general, and military expansion in particular, which generated new forms of insecurities and threats. This suggests that the transition reshaped the political landscape and brought significant changes that were felt in the gendered everyday. Importantly, these changes defy simplified assumptions of progress, instead encompassing a complex mix of improvements, continuities of war and new forms of insecurities.

In the life stories shared by our respondents, experiences of fleeing from armed attacks and of being subjected to torture and forced labour at the hands of the Tatmadaw were particularly widespread during periods of war. However, torture and forced labour continued after ceasefires brought an end to armed clashes. For example, a method of positional torture colloquially known as 'drying in the sun' (နေလှန်း) and 'drying in the snow' (နှင်းလှန်း), in which villagers – children, the elderly, women and men alike – would be forced to sit outside with their arms stretched out, sometime for periods as long as 24 hours, seemed to be a widespread practice up until the mid-2000s in the communities we visited in southern Mon state. In Kayah state, everyday life was equally violent during the same time period, with even the most basic necessities out of reach for most people living in rural areas targeted by fighting. Villagers would be forced to provide materials and food for soldiers, which meant that families could not regularly feed themselves; instead their labour and livelihoods would be diverted towards military needs. This placed an enormous strain on women in particular, as they had to both give the military what they required and feed their families, while many men hid, as illustrated in this quote from Mon state: 'My dad usually had to run or hide [from the Tatmadaw], he hardly stayed at home. Usually, taking care of the children, cooking, all household jobs, were the responsibility of my mum. We did not have an income.'[2] A woman we interviewed in Kayah state echoed these experiences:

> I would bring food to the jungle for my husband, when he was hiding from the Tatmadaw […] I would pretend I am going to take water or I am going to the jungle to cut the tree or something like that […] I went

2   Interview with two women, Mon state, 28 November 2019.

there even though I was really afraid, I had to go there in fear. When my husband was away I would do everything, shifting cultivation, taking care of the children, household chores. Sometimes my husband had to hide for a month, as the Tatmadaw could come and stay in the village, sleep in my house. They would steal our chickens and pigs [...] Some women, they also experienced rape by the Tatmadaw and also violence.[3]

Moreover, as ethnic minority areas were targeted by counterinsurgency campaigns, thousands of houses were burned down, and people were forcibly relocated to military-controlled villages where food and security was scarce. One woman told us that after the Tatmadaw burned down their village in Kayah state in the 1990s, her grandparents were so desperate for food that they tried to eat the rice that had been destroyed in the fire: 'They brought that black burned rice and they cooked it. The smell was so bad. They were sick a lot.' Everyday life in war thus exacerbated a gendered division of labour that saw women shouldering most of the responsibility for ensuring, or attempting to ensure, survival for families and communities.

These experiences of gendered labour and insecurity carried over into the post-ceasefire and transitional periods. Increased troop presence after ceasefire agreements meant that villagers were still required to provide materials, food and labour for troops now permanently stationed in their areas, making it hard for households, often headed by women, to survive and feed themselves. The 2014 census reveals that a majority of women in both Kayah and Mon state were still primarily engaged in informal, unpaid or underpaid reproductive work, including childrearing, subsistence farming, cooking and care work.

While there was a slow reduction in direct armed violence over time, other forms of structural violence continued. These forms of violence tend to disproportionally affect women, because they carry the largest reproductive responsibility for making everyday life sustainable as well as meaningful (Faxon 2020). This suggests that generations of conflict and under-development in rural communities have resulted in a stark gendered division of labour that continues to restrict women's socioeconomic and educational opportunities in the present (Hedström and Olivius 2020; Blomqvist, Olivius and Hedström 2021).

These embodied, gendered everyday experiences over time challenge the idea of an unambiguous transition from worse to better. This is not to

---

3   Woman in Kayah state, cited in Hedström and Olivius forthcoming.

disregard the significant transformations that took place, but it is important to remember that gendered insecurities, alongside the broader issues of ethnic minority inequality and violence, were reproduced, sometimes in new forms, in post-ceasefire life. For example, in Mon state, although outright fighting abated after 1995, the increase in troops meant that younger women still faced significant threats. In the past, young women would hide when the troops moved through their areas because 'The Tatmadaw came and brought them to their place.'[4] But once the ceasefire was in place women could no longer hide, as this quote illustrates:

> We can see that between 1995 and 2004 things got worse [for women]. Because before, [the Tatmadaw] only called for safeguards and human shields. But when they were building the Tatmadaw camps, they asked for the beautiful and young women and teenagers and made them sing for them. There was less fighting but more militarization.[5]

New forms of gender-based insecurities were not only emanating from the military, however. Ceasefire agreements and overall economic and political liberalization resulted in an influx of investors, crony companies (using military protection) and largescale infrastructural development. The fact that villagers primarily have customary access to land, and moreover might not be fluent in the legal, Bamar language needed to claim land rights, led to widespread loss of land and livelihoods: 'Because there is less fighting, the government is inviting so many investments, so people are really worried that if there is more investment, they will grab our lands.'[6] Women are especially vulnerable to dispossession because they are even less likely than men to have formal ownership of the land on which they work (Faxon 2017; Cornish 2017; Transnational Institute 2015; The Global Justice Center 2017).

Moreover, a spiraling drug epidemic has in recent years compounded women's heavy reproductive burden and continued to restrict their access to the public sphere. As described by this woman in Mon state: 'The drug issue is really bad, we are really afraid of it. As a woman, we don't dare to go out alone.'[7] Across Myanmar, and especially in ethnic rural areas, the use of heroin, methamphetamine and *yaba* is pervasive. This has been linked to ceasefire

---

4   Interview with six women and one man, Mon state, 28 November 2019.
5   Interview with eight women, Mon state, 27 November 2019.
6   Interview with two women and one man, Kayah state, 28 March 2019.
7   Interview with two women, Mon state, 28 November 2019.

arrangements in parts of eastern Myanmar, where militia groups and criminal enterprises enjoy a relative degree of freedom, producing 'conditions [that] are ideal for large-scale drug production' (International Crisis Group 2019: i). As the majority of drug users are men, women are straining to ensure everyone's survival, which simply does not leave enough time for them to participate in public, political life. In the words of one woman: '[Men] cannot work for the house income, and then women get many burdens [...] That is why they can't be [involved] in the community.'[8] These experiences, on the part of both women and men, raise the question of who exactly benefits from ceasefire deals and business investments.

To sum up, while the transition significantly reshaped the political landscape and brought positive improvements in some ways and for some people, the ways in which these changes were felt and experienced in the everyday by people living in conflict-affected communities are informed by broader gendered relations of power. These reproduce or produce new insecurities experienced by women living far away from the centres of power, in the rural borderlands.

The Past is in the Present: Temporal Complexity

People's experiences also challenge the temporality of conventional notions of transition. While life became better due to the absence of outright conflict in the particular areas we visited, past insecurities were reproduced or replaced by new uncertainties or threats. For many of the people we spoke to, it was difficult to clearly delineate between war and peace, or to identify a distinct 'before' and 'after' key macro-level events such as a ceasefire or the 2011 end of direct military rule. Instead, their narratives and ways of making sense of their lives were marked by temporal complexity (McLeod 2013), where time was not experienced as 'moving forward', but rather as recurring cycles of insecurity, fluctuating in intensity (see Wittekind 2018; Hyde 2015). In very tangible ways, past experiences of dispossession, displacement and violence framed decisions made in the present. In this way, the temporality of anticipation, in which what happened in the past might occur again, structured everyday life (Das 2007; Jefferson and Buch Segal 2019). This points to how the relationship between past, present and future

---

8   Interview with four women, 1 December 2019.

is experienced not as linear, but as complex and intertwined. In southern Kayah state, women from a Karen community explained that in their area:

> Women had a long experience with that really bad situation in the war. Women are still in fear until now. Only some women who are activists like us, only just a few women dare to speak out, or something like that, the rest they are still in fear because of past experiences.[9]

This exemplifies how the ways in which the past spills over into the present structures people's experiences of and opportunities to participate in post-war society. Many women we spoke to explained that fear and trauma kept them from involving themselves in politics, or making their voices heard in their communities. For women, restrictive legacies of fear were also compounded by the effects of a wartime division of labour that prevented them from acquiring education and language skills. In addition, as discussed above, the continuing care work demands placed on women due to the prevailing absence of state welfare provisioning eats up the time and energy that women could otherwise use for paid work or civic engagement. Thus, the ways in which the war casts long shadows over post-war everyday lives is also fundamentally gendered.

Moreover, past experiences of war, and the anticipation of recurring episodes of violence and threat, structure expectations for the future. Strikingly, in the light of the 2021 military coup, a group of civil society activists we interviewed in Kayah state were already arguing in 2019 that the military could, and probably would, take back power at any time:

> So, we have the same situation as in the past [...] [The military] already has the legitimacy to take power any time, whenever they want to take it back [...] that is why I just feel like [...] the past experience will happen again in the future also.[10]

This anticipation of recurrence, rather than progress and change, has material, direct effects in and on people's everyday lives. For example, farmers in Kayah state explained that there was no point for them to invest in housing, as they in any case expected to eventually lose their property to the military (Hedström and Olivius 2022). This experience of looming threat was eloquently described by an older man we met in Mon state: 'I

---

9   Interview with two women, 2 April 2019.
10 Interview with four women in Kayah state, cited in Hedström and Olivius 2022.

feel that all people, all groups, are holding a bomb. A time-bomb. Any time it can explode.'[11]

Thus, while the post-2011 transition period was not experienced as just a continuation of wartime dynamics, villager's everyday lives were still marked by both the anticipation and the actuality of recurring violence, displacement and dispossession. New political dynamics, issues and insecurities generated by post-war processes of change were not perceived as examples of progress and change, but as new manifestations of long-standing patterns of conflict and oppression. As a woman in Mon state notes, the end of war did not mean the end of fear and insecurity:

> Even though there is no fighting, it doesn't mean that we have peace in Mon areas. Because without fighting, people still have concerns and they have fear of different things, you know. From different situations. For example, business and development projects.[12]

While the causes changed – from counterinsurgency to development projects, for example – violations like forced dispossession and displacement have recurred across time. This is clear in the following narrative, where events and issues in Myanmar over 70 years were situated as illustrations of the same fundamental pattern:

> There is no peace since about 70 years already, and since we were born we have not seen any case of peace. And within 70 years there are so many conflicts in the area, and even though the government and the armed groups are doing the peace process […] there is no improvement, no process going forward. So in short we can say that there is no peace in the region. Regarding the conflict, another [problem] is always coming, one by one, for example such as land confiscation, land grabbing, and also exploitation of natural resources. And the current issue with General Aung San Statue.[13] So all of these things are big issues, so that's why it is still far from peace in our region.[14]

While the character of conflict and the issues in focus changed over time, overarching political and legal reforms did little to change people's experience of and relationship to the state, which continued to be largely perceived as

---

11   Interview with man in Mon state, cited in Hedström and Olivius 2022.
12   Interview with one woman, Mon state, 4 December 2019.
13   For an analysis of the Aung San Statue case, see Olivius and Hedström 2021.
14   Interview with three men, Kayah state, 28 March 2019.

predatory, extractive, and violent (Naw Wai Hnin Kyaw and Soe Soe Nwe 2019; Kyed 2020; Wittekind 2018). As one man in Kayah state explained, this means that people still did not feel secure, and were not able to trust that the relative stability of 2019 would last:

> There is no security when, if we go out at midnight or other times we still have a concern, we are still in fear. So as long as the government system is not reformed, we fear for the stability in the country.[15]

Here, continued military power and Bamar dominance were singled out as a reason why the transition was not trusted to lead to something genuinely new. In this way, wartime relationships and experiences spill into and shape postwar lives, challenging conventional ideas about linear transitional time. Exploring transitional processes through the lens of the gendered everyday allows us to make visible these continuities of violence across space and time, and to foreground an alternative temporal framework through which people make sense of their lives.

Conclusion

In the past decade, people's everyday lives in Mon and Kayah states have been affected by political and economic shifts caused by ceasefire agreements from the 1990s and onwards; and by political reforms, economic liberalization and renewed peace negotiations following the 2011 transition from military to semi-civilian rule. These transitional processes combined have brought a complex mix of improvements, new insecurities and threats, as well as a reproduction of wartime dynamics. These multifaceted, multidirectional post-war dynamics and their effects are intertwined with and conditioned by gendered relations and norms.

Notably, while armed violence and forms of forced labour that primarily targeted men were reduced over time, structural forms of violence that disproportionally affect women have persisted. Women's social reproductive burden continues to be overwhelming in the absence of state welfare provisioning. These legacies of war are compounded by new dynamics, such as male drug abuse and labour migration, thus continuing to leave women responsible for sustaining families and communities while unable to access education or paid labour opportunities. Due to gender norms as well as legal

---

15   Interview with one man, Kayah state, 1 April 2019.

frameworks, women are also particularly vulnerable to dispossession as a result of development-related land grabbing.

In the aftermath of the military coup, these patterns are being exacerbated, with women reporting both increased caring responsibilities and increased violence, resulting in negative coping mechanisms, including cutting down on food, savings and medicines, and staying inside (UN Women and UNDP 2022). These are gendered experiences and coping strategies that Agatha Ma and Kusakabe (2015) already found women to be adopting in 2011–2012 in their study on women living in Kayah state, suggesting that past experiences are being repeated in the present moment.

Our findings demonstrate, then, that, rather than constituting a straight-forward 'move from madness to sanity, or from evil to good' (Keen 2007: 9), post-war transitions are messy, multifaceted and multidirectional. Moreover, the knowledge gained from speaking to women and men living in conflict-affected areas trouble not only ideas about the progressive nature of transitional change; the lived experiences of our respondents also destabilizes conventional, linear temporal frameworks. In their lives, time has not been experienced as 'moving forward' towards the future, but rather as recurring cycles of insecurity, dispossession and displacement, where the past, present and future have been intertwined. This was visible in the way wartime gendered divisions of labour restricted women's political and economic opportunities in the post-war, and in how the anticipation that the past will 'return' in the future shaped investment decisions as well as political activism in the present. From this perspective, the 2021 military coup appears not as an anomalous interruption of a trajectory of progress, but as yet another cycle of insecurity that needs to be navigated in everyday life. This temporal complexity points to the relevance of the feminist assertion that war and peace are not dichotomous opposites, but exist on a continuum of gendered violence (Cockburn 2004). Moreover, it highlights the importance of approaching the post-war period as a con-tinued struggle against the enduring legacies of war, and of paying careful attention to how those legacies are manifested, navigated and transformed in the gendered everyday.

References

Agatha Ma and Kyoko Kusakabe. 2015. 'Gender analysis of fear and mobility in the context of ethnic conflict in Kayah State, Myanmar.' *Singapore Journal of Tropical Geography* 36 (3): 1–15.

Ardeth Maung Thawnghmung. 2011. 'The politics of everyday life in the twenty-first century.' *The Journal of Asian Studies* 70 (3): 641–656.

———. 2019. *Everyday Economic Survival in Myanmar*. Madison: University of Wisconsin Press.

Benjamin, Walter. 2007 [1968]. *Illuminations: Essays and Reflections*. Edited by Hannah Arendt, translated by Harry Zohn. New York: Schocken Books.

Berents, Helen. 2015. 'An embodied everyday peace in the midst of violence.' *Peacebuilding* 3 (2): 1–14. Available at: doi.org/10.1080/21647259.2015.1052632.

Bjarnegård, Elin. 2020. 'Introduction: Development challenges in Myanmar: Political development and politics of development intertwined.' *The European Journal of Development Research* 32: 255–273. Available at: doi.org/10.1057/s41287-020-00263-2.

Blomqvist, L., E. Olivius and J. Hedström. 2021. 'Care and silence in women's everyday peacebuilding in Myanmar.' *Conflict, Security & Development* 21 (3): 223–244.

Burke, Adam, Nicola Williams, Patrick Barron, Kim Jolliffe and Thomas Carr. 2017. *The Contested Areas of Myanmar: Subnational Conflict, Aid, and Development*. Yangon: Asia Foundation. Available at: asiafoundation.org/wp-content/uploads/2017/10/ContestedAreasMyanmarReport.pdf.

Callahan, Mary Patricia. 2012. 'The generals loosen their grip.' *Journal of Democracy* 23 (4): 120–131. Available at: doi.org/10.1353/jod.2012.0072.

Choi, Shine. (2021). 'Everyday peace in critical feminist theory.' In *Routledge Handbook of Feminist Peace Research*, pp. 60–69. London: Routledge.

Cockburn, Cynthia. 2004. 'The continuum of violence: A gender perspective on war and peace.' In W. Giles and J. Hyndman (eds), *Sites of Violence. Gender and Conflict Zones*, pp. 24–44. Berkeley and Los Angeles: University of California Press.

———. 2010. 'Gender relations as causal in militarization and war.' *International Feminist Journal of Politics* 12 (2): 139–157. Available at: doi.org/10.1080/14616741003665169.

Cornish, Gillian. 2017. 'Women and Resettlement. A Case Study on Gender Aspects at the Upper Paunglaung Hydropower Dam.' Yangon: Spectrum.

Das, Veena. 2007. *Life and Words: Violence and the Descent into the Ordinary*. Berkeley and Los Angeles: University of California Press.

Décobert, Anne. 2020. '"The struggle isn't over": Shifting aid paradigms and rede-fining "development" in eastern Myanmar.' *World Development* 127: 104768. Available at: doi.org/10.1016/j.worlddev.2019.104768.

Diamond, Larry. 2012. 'The need for a political pact.' *Journal of Democracy* 23 (4): 138–149.

Elias, Juanita and Shirin Rai. 2015. 'The everyday gendered political economy of violence.' *Politics & Gender* 11 (02): 424–29. Available at: doi.org/10.1017/ S1743923X15000148.

———. 2018. 'Feminist everyday political economy: Space, time and violence.' *Review of International Studies* 45 (2): 201–220. Available at: doi.org/10.1017/ S0260210518000323.

Enloe, Cynthia. 1990. *Bananas, Beaches and Bases: Making Feminist Sense of International Politics.* Berkeley and Los Angeles: University of California Press.

———. 2000. *Maneuvers: The International Politics of Militarizing Women's Lives.* Berkeley, CA: University of California Press.

Faxon, Hilary Oliva. 2017. 'In the law and on the land: Finding the female farm-er in Myanmar's national land use policy.' *Journal of Peasant Studies* 44 (6): 1199–1216. Available at: doi.org/10.1080/03066150.2017.1324424.

———. 2020. 'Securing meaningful life: Women's work and land rights in rural Myanmar.' *Journal of Rural Studies* 76 (March): 76–84. Available at: doi.org/ 10.1016/j.jrurstud.2020.03.011.

Ferguson, Jane M. 2014. 'The scramble for the waste lands: Tracking colonial legacies, counterinsurgency and international investment through the lens of land laws in Burma/Myanmar.' *Singapore Journal of Tropical Geography* 35 (3): 295–311. Available at: doi.org/10.1111/sjtg.12078.

Gusic, Ivan. 2019. 'The relational spatiality of the postwar condition: A study of the city of Mitrovica.' *Political Geography* 71 (February): 47–55.

———. 2020. *Contesting Peace in the Postwar City: Belfast, Mitrovica, and Mostar.* Cham, Switzerland: Palgrave/Springer.

Hedström, Jenny. 2021. 'On violence, the everyday and social reproduction: Agnes and Myanmar's transition peacebuilding.' *Peacebuilding* 9 (4): 371–386. Available at: doi.org/10.1080/21647259.2021.1881329.

Hedström, Jenny and Elisabeth Olivius. 2020. 'Insecurity, dispossession, depletion: Women's experiences of post-war development in Myanmar.' *The European Journal of Development Research* 32: 379–403. Available at: doi.org/10.1057/ s41287-020-00255-2.

———. 2022. 'Tracing temporal conflicts in transitional Myanmar: Life history diagrams as methodological tool.' *Conflict, Security & Development.*

Hmung, Samuel. 2021. 'New Friends, Old Enemies: Politics of Ethnic Armed Organisations after the Myanmar Coup.' Policy Briefing – SEARBO. Canberra: New Mandala.

Hom, Andrew. R. 2010. 'Hegemonic metronome: the ascendancy of Western standard time.' *Review of International Studies* 36 (4): 1145–1170.

Hyde, Alexandra. 2015. 'The present tense of Afghanistan: Accounting for space, time and gender in processes of militarisation.' *Gender, Place & Culture* 0524 (July): 1–12. Available at: doi.org/10.1080/0966369X.2015.1058759.

International Crisis Group. 2019. *Fire and Ice: Conflict and Drugs in Myanmar's Shan State*. International Crisis Group: Yangon, Jakarta and Brussels. Available at: www.crisisgroup.org/asia/south-east-asia/myanmar/299-fire-and-ice-conflict-and-drugs-myanmars-shan-state.

Jefferson, Andrew M. and Lotte Buch Segal. 2019. 'The confines of time – On the ebbing away of futures in Sierra Leone and Palestine.' *Ethnos* 84 (1): 96–112. Available at: doi.org/10.1080/00141844.2018.1548497.

Jones, Lee. 2014. 'Explaining Myanmar's regime transition: The periphery is central.' *Democratization* 21 (5): 780–802.

Keen, David. 2007. 'War and peace: What's the difference?' *International Peacekeeping* 7 (4): 1–22.

Klem, Bart. 2018. 'The problem of peace and the meaning of post-war.' *Conflict, Security & Development* 18 (3): 233–255.

Kyed, Helene Maria (ed.). 2020. *Everyday Justice in Myanmar: Informal Resolutions and State Evasion in a Time of Contested Transition*. Copenhagen: NIAS Press.

L. Gum Ja Htung. 2018. *Land Grabbing as a Process of State-Building in Kachin Areas, North Shan State, Myanmar*. Chiang Mai: Chiang Mai University Press.

Linz, J. and A. Stephan. 1996. *Problems of Democratic Transition and Consolidation: Southern Europe, South America and Post-Communist Europe*. Baltimore: John Hopkins University Press.

Lyytikäinen, Minna, Punam Yadav, Annick T. R. Wibben, Marjaana Jauhola and Catia Cecilia Confortini. 2020. 'Unruly wives in the household: Toward feminist genealogies for peace research.' *Cooperation and Conflict* 56 (1): 3–25.

Marijan, Branka. 2017. 'The politics of everyday peace in Bosnia and Herzegovina and Northern Ireland.' *Peacebuilding* 5 (1): 67–81.

McLeod, Laura. 2013. 'Back to the future: Temporality and gender security narratives in Serbia.' *Security Dialogue* 44 (2): 165–181.

Meehan, Patrick and Mandy Sadan. 2017. 'Borderlands.' In Adam Simpson, Nicholas Farrelly and Ian Holliday (eds), *Routledge Handbook of Contemporary Myanmar*. London: Routledge, pp. 83–91. Available at: doi.org/10.4324/9781315743677.

Mi Thang Sorn Poine. 2018. 'Gendered aspects of access to justice in southern Mon State.' *Independent Journal of Burmese Scholarship* 1 (2). Available at: journalofburmesescholarship.org/issues/v1n2/01ThangSorn.pdf.

Myanmar Now. 2021. *Myanmar Military Launches Airstrikes against Karenni Resistance.* Available at: www.myanmar-now.org/en/news/myanmar-military-launches-airstrikes-against-karenni-resistance. Accessed 9 June 2021.

Naw Wai Hnin Kyaw and Soe Soe Nwe. 2019. 'From Margin to Center: Experiences of Political and Social Marginalization of Ethnic Minorities in Karenni State.' Yangon: Friedrich-Ebert-Stiftung Myanmar Office and Peace Leadership and Research Institute.

New Mon State Party. 1985. *Answers to Questionnaire on Mon Freedom Movement.* Mon National University.

Olivius, Elisabeth and Jenny Hedström. 2021. 'Spatial struggles and the politics of peace: The Aung San statue as a site for post-war conflict in Myanmar's Kayah State.' *Journal of Peacebuilding & Development* 16 (3): 275–288. Available at: doi.org/10.1177/1542316620986133.

Rahman, Farhana. 2021. '"I find comfort here": Rohingya women and taleems in Bangladesh's refugee camps.' *Journal of Refugee Studies* 34 (1): 874–889. Available at: doi.org/10.1093/jrs/fez054.

Rhoads, Elizabeth L. and Courtney T. Wittekind. 2019. 'Rethinking land and property in a "transitioning" Myanmar: Representations of isolation, neglect and natural decline.' *Journal of Burma Studies* 22 (2): 171–213. Available at: doi.org/10.1353/jbs.2018.0011.

Scheper-Hughes, Nancy. 1992. *Death Without Weeping: The Violence of Everyday Life in Brazil.* Berkeley: University of California Press.

Simpson, Adam. and Nicholas Farrelly (eds). 2020. *Myanmar: Politics, Economy and Society.* London: Routledge.

Skidmore, Monique. 2009. 'Secrecy and trust in the affective field: Conducting fieldwork in Burma.' In Martha K. Huggins and Marie-Louise Glebbeek (eds), *Women Fielding Danger: Negotiating Ethnographic Identities in Field Research*, pp. 301–325. Plymouth: Rowman and Littlefield.

Söderström, Johanna. 2020. 'Life diagrams: A methodological and analytical tool for accessing life histories.' *Qualitative Research* 20 (1): 3–21. Available at: doi.org/10.1177/1468794118819068.

South, Ashley. (2008). *Ethnic politics in Burma: States of conflict.* London: Routledge.

Sylvester, Christine. 2012. 'War experiences/war practices/war theory.' *Millennium: Journal of International Studies* 40 (3): 483–503. Available at: doi.org/10.1177/0305829812442211.

Tin Maung Maung Than. 2014. 'Introductory overview: Myanmar's economic reforms.' *Southeast Asian Economies* 31 (2): 165.

The Global Justice Center. 2017. 'Vulnerable land, vulnerable women. Gender dimensions of land grabbing in Myanmar.' Berkeley: Goldman School of Public Policy, University of California in collaboration with The Global Justice Center, May issue.

Transnational Institute. 2015. Linking Women and Land in Myanmar: Recognising Gender in the National Land Use Policy. Amsterdam: Transnational Institute.

Väyrynen, Tarja. 2019. 'Mundane peace and the politics of vulnerability: A nonsolid feminist research agenda.' *Peacebuilding* 7 (2): 146–159.

Wibben, Annick. T., Confortini, Catia. C., Roohi, Sanam., Aharoni, Sarai. B., Vastapuu, Leena., & Vaittinen, Tiina. (2019). "Collective discussion: piecing-up feminist peace research." *International Political Sociology*, 13 (1): 86–107.

Women's League of Burma (WLB). (2011). The Founding and Development of the Women's League of Burma: A Herstory. Available at: womenofburma.org/the-founding-anddevelopment-of-the-womens-league-of-burma-a-herstory/.

Wittekind, Courtney T. (2018). "Road plans and planned roads: entangled geographies, spatiotemporal frames, and territorial claims-making in Myanmar's Southern Shan State." *Journal of Burma Studies*, 22 (2): 273–319.

UN Women and UNDP. 2022. 'Regressing Gender Equality in Myanmar: Women living under the Pandemic and Military Rule.' New York: United Nations Development Programme and the United Nations Entity for Gender Equality and the Empowerment of Women.

Yadav, P., & Horn, D. M. (2021). 'Continuums of violence: Feminist peace research and gender-based violence.' In *Routledge handbook of feminist peace research*, pp. 105–114. London: Routledge.

CHAPTER 10

From Mutual Aid to Charity

Violence and Women's Changing Interethnic Relationships in Rakhine State

Shae Frydenlund and Wai Wai Nu

*M*yanmar's post-war transition is generally conceptualized as the period after 2011, when a nominally civilian government tilted away from authoritarian military rule towards the twin promises of democratization and development. Yet for non-Burman, minority women throughout the country, the transition was accompanied by entrenched – and especially gendered – violence that stripped women of resources, extended the working day, and led to greater insecurity (Faxon 2017; Frydenlund 2020a; Hedström 2016, 2021; Hedström and Olivius 2020). For Rohingya and Rakhine Buddhist women from Arakan (Rakhine) state, the year 2011 yielded few material benefits. Soon after, life was sharply cleaved into two parts: before and after 2012. In October of that year, racially motivated pogroms targeted Muslim community members, their homes and their businesses. Eight years later, over 120,000 Muslim people, mostly Rohingyas, remain imprisoned in inhumane camps outside the regional capital of Sittwe. Rohingyas have, it must be noted, been subjected to state-sanctioned violence since the 1970s, but the 2012 pogroms uniquely reorganized both interpersonal relationships between Rohingya and Rakhine Buddhist women and women's embodied positioning vis-à-vis the state. Beyond the loss of mobility and livelihoods, Rohingya women also lost relationships with Rakhine friends and community members. These changes in intimate life have, we argue, far-reaching and heretofore overlooked class consequences.

The gendered political and economic implications of anti-Muslim racism and violence are well-known, as women disproportionately bear the costs of forced displacement, denial of citizenship rights, and exclusion from formal labour markets (Chaudhury 2021; Farzana 2011, 2017; Frydenlund 2020a,

2020b; Rahman 2019). The impacts of violence on communal relations between Muslims and Buddhists are likewise well documented (McCarthy and Menager 2017; Moe Thuzar and Darren Cheong 2019; Prasse-Freeman and Mausert 2020; Schissler, Walton and Phyu Phyu Thi 2017; Thawnghmung 2016) Yet the broader effects of changing interpersonal relationships between Muslim and Buddhist women are not well understood.

Shifting the scale of inquiry from the national to the intimate spaces of everyday life, we approach interethnic personal relationships and cultural practices as politically and economically significant activities. These practices are simultaneously impacted by and productive of broader hegemonic processes. Specifically, we examine the ways in which Rohingya and Rakhine women's reconfigured friendships are relationally linked to the reproduction of Burman hegemony as a racial, gender and class project that benefits elites in Myanmar at the expense of lower-class women.

This chapter is organized into five sections, beginning with a brief discussion of critical literature situating Burman hegemony and communal violence within structures of ethnic, racial, gender and class oppression (and opportunity). We then discuss feminist political economy analyses of gendered dispossession and embodied exclusion. The third section discusses our feminist methodology and the use of feminist–materialist methods of interview and oral history. The next sections provide ethnographic accounts of Rohingya and Rakhine women's memories of inter-ethnic friendships, shared cultural practices and contemporary experiences of embodied securitization. These stories simultaneously reflect and shape women's explanations of the uneven distribution of material benefits and harms that have accompanied social, political and economic reform in Myanmar. We conclude with a discussion of the significance of Rohingya and Rakhine women's memories, experiences and views in building an understanding of the relationship between gendered relations of mutual care and changing class relations in Myanmar and post-war contexts more broadly.

Communal Violence and Burman Hegemony

By now it is well established that racialized ethnic categories, or ethnic identities imbued with assumed biological characteristics (Frydenlund 2017, 2018; Peake and Schein 2000), have become more, not less, salient in Myanmar since a nominally civilian government took power (Walton 2013;

Walton and Hayward 2014; Prasse-Freeman 2013). In particular, historical analyses of postwar politics and democratic transition in Myanmar foreground Burmanization as a political project aimed at resurrecting Burmese national unity through Burman Buddhist ethnic and cultural belonging (Tharaphi Than 2013a, 2013b; Charney 2009). Other scholars have used the Gramscian concept of hegemony, or the cultural and ideological control exerted by ruling classes, to theorize ethnic power relations in Myanmar (Campbell and Prasse-Freeman 2021, Cheesman 2017) As a chauvinist project, Burman hegemony is readily apparent as a baked-in feature of legal reforms to citizenship (Cheesman 2017) and the 'race and religion laws', rendering ethnic minorities, especially Muslims, racialized non-citizens who are deviant and dangerous to the Burmese Buddhist nation (Nyi Nyi Kyaw 2016).

In tandem with racialized oppression, Burman hegemony is also an expression of patriarchal power. This is demonstrated, for example, in Tharaphi Than's (2013a) and Chie Ikeya's (2011) pathbreaking histories of women in Burma, which locate the cultural politics of women's bodily practices within the struggle to articulate a cohesive Burmese tradition and national identity in contrast to foreign modernity. As early as the 1930s, Burman women in interracial marriages were shamed for corrupting an imagined 'Burman bloodline' (Tharaphi Than 2013a: 125), while the present-day 'race and religion' laws represent Muslim men as uniquely threatening to the wellbeing of a Burman Buddhist citizenry. Muslim women are represented as oppressed by a patriarchal culture and Buddhist women come to stand for the vulnerable body of the Bamar Buddhist nation (McCarthy and Menager 2017; Nyi Nyi Kyaw 2016). In Rakhine state, the violent pogroms of 2012 exemplified this relationship between Burman hegemony, racial violence and patriarchy in Myanmar. The rape and murder of Ma Thida Htwe, and the subsequent scapegoating of Muslim men for the crime, ignited mass violence against mostly Rohingya community members, who were accused of violating Buddhism and the Burmese nation itself.

Where various international media analyses and academic writing (see, for example Ware and Laoutides 2018) explained the 2012 pogroms as the result of longstanding ethnic group enmity and religious tension, Indian feminist scholars long ago dispelled this myth through studies of far-right Hindutva communalism and anti-Muslim violence in India. Indeed, Gyanedra Pandey (2006), Charu Gupta ([ed.] 2012), Urvashi Butalia (1994,

2015 [ed.]) and Veena Das (2006) show that communalism and communal violence pivot on racialized othering and the exploitation of subjugated groups rather than on outmoded ideas about ethnic enmity. Given these key interventions, analyses of Myanmar's fraught transition must account for the fact that communal violence is ineluctable from race, gender, and *class* oppression in wider Myanmar.

Extending Stephen Campbell and Elliott Prasse-Freeman's reading of Gramsci and W.E.B Du Bois, we approach Burman hegemony as a *class* project. They argue that a singular focus on the ethno-racial dimensions of Burman hegemony precludes the essential role of class politics in shaping Burman-ness itself. Mapping liberal white privilege theory onto Myanmar likewise fails to consider how Burman hegemonic social relations reproduce racial capitalism – understood as capitalism's systemic dependence on racialized inequality (Robinson 2020; Melamed 2015). Rather, Burman privilege operates to divide an ethnically diverse proletariat. Taken alongside Indian and Burmese feminist analyses, this argument provides an instructive framework for exploring the class implications of racial and gendered violence for minority women in Arakan. We define Burman hegemony as the forms of social-cultural control that promote the class domination of proletarians by elites in Burma. These forms of control include segregation, exclusion from education and employment, racial discrimination and, we argue, the restructuring of intimate personal relationships.

This chapter considers how Burman hegemony is re/produced through the reorganization of women's friendships and mutual relations of care. In the next section we draw on feminist political economy frameworks to consider how Burman hegemony becomes visible in the replacement of women's mutual relations of care with dependence, the securitization of women's bodies, and the formation of new gendered and racialized divisions of labour that benefit Rakhines and elites in Arakan.

Gendered Dispossession in Myanmar

A feminist political economy approach illuminates linkages between state-led economic reform and gendered dispossession (Faxon 2017; Hedström and Olivius 2020; Frydenlund 2020b). This approach has been used to show that as state-led violence continues to ravage Myanmar's northern uplands, women face increased precarity as they become sole household providers and are pushed into dangerous, low-wage work (Hedström and Olivius 2020). Similarly, Hilary Faxon (2017, 2020) demonstrates how post-2011 state land reforms pivot on patriarchal Burman discourses of nonexistent gendered inequality that subjectivizes an imagined female farmer, obscuring women's proletarian identities as rural workers and consolidating power among elite rural women.

Feminist ethnographic scholarship and feminist political economy scholarship have also mapped the contours of anti-Muslim violence and Burman hegemony through both Rohingya women's experiences of exclusion and dispossession *and* their practices of making dignified lives in displacement (Rahman 2019; Farzana 2011, 2017; Frydenlund 2020a). Specifically, Burmanized spaces such as schools, police offices and formal workplaces forcibly exclude Muslim women who wear *pa'wa*, or headscarves. Reflecting Chie Ikeya's (2011) research on gender and modernity in postwar Myanmar, Muslim women's bodily practices hold a broader political significance. While Ikeya's focus on embodied struggle reveals a crisis of masculinity and competing visions of modernity in a changing nation, recent studies of Muslim women's experiences of embodied exclusion and dispossession illuminate broader linkages between racialized ethnic hierarchies, patriarchy and class oppression in transitional Myanmar (Farzana 2017; Frydenlund and Shunn Lei 2021). Here, Burman hegemonic spaces not only racialize *hijabi* women as deviant Others, but also silo Muslim women in low-paid, insecure and flexibilized work. Meanwhile, confinement to rural IDP and refugee camps expands Rohingya women's care work burdens and limits women's ability to reproduce each other through social solidarity, mutual aid and spiritual connection.

In her striking study of *taleem*, or women-only religious spaces, Farhana Rahman (2019) reveals the inefficacy of international 'women-friendly spaces' in the camps. Instead, Rohingya women prefer faith-based spaces, which provide women with friendship, comfort and joy amid daily struggle. In particular, women can justify leaving the safety of their own shelters to participate in religious activities with other women. For Rohingya women confined to villages and camps in Rakhine state, state-sanctioned immobility curtails women's ability to participate in both faith-based group activities and interethnic women-only social activities deemed appropriate by relatives. As the following sections will show, this loss has interconnected gender, racial and class consequences.

More broadly, feminist political economy literature brings the gendered social, political and economic effects of violence and displacement into clear relief; however, women's everyday practices at the scale of the home are also *constitutive* of politics and economic processes (Fluri 2009; Hedström 2018; Massaro and Williams 2013). We therefore draw attention to the ways in which interethnic cultural ties and friendships – and the absence of these social relations – instantiate the social reproduction of communities, the reproduction of agricultural labour and the reproduction of Burman hegemonic social relations.

Methodology

Our collaboration, through which the legal expertise and embodied experiences of Rohingya legal scholar Wai Wai Nu meets Shae Frydenlund's Marxist-feminist approach to labour geography, is built on the authors' friendship and mutual desire to improve the material lives of marginalized women in Myanmar and Bangladesh. Our project shares firsthand history of interethnic communal relations in Arakan as remembered and explained by a small sample of both Rohingya and Rakhine women from across the region. We draw on the foundational insights of postcolonial feminism (Faria and Mollett 2016; Hiemstra and Billo 2017; Moss, Al-Hindi and Kawabata 2002; Nagar 2013) and Third World feminism (Herr 2014; Mohanty 2003; Mohanty, Russo and Torres 1991). The analytical strength of Third World feminism lies in approaching poor, rural and minoritized women – those positioned as Third World women – as bearers of knowledge and an epistemic advantage located in their grounded, geographically specific experiences. Looking to Rohingya and Rakhine women's experiences illuminates new ways of viewing inter-ethnic relationships, ethnic and political identities, and economic lives lived in Arakan.

A Postcolonial and Third World feminist methodology also helped us approach the diversity of women's experiences and narratives with reflexivity about how our own subjectivity shapes the interviews, oral histories and focus groups – and the information and omissions therein – as a result of the authors' educational status, race and affiliation with elite international feminist organizations. Our methods of feminist interview and oral history are grounded in geographically specific knowledge to generate a broad understanding of the history of interdependence and of the mutual relations of care that link Rohingyas and Rakhines. Moreover, building on the theo-retical contributions of Saba Mahmood (2006), we emphasize the fact that Rohingya women's frequent embrace of Islamic practices that subordinate women, such as the requirement to submit to a husband's authority, are not the product of ignorance or false consciousness. Rohingya women are not a monolith, and they have multiple ways of engaging with (or modifying) deeply held religious and cultural values that inflect their lives with meaning and satisfaction.

The research team conducted fieldwork for a total of eight weeks between October 2017 and January 2018 in two Rohingya villages near Sittwe and in the three largest refugee camps in Cox's Bazar. Research activities included 30 semi-structured interviews with Rohingya and Rakhine Buddhist wom-en; 10 oral histories (five Rohingya and five Rakhine); three focus groups with Rohingya women in Myanmar and Bangladesh; and one focus group with Rakhine Buddhist women in Myanmar. Interviews explored subjects' memories of life before 2012, relationships with Rakhine or Rohingya neigh-bours, community members and officials, and opinions about the causes and conditions of the contemporary crisis in Rakhine. Interviewers provided (or arranged for) a private space for informants to share their personal views and memories, which subjects might not have felt comfortable sharing in a group setting. This also allowed the researcher to ask specific questions about experiences, memories, and opinions. Oral histories complemented interviews by providing space for subjects to structure their own narratives and to share their life stories with minimal researcher involvement.

Feminist oral history shifts the focus from current events and traumas, which are the focus of most journalistic accounts of the Rohingya tragedy and Rakhine conflict, to a richer and more complex past life. This opens possibil-ities for understanding the historical context of contemporary Arakan from the perspective of the everyday lives and relationships that colour people's memories of life there. Focus groups provide the opportunity to observe the synthesis and diversity of views held by subjects, which may support or contradict findings from interviews and oral histories. Focus groups also create space for women who have suffered trauma to connect, share stories, make friends and benefit from the support of other women. There are certainly limitations and downsides to this approach: for example, power dynamics between co-ethnic women who are unevenly positioned according to class or family status can come into play, with the voices of more educated and confident women drowning out those of other women. We observed this to a certain extent in our focus groups. We therefore acknowledge the limited generalizability of the findings from our small sample, and we would like to highlight the importance of triangulating between multiple methods.

Before We were Refugees: Rohingya Women's Memories of 'Pre-Transition' Life

On a cold January morning in 2018, the authors visited a small Rohingya settlement near Kutupalong-Balukhali camp in Cox's Bazar, Bangladesh. The camp was constructed in the early 1990s. We crossed a busy road and entered lush wet-rice paddies, walking on the packed dirt partitions and hopping over irrigation ditches until we reached a long row of bamboo houses constructed on flat, elevated ground. The houses were small, only two rooms, and each row of 15 or so homes was separated by a narrow path. Arriving at Shafika's home, we were met with the sweet, smoky smell of roasting chicken and the sound of many women's voices. Although she left Myanmar with her family nearly 25 years ago as military-led violence, forced labour, and extrajudicial arrests and killings spurred an exodus of some 250,000 Rohingyas into Bangladesh, Shafika still wore the *thamein* – a marker of her Burmese identity. As Shafika cooked, a group of five Rohingya women between the ages of 18 and 50 sat on the doorstep and sewed decorations made from tiny iridescent squares of ramen packaging, brightly coloured cotton buds and precisely cut soda cans, for an upcoming wedding. 'It will be beautiful', one of the women remarked, adding that she loved the Rohingya wedding traditions of her Burmese homeland. Though weddings in the Bangladesh refugee settlements and camps often take on a local aesthetic, the women were emphatic in making a distinction between a 'real' Rohingya wedding in Myanmar and the colourful, hybrid weddings of Cox's Bazar, which are more likely to feature Bengali and Hindi pop than Rohingya folk songs.

When asked to tell the stories of their lives lived thus far, the women reflected on what they missed most: their land and animals, their security and their friendships. Many of their most cherished relationships were with Rakhine Buddhist schoolgirls and neighbours. Shafika, who attended school until fleeing Myanmar at age 14, told us about her life growing up in a small town near Maungdaw: 'I even miss the soil. I miss the air. I miss my young life. I miss my friends.' She had two close Rakhine friends as a young girl

– she recalled their names without hesitation: Chyo Ma Win and Hla Hla Min – 'We played together, we went to each other's homes, we helped each other, we ate each other's food. I was happy.'[1]

It is worth noting that those who could attend school were significantly more likely to have Buddhist friends. This highlights the role of education not only in improving girls' life chance, but also as a space that fosters mutual relations of care in wider society. Many women from more rural areas did not have access to nearby schools and were significantly more likely to say that they did not have Rakhine friends, mostly because they did not speak Burmese. Since 2012, Rohingya women's access to education has been dramatically curtailed, leading to greater isolation, earlier marriages, and greater insecurity (Fortify Rights 2019). Most Rohingya girls are not kept out of school as a result of 'conservative' or 'fundamentalist' Islamic values; rather, it is fear of sexual assault incurred on long walks to school, assault or unwanted marriage proposals from boys at a co-ed state school, sexual assault from Tatmadaw soldiers, or military mobility restrictions.[2] Women's experiences of immobility demonstrate one of the key facets of Myanmar's post-war transition, where securitization produces new vulnerabilities for Rohingya women, who lack access to education, socialization and the material benefits of inter-ethnic friendships. We also argue that a lack of access to inter-ethnic friendships is also accompanied by reduced access to material and emotional support, further entrenching gendered disparities in life chances and weakening women's position relative to men, employers and landlords.

Aisha, 42, came from a modest farming family in Bauthidaung. Growing up, her best friend was Rakhine Buddhist. This friend was also the daughter of a Na Sa Ka border police officer. The Na Sa Ka was, and is, infamous for its brutality. Aisha and her friend visited each other's houses and often had picnics together with their families – she recalled what they would eat and her joy in preparing food for the gatherings: 'We would get together and cook whole chickens at my family's house for our picnic parties. I would visit her house and we would play together.'[3] For Rohingyas, sharing a cooked whole chicken is different from sharing a chicken curry. This dish marks important Rohingya gatherings such as weddings and the welcoming of honoured

1   Shafika, Cox's Bazar, 8 January 2018.
2   Military mobility restrictions have affected Rohingya villages since the 1970s, though have accelerated significantly in scope and effect since 2012.
3   Aisha, Cox's Bazar, 8 January 2018.

guests. A whole chicken fried and surrounded by golden-fried boiled eggs also Islamic values of communal sharing and respect for neighbours. Aisha's memory of her friendship is significant because it enhances our understanding of the diverse ways that Rohingya and Rakhine families supported each others' livelihoods and wellbeing through mutual relations of care. These relations included cultural rituals and sharing before communal relations deteriorated and Rohingyas were dispossessed (see also Green, McManus and de la Cour Venning 2015). It also underscores the fact that Rohingyas and Rakhine Buddhists once shared a similar class status, as rural people for whom inter-ethnic picnic parties and culturally-significant celebratory foods were a part of everyday life.

Reflecting on Aisha's memory also offers some insight into a figure who embodies Burman supremacy and performs the military-state but is too often oversimplified: the Tatmadaw soldier. Though the Na Sa Ka border police officer who was the father of Aisha's friend undoubtedly knew of, and likely even participated in, acts of discrimination and violence that targeted Rohingyas in the 1990s, this soldier and his family shared picnic parties with Rohingya neighbours. Of course, many of the perpetrators of unspeakable violence have, throughout history, also shared intimacies of varying kinds with members of the groups they have persecuted. These relationships do not change the structurally violent relations of domination that subjugate Rohingyas and disproportionately disenfranchise Rohingya women in Myanmar. However, this memory does present a more complex picture of intimate everyday relationships between people who were positioned drastically differently vis-à-vis military-state power in Myanmar in the tumultuous 1990s, and suggests mutual relations of care and social reproduction activities linking Rohingyas and Rakhines.

In contrast with childhood memories of peaceful life lived alongside Rakhine friends and neighbours, Rohingya women's stories of their life in the present in Arakan located their anxiety, unhappiness, poverty and insecurity in relation to new imperatives to participate in wage work for family survival. Maria Begum, 36, joined her husband to work outside the home after bans on travel after 2012 left them unable to procure necessary farming equipment, seeds, and fertilizer and prevented workers and relatives from coming to their small farm to plant and harvest.

I was educated to the fifth grade, and I can read and write the Qur'an. Before 2012 my husband and I were living happily together. When I learned to sew, he wouldn't let me work. I was happy with this – he provided everything and I could stay at home with the children. When he couldn't farm or work here after 2012, he went to Malaysia for work. I haven't seen him since. Some people say he was arrested and detained, some people say he has died. Now I have to work but it's not enough to survive anymore. When the Myittar Resource Foundation was here in the village, I worked as a tailor and got 160,000 per month. But then they left, and other villagers aren't buying or tailoring clothes. Now I can only get 1000 per month, and I have to depend on my parents to survive. If my children are sick, I need money for medicine. I used to have a best friend, Phyu Phyu Thein. She was Rakhine, and when I needed money when my children were sick, she would help me, and when I could I would help her. Now we can't leave the village and I don't know where she lives. It makes me sad. I often feel alone and anxious. I have to go out to work and make sure my children are happy, so they don't cry because they miss their father. The international community and the Rakhine community should know that we just want to live together in peace like we did before 2012. That is all we want.[4]

When asked if she currently has any friendships with Rakhine women, Maria said no. Then she thought for a moment and added: 'The brickfield owners are Mog [Rakhine Buddhist]. When I am facing hardship, the owner gives me money, she gives me clothing. That is our relationship.' Maria's experience is significant because it draws attention to a reversal in intimate and communal relations between Rohingyas and Rakhines in the region, as well as to the ways in which women's inter-ethnic friendships and communal relations are sutured to their labour activities, their class status and to the wider economic landscape within the region. When Maria had a similar class status to her Rakhine friend, they were able to fill gaps in household income and, to a degree, support each other's livelihoods *and* the regional agricultural economy. As the class positioning of the Rohingyas erodes relative to that of the Rakhines, women's mutual relations of care are upended and replaced by conditions of dependence and vulnerability.

This repositioning not only reflects a broader shift toward Burman hegemonic social relations that shore up the livelihoods of more privileged citizens, but also reproduces these hegemonic relations on a daily basis through intimate interactions at the scale of the community and of the

4   Maria Begum, Cox's Bazar, 9 January 2018.

individual body. As the class status of rural Rakhine women improves and is guaranteed through police and state practices that favour those who share class status with Bamar Buddhist elites, such as wealthy Muslim capitalists, Rohingya women's status worsens as they work in low-wage jobs to make up shortfalls in household income and take on additional care work burdens to ensure the family's survival.

Moreover, as a Rohingya reserve army of labour grows in relation to dispossession – including the loss of fishing licenses (Saw Eh Htoo 2016), the loss of land and the ability to farm, and pillaged businesses – those with increased access to the means of production accelerate the devaluation of Rohingya work and induce conditions of hyper-exploitation as once-narrow gaps in class status widen (Frydenlund 2020a, 2020b; Wolpe 1976, cited in Campbell 2018). Put another way, Rohingya and Rakhine women's intimate social relations are both shaped by and constitutive of structural shifts in the political economy of the region and Myanmar writ large, in which Buddhists and elites are more likely than ever to own the means of production and benefit from the debts and poverty of the poor.

'We Lived Peacefully Together': Rakhine Women's Experiences

Hla Hla Win, 25, is from a farming family in Bauthidaung. She began work for a Sittwe nonprofit after finishing her university degree, though her parents disapprove of her work and encourage her to take a more stable, permanent job with the government. She joined a group of four other young women, most of whom held high school or university diplomas, at an office in downtown Sittwe for a focus group discussion. The women grew up at a later time than most of the Rohingya women interviewed in Bangladesh and elsewhere in Sittwe, as most were born after 1990, but their memories also echoed the Rohingya stories about experiences of peaceful interethnic relations before 2012:

> I had many Muslim friends growing up, especially my friend Rafik. We knew each other from school and would go to festivals together. [Rakhines and Rohingyas] lived peacefully together for generations. We now hear a lot about killings, so now the communities are afraid of each other. Before the conflict, if there were religious festivals, we would go

211

together. Especially for Eid. Eid was so much fun. We would visit each other. It was really peaceful.[5]

Like Shafika's memories of cooking chickens, picnicking and sharing meals with Rakhine neighbours and friends before she fled to Bangladesh, Hla Hla Win's experiences also reflect a certain fluidity of ethnic boundaries, which characterized multi-ethnic communities in the recent past. As historically interlinked and interdependent peoples from Arakan, Rohingyas and Rakhines are, as Prasse-Freeman and Mausert argue, 'two sides of the same Arakanese coin' (2020: 1), with ethnic identities marked by shared politics, economies and cultural traditions. Rakhine memories of peace and friendship and of participation in Muslim religious and cultural activities such as Eid emphasize the permeability of supposedly fixed, irreconcilable ethnic differences. Hla Hla Win's life course contrasts sharply with the Rohingya women with respect to material wellbeing and security. Though some grew up in agricultural families in the Bauthidaung area, the Rakhine women accessed higher education and have freedom of mobility and economic security. For them, the disappearance of community relations and interethnic friendships is not a material loss and does not affect their ability to support themselves or their communities. Rather, we argue that Rakhine women's repositioning as more privileged citizens and occasional providers of charity to Rohingyas – albeit at the cost of social sanctions, as in the case of the Rakhine woman who was publicly beaten when her husband delivered aid to Rohingyas in displacement camps (Beech 2017) – reflects the role of intimate inter-ethnic relationships at the scale of the body, the home and the community as a site where Bamar hegemonic social relations and politics are produced and reproduced.

The Rakhine women were eager to share their views of the reasons why relations between Muslims and Buddhists are no longer peaceable. Phyu Phyu Tin, 21, explained that 'in my village [in central Arakan], relations between Muslims and Buddhists were very good – there were never any problems – but now, after 2012, Buddhists and Muslims are afraid of each other'. Moe Chit, 19, added that media and rapid communication played a large role in destroying trust between the two groups, stoking fear, misunderstanding and resentment: 'Because of the development of technology, news can spread very easily. Pictures and videos make it easy for people to

5   Hla Hla Win, Sittwe 15 October 2017

believe things are true. Fake news is a problem.' The women make a good point. Social media, especially Facebook, was instrumental in instigating communal violence that targeted Rohingyas and other Muslims. Reflecting findings from research conducted by the International State Crime Initiative, the women emphasized that it was not just internet denizens, but political and community leaders and elites who were to blame for spreading false information (Green, McManus and de la Cour Venning 2015: 59).

Ma Ein Myo is 28, and recently finished an internship in Myitkyina. She reflected on life before 2012 and emphasized the role of communication and spatial proximity between members of different ethnic groups in creating peaceful communal relations:

> There are both Rakhines and Muslims in my village, but I don't remember any conflict with Muslims before 2012. Now they are afraid of each other. The main problem is that [Buddhists and Muslims] don't speak. They have become closed. Rakhine students are afraid when they see Muslims with beards or women with veils. The Muslims are also living only with Muslims. In Myitkyina, there is a lot of diversity – Kachin, Chinese, Pao, Bamar – they are together all the time![6]

There were, of course, conflicts between the military and Rohingyas before 2012, but Rakhine villages far from the northwest were unlikely to have been affected in the same way as those closer to Rohingya-majority communities. Ma Ein Myo believes that Rohingyas, Myanmar Muslims and Buddhists have become strangers, and that distance has led to fear and violence. However, her perspective is also indicative of a broader erasure of the role of communal and military violence in separating Rohingya and Rakhine groups in the region. Distrust between the two communities is inseparable from the dispossession of the Rohingyas and from the ongoing consequences of military-led mobility restrictions and internal imprisonment.

It is noteworthy that Rakhine women understand fear and mistrust as the root cause of shifting communal relations and the disappearance of friendships between Rakhines and Muslims. This framing occludes the devastating impacts of both military and communal violence and overlooks the material links between mutual relations of care and the chasmic class inequalities that have opened between themselves and their Muslim former neighbours. When the women talk about coming together and living alongside people

---

6   Ma Ein Myo, Sittwe, 16 October 2017.

from different ethnic groups as beneficial in the struggle against discrimination and racially-motivated violence, they also index a liberal understanding of the causes and conditions of such discrimination and violence, in which misrecognition and ignorance, rather than racial hierarchies and violent political economies, converge to produce subjugation. As critical feminist and anti-racist scholars have argued, diversity and multiculturalism alone is not the antivenom to race, class and gender-based hierarchies (Coulthard 2014). Rather, the racial and gendered hierarchies that form the scaffolding of racial capitalism must be attacked, for equity and peaceful communal relations to thrive.

Rakhine women's experiences also underscore the racialized and gendered securitization of Muslim women's bodies in Arakan. While sharing the story of her life after moving out of her parents' house and meeting her boyfriend – Zinn Zinn recalled her repeated experiences of harassment in the street after being mistakenly identified as a Muslim woman:

> Here in Sittwe if I wear a scarf to protect my face from the sun, men yell *'kalar ma!'* [a gendered racial slur used to refer to women with South Asian physiogymy]. This has happened three times. Once at the market, and twice in the street. It was scary. My boyfriend tells me I shouldn't wear a scarf at all here because it's dangerous for Muslim women.[7]

Zinn Zinn and the other young Rakhine women talked at length about the structural forms of sexism that shaped their lives and limited their opportunities, including the preference for male children and the discriminatory state practice of increasing the test score required to enter medical school for women. Yet Zinn Zinn also recognized that being perceived as Buddhist or Muslim affected her ability to safely move through public space – Muslim women's confinement to villages and displacement camps notwithstanding – and points to the interlocking forms of oppression that Muslim women face in contemporary Myanmar. Her momentary experience as an out-of-place Muslim woman made embodied securitization visible as a spatial expression of Burman hegemony, where bodies are marked as 'appropriate' or 'inappropriate' for specific places based on gendered and racialized spatial imaginaries. As Mona Domosh (2017) argues of Black experiences of spatial containment in Jim Crow America, white spatial imaginaries that kept Black people in place were bound up with racial divisions of labour that

---

7   Zinn Zinn, Sittwe, 16 October 2017.

generated profit for white cotton capitalists. Considered alongside the new positioning of Rohingya women as precarious workers who are kept in place, the isolation of these women from Rakhine women and their loss of access to mutual relations of care posit future class-attuned analyses of the Burman spatial imaginaries that justify the subjugation of Muslims.

Conclusion

Data from oral histories, focus groups and interviews with Rohingya and Rakhine women from Arakan shed light on the ways in which Rohingya and Rakhine women have been repositioned not only in relation to each other, but in relation to local labour markets, the national economy, and the military-state. The material lives of Rohingya and Rakhine women are unevenly impacted by state practices and policies that entrench racial, gender and class inequality. While Rakhine women respondents from agricultural backgrounds gained access to higher education, Rohingya women are barred from university and Rohingya work is devalued. Yet these structural changes have also been accompanied by the disappearance of shared cultural practices, lost inter-ethnic friendships, and the securitization of the gendered and racialized bodies of Muslims. Shifting the scale and the site of inquiry from state spaces and places of employment to the body, home and community makes interethnic friendships and relations of mutual care between women visible, as crucial sites where Burman hegemony is actively reproduced.

In addition to recentring intimate relations as important sites productive of post-conflict politics and political economies, a class-attuned analysis of the views of Rohingya and Rakhine women has the added benefit of unsettling dominant discourses about Arakan history. Specifically, their experiences of shared cultural practices, relations of mutual care and peace challenge the argument that conflict between Muslims and Buddhists is a defining feature of Arakanese history. Recalling Shafika's fond memories of the air, soil, animals and friendships that characterized her life before displacement, the violent and segregated landscape of Arakan becomes peculiar rather than a historical status quo. Women's memories of interethnic friendship, home and community offer additional empirical evidence in support of the argument that conflict and communal violence between Rohingyas and Rakhine Buddhists is not the product of long-simmering tensions that have existed since time immemorial – they emerged at specific historical conjunctures where political, state and military interests articulated with Rakhine nationalist political interests, broadly construed, to marginalize and dispossess Rohingyas and reaffirm elite livelihoods in Arakan and Myanmar writ large. In particular, Myanmar's transition to semi-civilian rule and a market economy was embedded within a broader Burman hegemonic project that marginalized the poor and non-Buddhist minorities and prioritized the livelihoods of elites, Bamars and culturally Burmese minorities at the expense of those targeted as anti-Burmese (Campbell and Prasse-Freeman 2022). The violent pogroms of 2012 reflect an alignment between neoliberalization and Burman chauvinism. Paying attention to Rohingya and Rakhine women's memories of life before mass displacement and violence, their changing or unchanging relationships with people from different ethnic and class backgrounds, and their everyday, material experiences illuminates not only the complexity of relations between Buddhists and Muslims in Rakhine – even a Na Sa Ka officer once picnicked with Rohingyas – but also undermines the popular, though debunked narrative that communal violence is the result of longstanding ethnic group enmity rather than state and military violence (see also Green, McManus and de la Cour Venning 2015: 31).

Set against a background of entrenched gendered, ethno-racial and class inequality at the national scale, Rakhine and Rohingya women's memories and explanations of inter-ethnic peace and conflict draw attention to the relationship between cultural and social ties and women's economic lives in contemporary Myanmar and in post-war contexts more broadly. Once positioned as both givers and recipients of aid and loans, Rohingya women are now positioned as recipients of charity in relation to Rakhine women. We argue that this rearrangement of ethnic and cultural relations is not only the result of national-scale political economic changes and ethnic politics, in which Buddhists and elites become more wealthy and secure as minoritized groups are dispossessed, but also of changes in intimate relationships at the scale of the everyday. Rohingya women's experiences of shifting relationships, cultural landscapes and labour market positioning also reveal that Burman hegemony is advanced not just through national-scale politics, but through everyday interpersonal relationships. Inter-ethnic friendships alone are not sufficient to repair a violent political economy, but solidarities built on mutual relations of care and resource-sharing are powerful salves for countering poverty and marginality. Without them, marginalized women become more marginal and those in closer proximity to elites gain access to improved livelihoods.

References

Beech, Hannah. 2017. 'I'm struggling to survive: For Rohingya women, abuse continues in camps. *New York Times*. 23 December.

Butalia, Urvashi. 1994. 'Community, state and gender: Some reflections on the partition of India.' *Oxford Literary Review* 16 (1): 33–67.

Butalia, Urvashi (ed.). 2015. *Partition: The Long Shadow*. London: Penguin.

Campbell, Stephen. 2018. *Border Capitalism, Disrupted*. Ithaca, NY: Cornell University Press.

Campbell, Stephen. and Elliott Prasse-Freeman. 2022. 'Revisiting the wages of Burman-ness: Contradictions of privilege in Myanmar. *Journal of Contemporary Asia* 52 (2): 175–199.

Charney, Michael. 2009. *A History of Modern Burma*. Cambridge: Cambridge University Press.

Chaudhury, Sabyasachi Basu Ray. 2021. 'Dispossession, un-freedom, precarity: Negotiating citizenship laws in postcolonial South Asia.' *South Atlantic Quarterly* 120 (1): 209–219.

Cheesman, Nick. 2017. 'How in Myanmar "national races" came to surpass citizenship and exclude Rohingya.' *Journal of Contemporary Asia* 47 (3): 461–83.

Coulthard, Glen Sean. 2014. *Red Skin, White Masks: Rejecting the Colonial Politics of Recognition*. Minneapolis: University of Minnesota Press.

Das, Veena. 2006. *Life and Words: Violence and the Descent into the Ordinary*. Berkeley: University of California Press.

Domosh, Mona. 2017. 'Genealogies of race, gender, and place.' *Annals of the American Association of Geographers* 107 (3): 765–778.

Faria, Caroline and Sharlene Mollett. 2016. 'Critical feminist reflexivity and the politics of whiteness in the "field".' *Gender, Place & Culture* 23 (1): 79–93.

Farzana, Kazi Fahmida. 2011. 'Music and artistic artefacts: Symbols of Rohingya identity and everyday resistance in borderlands.' *ASEAS – Austrian Journal of South-East Asian Studies* 4 (2): 215–236.

———. 2017. *Memories of Burmese Rohingya Refugees: Contested Identity and Belonging*. London: Springer.

Faxon, Hilary Oliva. 2017. In the law & on the land: Finding the female farmer in Myanmar's National Land Use Policy. *The Journal of Peasant Studies*, 44 (6), 1197–1214.

Faxon, Hilary Oliva. 2020. 'Securing meaningful life: Women's work and land rights in rural Myanmar'. *Journal of Rural Studies*, 76 (1), 76–84.

Fortify Rights. 2019. *End Child Marriage, Protect Rohingya Refugee Girls*. 21 February. Available at: www.fortifyrights.org.

Fluri, Jennifer L. 2009. 'Geopolitics of gender and violence "from below".' *Political Geography* 28 (4): 259–65.

Frydenlund, Shae. 2017. 'Labor and race in Nepal's indigenous nationalities discourse: Beyond "tribal" vs "peasant" categories.' *HIMALAYA, The Journal of the Association for Nepal and Himalayan Studies* 37 (1): 8.

———. 2020a. 'Motherhood, home, and the political economy of Rohingya women's labor.' In Pavin Chachavalpongpun, Elliott Prasse-Freeman and Patrick Strefford (eds), *Unraveling Myanmar's Transition: Progress, Retrenchment, and Ambiguity Amid Liberalisation*, pp. 235–260. Kyoto: Kyoto University Press.

———. 2020b. 'Support from the South: How Refugee Labor Reproduces Cities.' Doctoral dissertation, University of Colorado at Boulder.

Frydenlund, Shae and Shunn Lei. 2021. 'Hawkers and Hijabi Cyberspace: Muslim Women's Labor Subjectivities in Yangon.' *Independent Journal of Burmese Scholarship, Special Issue on the Rohingya: Politics of Inclusion and Exclusion in Myanmar* 1: 282–318.

Green, Penny, Thomas McManus and Alicia de la Cour Venning. 2015. *Countdown to Annihilation: Genocide in Myanmar*. London: School of Law, Queen Mary University. International State Crime Initiative.

Gupta, Charu (ed.). 2012. *Gendering Colonial India: Reforms, Print, Caste and Communalism*. New Delhi: Orient Blackswan.

Hedström, Jenny. 2018. 'Reproducing Revolution: A Feminist Political Economy Analysis of the Conflict in Kachinland.' Doctoral dissertation, Monash University.

———. 2021. 'On violence, the everyday, and social reproduction: Agnes and Myanmar's transition.' *Peacebuilding* 9 (4): 371–386. Available at: doi.org/10.1080/21647259.2021.1881329.

Hedström, Jenny and Elisabeth Olivius. 2020. 'Insecurity, dispossession, depletion: Women's experiences of post-war development in Myanmar.' *The European Journal of Development Research* 32: 379–403. Available at: doi.org/10.1057/s41287-020-00255-2.

Herr, Ranjoo Seodu. 2014. 'Reclaiming Third World feminism.' *Meridians* 12 (1): 1–30.

Hiemstra, Nancy and Emily Billo. 2017. 'Introduction to focus section: Feminist research and knowledge production in geography.' *The Professional Geographer* 69 (2): 284–90.

Ikeya, Chie. 2011. *Refiguring Women, Colonialism and Modernity in Burma*. Honolulu: University of Hawai'i Press.

Mahmood, Saba. 2011. *Politics of Piety: The Islamic revival and the feminist subject*. Princeton: Princeton University Press.

Massaro, Vanessa A. and Jill Williams. 2013. 'Feminist geopolitics.' *Geography Compass* 7 (8): 567–577.

McCarthy, Gerard and Jacqueline Menager. 2017. 'Gendered rumours and the Muslim scapegoat in Myanmar's transition.' *Journal of Contemporary Asia* 47 (3): 396–412

Melamed, Jodi. 2015. 'Racial capitalism.' *Critical Ethnic Studies* 1 (1): 76–85.

Moe Thuzar and Darren Cheong. 2019. 'Ethnicity, citizenship and identity in post-2016 Myanmar.' In: Daljit Singh and Malcolm Cook (eds), *Southeast Asian Affairs 2019*, pp. 243–258.

Mohanty, Chandra. 2003. *Feminism without Borders: Decolonizing Theory, Practicing Solidarity.* Duke University Press.

Mohanty, Chandra, Ann Russo and Lourdes Torres. 1991. *Third World Women and the Politics of Feminism.* Bloomington: University of Indiana Press.

Moss, Pamela, Karen Falconer Al-Hindi and Hope Kawabata. 2002. *Feminist Geography in Practice: Research and Methods.* Malden: Wiley-Blackwell.

Nagar, Richa. 2013. 'Storytelling and co-authorship in feminist alliance work: Reflections from a journey.' *Gender, Place & Culture* 20 (1): 1–18.

Nyi Nyi Kyaw. 2016. "The 969 Movement and Anti-Muslim Violence." In *Islam and the State in Myanmar : Muslim-Buddhist Relations and the Politics of Belonging,* Oxford: Oxford University Press.

Pandey, Gyanendra. 2006. *Routine Violence: Nations, Fragments, Histories.* Stanford University Press.

Peake, Linda, & Harold Schein. 2000. 'Racing geography into the new millennium: Studies of race and North American geographies'. *Social & Cultural Geography,* 1 (2), 133–142.

Prasse-Freeman, Elliott. 2013. Scapegoating in Burma. *Anthropology Today,* 29 (4), 2–3.

Prasse-Freeman, Elliott and Kirt Mausert. 2020. 'Two sides of the same Arakanese coin: "Rakhine", "Rohingya" and ethnogenesis as schismogenesis.' In: Pavin Chachavalpongpun, Elliott Prasse-Freeman and Patrick Strefford (eds), *Unravelling Myanmar's Transition: Progress, Retrenchment, and Ambiguity Amidst Liberalization.* Singapore: NUS Press.

Rahman, Farhana. 2019. '"I find comfort here": Rohingya women and taleems in Bangladesh's refugee camps.' *Journal of Refugee Studies* 34 (1): 874–889. Available at: doi.org/10.1093/jrs/fez054.

Robinson, Cedric J. 2020. *Black Marxism: The making of the black radical tradition.* Durham: UNC Press.

Saw Eh Htoo. 2016. 'Small-scale fisherman in Rakhine state.' *Independent Journal of Burmese Scholarship* 1 (1): 9–33.

Schissler, Matt, Matthew J. Walton and Phyu Phyu Thi. 2017. 'Reconciling contradictions: Buddhist–Muslim violence, narrative making and memory in
Myanmar.' *Journal of Contemporary Asia* 47 (3): 376–395.

Tharaphi Than. 2013a. *Women in modern Burma*. London: Routledge.

Tharaphi Than. 2013b. 'The languages of Pyidawtha and the Burmese approach to
national development'. *South East Asia Research*, 21 (4), 639–654.

Thawnghmung, Ardeth Maung. 2016. 'The politics of indigeneity in Myanmar:
Competing narratives in Rakhine state.' *Asian Ethnicity* 17 (4): 527–547.

Walton, Matthew J. 2013. "The 'Wages of Burman-Ness:' Ethnicity and Burman
Privilege in Contemporary Myanmar." *Journal of Contemporary Asia* 43 (1):
1–27.

Walton, Matthew J., and Susan. Hayward. 2014. *Contesting Buddhist Narratives :
Democratization, Nationalism, and Communal Violence in Myanmar*. Honolulu:
East-West Center.

Ware, Anthony and Costas Laoutides. 2018. *Myanmar's 'Rohingya' Conflict*. Oxford:
Oxford University Press.

Wolpe, Harold. 1976. 'The "white working class" in South Africa.' *Economy and
Society*, 5 (2), 197–240, Cited in Campbell, 2018.

CHAPTER 11

Gender, disabilities and displacement in Kachin State

Dan Seng Lawn, Jana Naujoks and Henri Myrttinen

Introduction

C lashes in June 2011 between the Myanmar armed forces, known as the Tatmadaw, and the armed wing of the Kachin Independence Organisation (KIO) re-ignited the armed conflict in Kachin State, ending a 17-year ceasefire.[1] The conflict has led to the deaths of thousands of civilians, and civilians have suffered from conflict-related sexual violence, forced recruitment (including of minors) and exposure to landmines (Human Rights Watch 2012). In December 2020, approximately 97,000 civilians in Kachin State were registered as internally displaced persons (IDPs), both in government-controlled and KIO-controlled areas (Myanmar Information Management Unit 2020; for gender dynamics in Kachin State, see also Cardènas, this volume). The February 1, 2021 coup d'état has escalated the fighting, leading to further casualties and displacement in the state. This chapter examines a grim legacy of this armed violence, namely the civilians and former combatants living with disabilities caused by the war. Furthermore, we also examine the impacts of war and displacement on people with non-conflict related disabilities. We do this by drawing on data collected in Kachin State in 2018 (Lawn and Naujoks 2018), and analyse the findings from a gender perspective. We thereby highlight the experiences of people who have often been left out or marginalized in the processes of transformation in Myanmar as well as in the narratives about it. While the opening up of new political spaces created avenues for civil society actors to advocate for gender-related issues both nationally and sub-nationally (as discussed in the chapters by Faxon and Aye Thiri Kyaw in this volume), the intersections of gender, disability

---

1   On the breakdown of the ceasefire, see Sadan (ed.) 2016.

and conflict have received comparatively little attention. The voices of both displaced persons and persons with disabilities themselves have often been largely absent from these debates.

This chapter is structured as follows. After a brief overview of the research methodology and the state of research on gender and disabilities, we discuss the various concerns raised by our interviewees, as well as giving an overview of services available to persons living with disabilities. We then discuss the gendered dimensions of disabilities in Kachin State and end with conclusions.

Gender, Disability and Conflict

This chapter is based on qualitative research conducted in September–October 2018, consisting of 161 interviews and six focus group discussions (FGDs). Our respondents were primarily men and women with mobility-related and visual disabilities. In addition, we conducted 19 key stakeholder interviews in government- and KIO-controlled areas,[2] including in IDPs camps (Lawn and Naujoks 2018). Of the interviewees, 45 per cent (64 respondents) were women and 55 per cent (77 respondents) were men. Most were internally displaced persons, including veterans of the Kachin Independence Army (KIA). Additional interviews were conducted for comparison with persons living with disabilities in Laiza and Myitkyina, who had not been displaced. Many of the disabilities in KIO-controlled areas were conflict-related, incurred through landmines, conflict violence, while fleeing from fighting, or due to lack of timely medical support. In the government-controlled areas, most of the respondents reported that their disabilities were congenital or stemming from accidents. The issues covered included safety and security; livelihoods; stigmatization and discrimination; services available to persons living with disabilities in Kachin State; and gendered expectations and changes.

While much of the research on the various armed conflicts in Myanmar continues to be gender-blind, there is a growing body of both academic and 'grey' literature on women and girls in conflict (see also chapters by

---

2   Key stakeholders included ethnic and community-based organizations, faith-based organizations, national organizations focused on supporting people living with disabilities, camp management structures and relevant local authorities on both the government and the KIO sides.

Pepper, Zin Mar Phyo and Mi Sue Pwint and Hedström, Olivius and Zin Mar Phyo in this volume). The gendered experiences of civilian of men and boys in conflict have been far less researched in Myanmar (Naujoks and Myat Thandar Ko 2018). In the case of the Kachin conflict, Jenny Hedström (2016a, 2016b and 2020) and Nhkum Bu Lu (2016) have studied women active in the KIO and its armed wing, the KIA. The impacts of the conflict on displaced women, and on civilian women more broadly, have been documented by various non-governmental organizations (NGOs) and humanitarian agencies, and to a lesser extent in academic research (for example Gender Equality Network and Kachin Women's Peace Network 2013; Gender in Humanitarian Action Workstream 2020; Johnston and Lingham 2020; McLaughlin and Seng 2018; Pistor 2017).

Globally, and in the Myanmar context as well, the interplay of gender and disability in contexts of displacement and conflict has remained understudied. Much of the existing literature on gender and disability draws on research in the Global North, in non-conflict and non-displacement situations (Grech and Pisani 2015; Mohamed and Shefer 2015; Shuttleworth, Wedgwood and Wilson 2012). Examining what literature is available on gender, conflict, displacement and disability, we do however see key similarities between Kachin State and other conflict contexts. These similarities include the need to differentiate between congenital/disease-related and conflict-/accident-related disabilities and how these impact gender (Shuttleworth, Wedgwood and Wilson 2012); the differential impacts of conflict-related disabilities on civilians and former combatants (Hartley 2013); and the need to approach the interplay of gender, disabilities and displacement as dynamic rather than static (Muhanna-Matar 2020).

The concept of 'disability' has historically been understood in different ways. Dan Goodley (2017: 8–20) outlined several ways in which disability or impairment is framed. These include moral framings of disability as a form of punishment or retribution for past misdeeds; medical understandings focusing on disability as a condition to be addressed; social understanding of disabilities focusing on how society creates barriers; and the biopsychosocial model, which seeks to bridge the gap between the medical and social models.

For the purposes of our research, we sought to use a biopsychosocial approach. While not officially espoused by any service providers or faith leaders, nor directly endorsed by any respondents, our research did hint at echoes of a 'moral' framing of disability among some community members and possibly some respondents as well (i.e. of it being a punishment for past bad deeds – see Goodley 2017), along with various forms of discrimination linked to superstitious beliefs. Service providers tended to take a medical approach, though increasingly also a social – or biopsychosocial – understanding of disabilities is beginning to take root as well, especially among CSOs. What is, however, often missing is a deeper gender analysis as well.

Key Concerns of Persons Living with Disabilities

Conflict and displacement expose people to the risks of direct violence, create livelihood-related concerns and concerns about a lack of control over one's life situation, as well as emotional and psychological stress. Furthermore, being displaced can become a source of social stigma. Some of these impacts take on particular gender dimensions. For example, women are expected to take care of both reproductive and productive labour, and face higher risks of various forms of sexual harassment, exploitation and abuse as well as of domestic and intimate partner violence, with little recourse to justice in such cases (Gender Equality Network and Kachin Women's Peace Network 2013; Hedström and Olivius 2020; Johnston and Lingham 2020; Pistor 2017). Men and boys may be more impacted by the frustrations associated with not being able to live up to expectations of being an economic provider; are more likely to come under suspicion of being a potential combatant; and also have higher rates of drug and alcohol abuse (Gender in Humanitarian Action Workstream 2020; McLaughlin and Seng 2018; Naujoks and Myat Thandar Ko 2018). Men, both in uniform and civilians, also form the majority of landmine victims in Myanmar, as they are more likely to be in combat or, in the case of civilians, to undertake activities that place them at higher risk, such as using heavy farming equipment in mine-contaminated areas (International Campaign to Ban Landmines 2014).

While displaced persons across the board face the above risks and vulnerabilities, they are often even more pronounced for those living with disabilities. These risks and vulnerabilities can extend to those caring for them, which tends to be women family members. In addition, the marginalization of those living with disabilities is compounded by physical barriers, stigma and discriminatory attitudes, including internalized stigma and fears of embarrassment or pity in public interactions (Naujoks and Lawn 2018). These both lead to and can be further exacerbated by reduced opportunities to gain skills and education and to participate in the work force (Khaing Khaing Soe 2017).

The key concerns raised by our respondents related to safety and security; concerns related to livelihoods; and discrimination and stigmatization. We will next explore these and their gendered dimensions in more depth.

Safety and Security

The most direct impact of armed conflict on people's lives is their increased exposure to violence, injury and death. Gender is one of the main factors affecting people's scope for action and decision-making as well as their vulnerabilities in times of violent conflict. Many gendered risks and vulnerabilities are exacerbated for those living with disabilities. For example, security threats faced while fleeing from their villages are often heightened for those living with disabilities due to their limited mobility. In the IDP camps, many threats remain, particularly as camps have at times been targeted by shelling and aerial bombardment and as there are often landmines in the areas around the camps. In addition, it is often difficult to meet basic needs including food, safe drinking water and primary healthcare.

Key security risks for civilian men and boys in Myanmar's conflict zones include being targeted by armed groups, including the Tatmadaw, as suspected combatants. Men with physical impairments are often suspected of being former combatants and face frequent interrogation at military checkpoints. This was mentioned as being a major barrier preventing them from accessing medical and educational services.[3]

For women and girls, various forms of sexual and gender-based violence (SGBV), committed both by armed actors and civilians, are a major risk in conflict-affected areas. Survivors and their families may not want to make cases public and visible for fear of stigmatization, and camp management committees in Kachin and elsewhere in Myanmar have been known to suppress reporting (Gender in Humanitarian Action Workstream 2020). Young women and girls with disabilities are particularly vulnerable to harassment when their parents or carers go out of the camp to work as daily labourers. A mother of one such victim stated:

---

3   Interview in Shwe Zet IDP Camp (Myitkyina), 18 October 2018. 47-year-old man, paralysed due to lack of medical support.

It is a shameful thing to tell. A bad guy from the neighbourhood tried to harass [my daughter]. So she was quite afraid and ran around. But the neighbourhood kept saying that nothing had happened. It happened when my husband and I went outside the camp to work as daily waged labourers, and we left her with the younger children. We did not know how to express [what happened]. The neighbourhood blamed us instead. They said that nothing had happened, though it was just too obvious.[4]

Men and boys with disabilities, especially those who are mute or have cognitive disabilities, may also be targets of SGBV, as it is assumed that they cannot report incidents of abuse or that they will not be believed. Domestic violence, physical and verbal abuse of those with disabilities by other family or community members is a further risk faced by persons living with disabilities, regardless of gender. Our findings included a case of a man who kept violently attacking his stepfather despite the latter's disabilities, beating him and cutting his neck with a knife. The stepfather had to stay at a monastery for his safety.

Livelihoods and Disabilities

Livelihoods are a major issue of concern across the board for internally displaced persons, but especially for men, whose sense of self-esteem and social standing in Myanmar is often linked to expectations of being the primary breadwinner, an expectation made all the more difficult to fulfil in a context of conflict and displacement (see also Naujoks and Myat Thandar Ko 2018). For women in families with members with disabilities, the loss of the male provider in a household often means that they face the burden of having to work more to sustaining the family economically, in addition to which they are often expected to care for the family member with disabilities (see also Johnston and Lingham 2020). Women with disabilities themselves may struggle to get help from other family members, as caring is seen as mainly a 'feminine task', which male household members may be unwilling to undertake:

The main problem in the households in the camp is when the primary breadwinner of the household gets ill or getting old. The family members have to look after him/her the whole time since he/she became disabled.

---

4   Interview, Padaukmyaing IDP Camp (Myitkyina), 16 October 2018. The young woman concerned was 19 years old and had polio-related disabilities.

In some households those living with disabilities are alone without any support from the relatives and neighbours.[5]

Displaced persons living with disabilities often face greater difficulty than other displaced peoples in finding livelihood opportunities, which can result in frustration, and this may then lead to negative coping mechanisms such as substance abuse,[6] but also, potentially, to domestic violence. Substance abuse is more likely among men, given gender norms that proscribe women from drinking alcohol or using drugs, but are more lenient in relation to this among men (Gender in Humanitarian Action Workstream 2020).

The respondents' perceptions around disabilities and gender roles are closely linked to their ability to generate income and get married, which in turn affects their sense of self-worth and position in their communities. Men living with disabilities, in particular, felt more socially integrated when they could generate income and provide for the family. Answers to whether respondents saw themselves as 'being disabled' varied accordingly: those who were able to earn an income and generate a livelihood often did not self-identify as living with a disability, in spite of impairments such as missing limbs. Those who were unable to make a living were more likely to self-identify as living with a disability. In a focus group discussion with visually impaired respondents, men highlighted their ability to navigate through life and to learn and earn as evidence that they were not disabled.[7] This is in line with expectations of strength, independence and being the breadwinner for Kachin men. Visually impaired women participants, meanwhile, talked less about how they saw themselves, and spoke more on behalf of blind children, in line with gendered expectations of being a caregiver. But even among women, the ability to contribute to the household income was a key indicator of social acceptance, with one woman living with a disability, for example, reporting problems with her in-laws until she started earning money, upon which she was respected by them.

Livelihood-related concerns were more acute among disabled respondents living in IDP camps. Apart from the monthly support that they receive from the camp leadership, they have little or no income and no job

---

5   Interview with service provider.
6   Methamphetamine and opiates are widely available in Kachin State.
7   Focus group discussion, Jan Mai Kawng School for the Blind (Myitkyina), 26 October 2018.

opportunities. Available jobs, which are mainly in banana, sugarcane and tea plantations, tend to be seasonal and temporary. Women are preferred as employees in tea plantations, mainly on the Chinese side, in order to pick tea leaves, as women have been socialized more to carry out monotonous work that requires attention to detail. In banana plantations, the main job is to carry banana bundles and spray pesticides, which is considered suitable for men due to the requirement for physical strength. Sugarcane plantations, on the other hand, mostly employ women. None of these jobs are easily accessible to persons living with disabilities. The jobs are physical and the terrain is hilly. A woman living in an IDP camp in Myitkyina related her struggles as a wife and mother, unable to get a permanent job even after living in the camp for seven years:

> Initially we received 100% of our share of aid from the camp. Since I am now able to do temporary jobs they have cut our share down to 70%. Now I have to work to support my husband and children. Since my husband is a drug addict he is doing nothing. As he is likely to create more problems when he goes out, I convince him to stay at home. It is extremely difficult to get a job, even for other displaced persons, let alone for us. Though I have lived in the IDP camps for something like six or seven years, I still have not got a permanent job.[8]

A respondent using a prosthetic leg mentioned that it is extremely difficult to work more than 1.5 hours in the field as the sweat and heat make it extremely uncomfortable.[9] Respondents also raised concerns about the health impacts of the pesticides and fertilisers used on the monoculture plantations.[10]

The armed conflict has also affected persons living with disabilities in areas not directly affected by armed conflict, such as in Myitkyina. The President of Myitkyina School for the Blind explained how the conflict has impacted on the school's fund-raising:

> Due to the conflict the population of persons living with disabilities is increasing. Likewise, the volume of donations we received has dwindled; due to the conflict our music band cannot go out and do fundraising shows across the region.[11]

---

8   Interview, Bethlehem IDP Camp (Myitkyina), 22 October 2018. 36-year-old woman with polio-related disabilities.

9   Ibid.

10 Interviews in Je Yang IDP Camps, 2018.

11 Interview, Mytikyina, 2018.

Thus, even beyond the direct impact of violence and displacement, as summed up by an NGO respondent, 'the conflict has made disabled persons more disabled', and has added new barriers to their livelihoods.[12]

For the majority of respondents, who have come from agricultural communities, access to land was central to their livelihoods and identity. Most of our respondents wanted to return to their home villages, but only if it was safe. As long as military troops remain stationed in the vicinity of their villages and landmine incidents continued, they did not dare to go back. Research on internally-displaced Kachin has shown differences between women and men in wanting to return or resettle (Gender Profile for Humanitarian Action 2020). Women were found to attribute more importance to living conditions, family cohesion, identity, education and health services, while for men fear of losing their land and houses in their place of origin was their main preoccupation. Respondents expressed concern that their land had been confiscated in their absence. This was echoed in our research as well. A displaced man with disabilities, for example, stated that he could no longer protect his property in the village, explaining how ethnicity intersects with his disability to shape the impact of the conflict on him:

> Since I have acquired a disability I cannot go back and oversee our family's land, while other people could occasionally go back and do short-term farming and come back. What made me despair most has been that I could not even go back and clear our family compound. [...]. As a result, some of my neighbours have confiscated some of our family land in our absence. Our neighbours did not need to flee. They are Tai Leng.[13]

Stigmatization and discrimination

Our research indicated that persons living with disabilities face different attitudes to different types of disabilities. There were, we found, traditional, positive attitudes to some types of disability, which are regarded as being auspicious or associated with good fortune. According to interviewees,

---

12 H. Nu Ra, 2018.

13 In multi-ethnic areas such as Tarlawgyi, ethnic Tai-Leng IDPs can return or did not need to flee, while ethnic Kachin IDPs face risks in returning home because they are more likely to be suspected of being KIA members or supporters, facing possible arrest. Interview in Shwe Zet IDP Camp (Myitkyina), 18 October 2018. 47-year-old man, paralysed due to lack of medical support

the presence of a child with autism or a cleft lip is sometimes considered auspicious for the family's wellbeing and wealth. However, stigma is attached to blind persons, to physically impaired persons, to deaf persons and to mentally- or intellectually-impaired persons. Persons with polio-related disabilities face discrimination due to unfounded fears of contagion. People with these kinds of disabilities are often considered inauspicious and are less valued as individuals, facing mocking and discrimination from others. There is also more stigma attached to congenital disabilities than to those caused by the conflict or an accident, while disabled veterans injured after 2011 are in some contexts perceived as heroes for having been injured in service.

Respondents recounted discrimination in the family, neighbourhood or community, the camps and the Church. A blind woman from Myitkyina School for the Blind recounted how she had been discriminated against by her family and neighbours:

> My family members and people in the neighbourhood looked down upon me when I was uneducated. I was an object of mockery for the kids in the neighbourhood. Now that I am an educated person, I no longer face this kind of thing.[14]

Thus, targeted support can positively shift the perceptions of persons with disabilities in the community and thereby also their own self-perception and quality of life. Our research also indicated that disabilities can have multiple interconnected impacts, such as blindness causing exclusion from educational opportunities, which then causes further exclusion socially or in the labour market.

Churches, as key social institutions in Kachin, can play a vital role in enhancing inclusion and social contact for persons living with disabilities, or, conversely, can also act as sites for social exclusion. The blind woman quoted above explained her experiences within the church congregation:

> I experienced discrimination while involved in the church activities. When I was a teenage girl I went to participate in the youth activities. While others were playing I had to stand alone doing nothing. I felt really small at that time.[15]

---

14 Interview, Jan Mai Kawng School for the Blind (Myitkyina), 26 October 2018. 34-year-old blind woman.

15 Ibid.

Another physically-impaired woman recounted how she had been looked down upon by the church members, explaining that 'some kind-hearted people included me in the choir competition last year. But some protested and rebuked them for including a physically disabled person.'[16] A displaced man with polio-related disabilities saw this discrimination as a fundamental failing of the congregation:

> The primary purpose of the Church is to look after the poor and down-trodden people, [...], depressed people, widows and outcasts. But the Church has forsaken those people. They only care about the rich people. Then who will look after those helpless people?[17]

Discrimination is also entrenched in some of the criteria for obtaining jobs, both in government- and KIO-controlled areas. One of the formal criteria for the post of a schoolteacher is that the applicant has to be 'a healthy person', which has been used to discriminate against persons living with disabilities:

> They do not want to give us jobs in the government sector. Just recently I asked a local school principal whether I could teach the children. He said no because he is afraid that the children will become like me. He is afraid that the children will imitate me. They do not want to employ us in any of the government jobs.[18]

Stigmatization does not only affect individuals directly, but can even lead to their children facing discrimination and harassment in the school and community. Some parents prevent their children from playing with the children of parents with disabilities. Children with disabilities are also discriminated against in other ways. For instance, blind children can study together with other students, but when they sit exams they have to sit under the stairs.[19] The general school curriculum and the exam questions are not accessible to blind students, as the exam questions include diagrams without proper descriptions. This indicates structurally-anchored discrimination within the education system,[20] but it also indicates clear entry points for

16 Interview, Maina RC camp, 8 October 2018.
17 Personal interview, Hpum Lum Yang IDP Camp (Laiza), 20 September 2018. 30-year-old man.
18 Ibid.
19 Focus group discussion, Jan Mai Kawng School for the Blind, (Myitkyina), 26 October 2018.
20 Ibid.

small but strategic changes that could enable better inclusion of learners with disabilities in the education system.

The conflict- and displacement-related concerns raised by our respondents in this section do not operate separately; in fact, they often have a cumulative effect and can be mutually reinforcing. For example, stigma and discrimination can be obstacles to education and employment, contributing to poverty and increased vulnerability, which in turn further exacerbates stigma. Ideally, support services can help break these cycles, but, as we explore next, these services are often thin on the ground.

Lack of Support Services

According to the Guiding Principles on Internal Displacement (UN Office for the Coordination of Humanitarian Affairs 2001), IDPs with disabilities are 'entitled to the protection and assistance required by their condition and to treatment which takes into account their special needs' (Principle 4) and they are to 'receive to the fullest extent practicable and with the least possible delay, the medical care and attention they require, [...] access to psychological and social services' (Principle 19). Nonetheless, support for displaced persons with disabilities is limited in Kachin State, and is provided by a handful of non-specialized organizations, which are often unable to offer additional support beyond providing general assistive devices[21] and monthly cash allocations.[22] Individuals with disabilities may get additional support through one-off donations, often mediated through faith-based organizations. Civil society organizations (CSOs) such as the Kachin Baptist Convention (KBC), Karuna Myanmar Social Services and the Nyein Foundation provide cash support of 80,000 MMK (equivalent to about US$51)[23] per person per month in government-controlled areas and 100,000 MMK (equivalent to about 64 USD) in KIO-controlled areas. The

---

21 These mostly consist of wheelchairs, tricycles, walking sticks and crutches, though availability depends on the location. For instance, eye protection glasses for the visually impaired or blind are only available in the government-controlled areas.

22 Interview, KBC Office Myitkyina, 15 October 2018 and interview, Nyein Foundation, Myitkyina, 12 October 2018. This was also mentioned by interviewees from Je Yang IDP camp, Myusha Hpyen Hpung (People's Militia) (MHH) from Laiza and from Maina IDP Camp in Waimaw.

23 Exchange rate during the data analysis in 2018.

prevailing approach to disabilities tends to be a charity-based one drawing on a medical model, rather than one that sees disabilities as socially-constructed.

CSOs and the government use divergent criteria for defining disabilities and providing support. While the government only recognizes four categories of disability (physical, visual, hearing and intellectual/learning impairments), other CSOs use the six Washington criteria,[24] and yet others apply broader definitions, which include people with HIV/AIDS. This leads to multiple, divergent lists of people living with disabilities between IDP camp leaders and CSOs, causing complications when different organizations distribute cash and other support but use different sets of criteria. Some respondents stated that they received less than the supposed amount as the local camp leadership agreed to split the total funds received for a smaller list of recipients between all persons listed as disabled on their own, which is a more comprehensive list. Furthermore, people with impairments may be listed as having disabilities by camp leaders against their will, as they feel they can function and earn their livelihood well enough and reject the label of 'being disabled'.

Currently, there is no dedicated psycho-social support available for persons living with disabilities in Kachin State. This is a significant gap for people who have survived traumatic violence related to the conflict, including displacement and, for some, loss of limbs to landmines. From the researchers' observations, traumas seemed more evident in KIO-controlled areas. This may be because KIO areas have experienced more and more recent violence than government-controlled areas. More of the disabilities were recent, with people still traumatized and adjusting to them, whereas in government-controlled areas there was a higher ratio of people with congenital disabilities, who were more reconciled to their disabilities.

Some IDP camps in the KIO-controlled areas have community halls that provide a place for persons living with disabilities to socialize and interact together, which serves the basic function of mutual support through exchange with others, to reduce feelings of isolation and depression. The community halls to some extent replicate the tea shop functionality as hubs for exchange and socializing. However, this also seemed to replicate the

---

24   The Washington Group Short Set of Questions on Disability, available at www. washingtongroup-disability.com/wp-content/uploads/2016/01/The-Washington-Group-Short-Set-of-Questions-on-Disability.pdf.

gendered patterns of tea shop use, with mostly men rather than women with disabilities using them.

Although persons living with disabilities have access to general health services through the camp clinics in KIO-controlled areas, the health services available at the clinics cannot address major sicknesses. IDPs in camps under government control can access medical services at the General Hospital in Myitkyina, which has better facilities than the KIO's General Hospital.

As we have highlighted thus far, the impacts of living with disabilities, of conflict and displacement, and of engaging with service providers are highly gendered. Next, we examine to what degree this has reinforced gendered roles and expectations and/or led to shifts in these.

Gendered Expectations and Shifting Gender Roles

The conflict has made it more difficult for men and women living in IDP camps in general to perform conventionally-assigned gender roles within the family and the community (see also Johnston and Lingham 2020). It is particularly challenging for displaced men and women with disabilities, as underscored by our respondents. In Kachin society, a man is traditionally expected to be the head of the family, the primary breadwinner, as well as the protector of the family and the land. In contrast, a woman is expected to be the homemaker, the mother and the organizer of family members and relatives, including caring for the old, young and sick. Both men and women are expected to marry and have children to continue the clan. However, the challenges of living with disabilities in situations of displacement and in an armed conflict create significant barriers to achieving these expectations.

For some, this has led to tensions in their relationships. A male respondent recounted how the conflict has upset the gender roles in the family, creating tensions for the couple:

> Though I am a disabled person, before the war broke out I could help my wife in many ways. When the war broke out in 2011 we had to flee to our swidden field, and she had to carry me on her back while fleeing. After that I think she was totally disappointed with me […] and we also lost all our family properties.[25]

---

25   Interview, Woi Chyai Camp, Laiza.

He was unable to protect his family and lands, and while they were fleeing his wife ended up protecting him by carrying him, in a reversal of gender role expectations. When the man could not play the expected gender role, his partner stopped recognizing his role, resulting in a strained relationship. He was unable to repair the broken relationship with his wife, in his view mainly because he could not perform the expected gender role as the protector of the family and of their property.[26]

In other cases, families with disabled members have accepted the shifts in conventional gender roles, but the disabled person's perception of themselves continues to be a challenge. Some men felt unable to live up to expectations as the primary breadwinners and heads of the family, even though other family members still viewed them as the head, resulting in stress, as this respondent said:

As a father, I feel really sad if I cannot fulfil or provide for their basic needs [...] I feel worried about not being able to help to improve my children's prospects. Because I am their father, I have the responsibility to support them to get better education, financial security and everything that they need. I do not want to think that I will not be able to support them in their lives in future because of being a disabled person.[27]

For another male veteran, the inability to fulfil gender role expectations had led to frustrations:

I am the head of the family. But my wife is now taking on most of those responsibilities. [...] I am not like other men who can do different work, and that is why I cannot earn much. The community expects that a man should be a hard-working person on behalf of their family, should have good social skills with people and the community, and should have a big heart and contribute to the needs of the community. Also, he must possess good health – that is what the community thinks of a good man. So I cannot contribute in many ways and because of this situation I feel upset.[28]

Especially among men, negative coping mechanisms may arise as a reaction to frustrations. While alcohol is banned in IDP camps, interviewees recounted male relatives smuggling in alcohol or drugs to men living with

26 Interview, Woi Chyai IDP Camp (Laiza), 18 September 2018. 51-year-old man with multiple disabilities, due to a bullet wound to his head in a battle before the ceasefire.
27 Older male veteran, Je Ying IDP camp, 15 September 2018.
28 Ibid.

disabilities, to alleviate depression and sadness. These efforts to help male family members can alleviate their symptoms, but they do not address real issues. There have also been cases of suicides, especially among disabled veterans. Some male respondents also recounted feeling anger due to their frustrations:

> When my children are going to attend school, my wife has to support them. I only have a nominal status in the family. When things don't happen as expected, I feel like blaming everyone verbally. If I see someone walking along, I feel like getting angry with them […] I feel I can't find the words to express myself. […] I can't express anything. […] I can only breathe and speak. […] That's why I feel I am a useless person.[29]

While male respondents often struggled with the loss of their status as main provider, women with disabilities struggled with living up to social and domestic obligations, feeling frustration and anger, and not wanting to be pitied:

> When my mother is away travelling, all the family responsibilities are on my shoulders. Things like social events, parties and funerals are my responsibilities. […] I feel embarrassed to wear clothes that are washed by my siblings. If I do these tasks, I face so many obstacles. I don't want to ask them to do them all the time. I don't want to give burdens to others because of me. I want to do things on my own. […] As I am not equal to others and I can't go anywhere, they look down on me. […] All the facial expressions of the neighbours [...] I feel like they are looking down on me. […] As I am the eldest daughter in my family, they would have many hopes for me if I were not a disabled person. Being an impaired person, they may have less hope for me.[30]

In some families, the impact of the conflict has been to exacerbate pre-existing issues of domestic violence. One woman with disabilities[31] interviewed used to work as a trained midwife in her community of origin. When she was raped and became pregnant, social pressure forced her to marry the rapist. Her husband is a violent alcoholic, but in their village she was able to earn money for the family and her husband 'could not trouble

---

29 Man with mobility impairments, Je Yang IDP Camp, 15 September 2018.
30 Woman with disabilities, Maina IDP camp, 8 October 2018.
31 Interview, Maina RC Camp, 9 October 2018. 46-year-old woman with disabilities related to polio due to lack of medical support as a child.

her much'. Due to the conflict, they had to flee and her younger son incurred a disability due to lack of medical support while fleeing. In the IDP camp, she has been unable to go out and find a job to support her family as she has to look after her disabled child. Her husband is rude to the community and violent when drunk, causing direct harm to the family and increasing the family's ostracization by others.

In spite of the extreme challenges, in some cases respondents had overcome traditional gender expectations, and adapted successfully to the new situation. One physically impaired man explained how he reviewed his role in the family after the conflict, saying:

> We no longer make any distinction between the husband's and the wife's family roles and responsibilities. I also help my wife in doing household chores.[32]

The transcending of gendered divisions was key for some in dealing with the new situation, making family life more stable and harmonious, despite the lack of income opportunities and the challenges of displacement. In the best of cases, the changes in gender roles were accompanied by a generally supportive approach to the person with disabilities, in spite of community pressure:

> I do experience some discrimination, such as people looking down on me; also, they bully my wife, as [the] wife of disabled husband. […]. I appreciate my wife so much, there are some families with members living with disabilities that have broken up because of that. […] We got married after I became a disabled person, but we knew each other before I became disabled […] After I became disabled, […] I explained to her that I was no longer able to do good business or to bring in income to the family, and that I was not even able any longer to take good care of our children, with my situation […] she responded that it was okay, that it was not my fault, and finally we got married. […] Even though she is a woman, she can take on men's responsibilities and things that are meant to be done by a man.[33]

In terms of the interplay between gender, displacement and disabilities, our findings echoed those of Muhanna-Matar's (2020) research on Syrian male refugees, who found different ways of coping with what Shuttleworth,

---

32   Interview, Je Yang IDP Camp (Laiza), 16 September 2018. 48-year-old man.
33   Older male veteran, Woi Chyai camp (Laiza), 18 September 2018.

Wedgwood and Wilson (2012) call the 'dilemma of disabled masculinity'. This dilemma arises from disability being 'associated with being dependent and helpless whereas masculinity is associated with being powerful and autonomous' (Shuttleworth, Wedgwood and Wilson 2012: 174). Echoing Gerschick and Miller (1994), some respondents continued to hold on to masculine ideals for their sense of self, for example by denying their disability status for as long as they could work. Some continued to struggle to reconcile their current life situation with their expectation that they should be a provider and the household head. Others, however, had reformulated their masculine self and their position in the household and the family. For women, many continued to live up to the expectation that they carry out household duties to the best of their ability, though often with deep frustration emanating from their physical limitations.

Conclusion

Our research sought to highlight the gendered experiences of conflict and displacement of persons living with disabilities in Kachin State. While Myanmar, pre-coup, was going through a major process of political and social transition, and in some areas through a post-conflict transition, most of our respondents were shut out of these processes. Especially for those in IDP camps, their lives are marked by economic precariousness and defined by constant exposure to armed conflict, violence and involuntary displacement. This displacement, intended to be temporary, has become a (semi-)permanent state of limbo, as some people have spent over a decade in the camps, including a younger generation, the members of which have been born, raised and spent the majority of their lives there. Even though they hope for a potential return to their home villages, many still fear being exposed to harassment by the military, to landmines and living in poverty. Displaced men struggle with their inability to live up to gendered expectations of being a provider and head of the family. As has also been discussed elsewhere (Hedström and Olivius 2020; Johnston and Lingham 2020), women in conflict zones, especially those who have been displaced, are burdened with multiple expectations of productive and reproductive labour.

While these gendered impacts affect all internally-displaced persons, the impacts are more acute and exacerbated for those with disabilities, whose lives and bodies will continue to be marked by the legacies of war even when it does eventually come to an end. Persons living with disabilities and their families face stigmatization and discrimination, some of which has been internalized, leading to depression and despair. Women with disabilities are not necessarily exempt from these, and they face frustrations and discrimination for not being able to fulfil roles that are expected of them. Women also tend to be the ones caring for family members with disabilities, thereby increasing their workload and raising the risk of depletion.

Nonetheless, the research also had some positive findings, highlighting the inter-relatedness and importance of change and social participation. Those men and women who were able to accept and embrace changed gender roles fared best, especially if this was coupled to being able to participate in social, economic and educational activities with others. Earning an income and getting an education were mechanisms for both men and women with disabilities to prove themselves to their families, earning respect and a positive self-identity alongside the income.

Both persons living with disabilities and displaced persons on the whole have to date been largely sidelined both in the pre-coup processes of positive change in Myanmar and the narratives about it, but they have borne the brunt of many of the negative changes, such as renewed conflict and increased economic insecurity. Their voices and concerns have also been largely sidelined in discussions about Myanmar's future, including in relation to their possible return home from camps. This sidelining has been greater for women than men, and for those with disabilities it has been greater than for those without. Ensuring that they can participate actively, and that they are able to address the social and physical barriers that prevent them from doing so, will not only lead to better policies relating to displaced persons, women's rights or disabilities issues; it will also allow men and women with disabilities to feel themselves to be the fully-fledged citizens that they should be, rather than to be social embarrassments or passive objects of charity. The coup and the escalation in violence in its aftermath and the socio-economic crisis it has triggered, compounded by the COVID-19 pandemic, have all further exacerbated the vulnerabilities of persons with disabilities, and made addressing these issues all the more pressing.

References

Gender Equality Network and Kachin Women's Peace Network. 2013. *Women's Needs Assessment in IDP Camps, Kachin State.* Yangon: Gender Equality Network and Kachin Women's Peace Network.

Gender in Humanitarian Action Workstream. 2020. *Gender Profile for Humanitarian Action: Rakhine, Kachin and Northern Shan, Myanmar, March 2020.* Yangon: Gender in Humanitarian Action Workstream.

Gerschick, Thomas and Adam Miller. 1994. 'Gender identities at the crossroads of masculinity and physical disability.' *Masculinities* 2: 34–55.

Goodley, Dan. 2017. *Disability Studies: An Interdisciplinary Introduction.* Los Angeles: Sage Publishers. Second Edition.

Grech, Shaun and Maria Pisani. 2015. 'Editorial: Towards a critical understanding of the disability/forced migration nexus.' *Disability and the Global South* 2 (1): 416–420.

Hartley, Julie. 2013. 'War-wounds: Disability, memory and narratives of war in a Lebanese disability rehabilitation hospital.' In Kevin McSorley (ed.), *War and the Body: Militarisation, Practice and Experience,* pp. 181–193. Abingdon: Routledge.

Hedström, Jenny. 2016a. '"Before I joined the army I was like a child": Militarism and women's rights in Kachinland.' In Mandy Sadan (ed.), *War and Peace in the Borderlands of Myanmar: The Kachin Ceasefire, 1994–2011,* pp. 236–256. Copenhagen: NIAS Press.

———. 2016b. 'The political economy of the Kachin revolutionary household.' *The Pacific Review* 30 (4): 581–595. Available at: doi:10.1080/09512748.2016.1273254.

———. 2020. 'Militarized social reproduction: Women's labour and para-state armed conflict.' *Critical Military Studies* 8 (1): 58–76. Available at: 10.1080/23337486.2020.1715056.

Hedström, Jenny and Elisabeth Olivius. 2020. 'Insecurity, dispossession, depletion: Women's experiences of post-war development in Myanmar.' *European Journal of Development Research* 32: 379–403.

Human Rights Watch. 2012. *'Untold Miseries' – Wartime Abuses and Forced Displacement in Burma's Kachin State.* New York: Human Rights Watch.

International Campaign to Ban Landmines. 2014. *Myanmar/Burma – Casualties and Victim Assistance, The Landmine and Cluster Munition Monitor 2014.* Geneva: International Campaign to Ban Landmines.

Johnston, Melissa and Jayanthi Lingham. 2020. *Inclusive Economies, Enduring Peace in Myanmar and Sri Lanka: Field Report.* Melbourne/Warwick, Monash University/University of Warwick.

Khaing Khaing Soe (2017). 'Disability Statistics in Myanmar: Highlight from 2014 Population and Housing Census provided in a presentation given at the United Nations Headquarters, New York, 9th March 2017.' Available at: unstats.un.org/unsd/statcom/48th-session/side-events/documents/20170309-2L-Khaing-Khaing-Soe.pdf

Lawn, Dan Seng and Jana Naujoks. 2018. *Conflict Impacts on Gender and Masculinities Expectations on People with Disabilities in Kachin State.* Myitkyina/Yangon: Kachinland Research Centre and International Alert.

McLaughlin, Rory and John Jeffry Seng. 2018. *Exploring Complexity: A Systemic Analysis of Social Cohesion in Kachin State.* Yangon: RAFT Myanmar.

Mohamed, Kharnita and Tamara Shefer. 2015. 'Gendering disability and disabling gender: Critical reflections on intersections of gender and disability.' *Agenda* 29 (2): 2–13.

Muhanna-Matar, Aitemad. 2020. *Beyond the Binary Understanding of Masculinities: Displaced Syrian Refugee Men Living with Disability and Chronic Illness in Jordan.* Occasional Paper No. 24. Doha: Center for International and Regional Studies (CIRS) Georgetown University in Qatar.

Myanmar Information Management Unit. 2020. *CCCM/ SHELTER/ NFI Cluster Analysis Report (CAR) – Kachin/ NSS, Myanmar. 1 Jan–29 Feb 2020.* Yangon: United Nations Myanmar Information Management Unit.

Naujoks, Jana and Myat Thandar Ko. 2018. *Behind the Masks – Masculinities, Gender, Peace and Security in Myanmar.* Yangon: International Alert.

Nhkum Bu Lu. 2016. 'A woman's life in war and peace.' In Mandy Sadan (ed.), *War and Peace in the Borderlands of Myanmar: The Kachin Ceasefire, 1994–2011,* pp. 291–307. Copenhagen: NIAS Press.

Pistor, Nora. 2017. *Life on Hold: Experiences of Women Displaced by Conflict in Kachin State, Myanmar.* Yangon: Trócaire/Oxfam.

Sadan, Mandy (ed.). 2016. *War and Peace in the Borderlands of Myanmar. The Kachin Ceasefire, 1994–2011.* Copenhagen: NIAS Press.

Shuttleworth, Russell, Nikki Wedgwood and Nathan J. Wilson. 2012. 'The dilemma of disabled masculinity.' *Men and Masculinities* 15 (2): 174–194.

UN Office for the Coordination of Humanitarian Affairs. (2001). *Guiding Principles on Internal Displacement.* Geneva: United Nations Office for the Coordination of Humanitarian Affairs.

CHAPTER 12

Involved but Not Included

Karen Women's Care Work as Transformative Vision for Peace

Terese Gagnon and Hsa Moo

*H*sa Moo is a Karen environmental and Indigenous activist and journalist working for the Karen Environmental and Social Action Network (KESAN), a leading non-profit environmental organization on the Thailand–Burma border. She has provided testimony to the International Criminal Court in support of charges of Crimes Against Humanity brought against the Myanmar Military. At the time of this conversation, Terese Gagnon was a PhD candidate in anthropology at Syracuse University where she was writing her dissertation, 'Seeding Sovereignty: Sensory Politics and Biodiversity in the Karen Diaspora'. In this conversation, conducted across multiple video chats between New York and Thailand, Hsa Moo and Terese discuss issues of women's gendered care work within the Karen revolution and ongoing struggle for just peace. They focus on new challenges and possibilities for gender dynamics, and for women's transformative visions of peace unfolding during Myanmar's fraught transition period.

Hsa Moo and Terese, in dialogue with the other authors of this volume, call into question dominant perceptions, held within Karen leadership and Myanmar studies alike, of who and what is worthy of being taken 'seriously' (Enloe 2013). They do so by taking seriously the work of Karen feminists who are engaged in the broader struggle for Karen self-determination, while continuing the decades-long work by Karen women of challenging patriarchal militarism and capitalism within this very struggle. Hsa Moo and Terese also discuss the ways in which Karen women push back against male efforts to (re)inscribe them into highly limited gendered scripts after the worst of the fighting has subsided. Such gendered scripts too often attempt to slot women into a narrow performance of social reproduction to preserve

242

the status quo. Hsa Moo and Terese discuss what such efforts to put women 'back in their place' after the war may tell us about the workings of militarized patriarchal and capitalist power in Myanmar more broadly. Drawing from their grounded experiences, Hsa Moo and Terese uncover ways in which Karen women have the power to transform conflict and to shape visions for just peace. As Hsa Moo notes of Karen women, 'we are involved, even though the men do not include us. In *Kawthoolei*,[1] for the women, if we don't get a chance, if we don't get recognized by our male leaders – we *don't care*. We have to serve our community anyway. That's the resilience of Karen women. If there is no woman, there is no peace.'

'Women Not Recognized as Front Line in the Revolution'

TG: Hsa Moo, it's wonderful to see you again! Thank you for taking time to have this conversation.

HsM: Yes! Although I'm not sure I can answer your questions. I'm just one of the activists in the community, the woman activists, no? I am working for the Karen community related to environmental issues, but my expertise is directly related to media work. For me, I was born in a refugee camp. I resettled to Canada for just a year and a half, but I was always thinking about coming back and helping my community. So in 2014 I came back to Thailand and started working for The Karen Environmental and Social Action Network (KESAN). That's just a little bit about my history, my background.

TG: Thank you. Related to this idea of commitment and your desire to return to work for your community, I've been thinking a lot about what it means to be engaged in struggle and committed to an effort even when there are many problems internal to that effort. I'm thinking especially about hierarchy and some of the negative consequences of top-down organization within a militarized context. I'm wondering if you could speak about any ways that you or others have pushed back against this, especially in male-dominated spaces.

HsM: In our community, we can see clearly that men dominate. Until now, in most of the Karen organizations the leaders are men. Women's organizations, the donors, they try to push them to include woman. But *still* this happens

---

1   Kawthoolie is the name of the free Karen homeland.

in our community, and it's really hard to change. I think things are getting better, but we still really need to push. We need to educate. However, it's really hard to educate our leaders. If you talk to the Karen Women's Organization (KWO) you will understand more about the woman's struggle.

For example, if we talk about this transition period, in the past, before the ceasefire, most of the village heads are women. Then, after the ceasefire, when things are getting a little bit better, then men get all in – they get their power. If we talk about the positives and negatives, there are both. I think for the woman, they really struggle as the village head. They really have to deal with the situations and also with the two different armed groups, the Burma army (the *Tatmadaw*) and the Karen National Liberation Army (KNLA). The women village chiefs had to go between the two groups, especially in mixed-control areas, where both armed groups were present. Now that things have gotten better, with less violence and less danger for village chiefs of getting killed or tortured, it is mostly men who are village heads. The former woman village heads, they are still struggling and working hard for their communities, but only without an official title now. They don't really care about their title but maybe they feel like they have no power anymore.

TG: A few years ago I read the KWO report about women village chiefs, 'Walking amongst Sharp Knives' (Karen Women's Organization 2010). That was a really eye-opening report. As you know, it draws on the testimonies of 95 former and current woman chiefs. It presents their stories of extreme hardship and struggle during their times as chief. These women village chiefs suffered a great deal from the brutal tactics the Myanmar military used against them and the members of their community. The report details numerous instances of torture and sexual violence against villagers and against the women chiefs, as well as murders committed by the Myanmar military. In addition to torture and abuse from the Myanmar military, the women chiefs also suffered great stress from the expectations placed on them by their husbands to fulfill their 'duties' to take care of their families, households, and farms. The report notes that several women chiefs were, 'blamed by their husbands for being "married" to Myanmar military "because they had to follow their orders"' (Karen Women's Organization 2010: 2).

HsM: It's true. The woman chiefs still had to deal with everything. They had to take care of the household work, take care of their kids, the cooking, gardening … everything. That's care work. But the men, they don't really care. That's part of our culture, Karen culture, this idea that men have to be the head of the household. But we really talk and try to explain to our new generation that this is the stereotype that men have to be the leaders. Actually, women can be leaders too!

TG: Yes! Also, the report was written in 2010, before men began taking over the role of chief again to the degree that they have now. So, it doesn't go into detail about this key occurrence. Do you know why it is that so many men have become village head after the ceasefire, after everything that the women chiefs endured on behalf of their communities?

HsM: It's really obvious, men dominate! The patriarchy style. Before the ceasefire, in the most difficult time of the conflict, the men are not there to be a leader, to deal with the army. So the woman has to lead, has to take risks. And then now, in the ceasefire times, and men became village heads again.

TG: What you say reminds me so much of what feminist political scientist Cynthia Enloe has said about how again and again, across different parts of the world, women are mobilized only 'for the duration' (2013: 11) of the war-waging or the revolution. She points out that during the war and during the revolution, women are called on to step up and make sacrifices, to do what men need them to do. But when the fighting's done they're told (and I'm paraphrasing), 'Enough. We needed your help just for the war, just for the revolution. Now you have to go back to your house, back to the kitchen, back to the care work.' I was thinking about this, and also considering the fact that the Karen revolution is such a specific example because this war has gone on for so long. Because it's been more than 70 years since the Karen revolution began, do you think it's harder for the men to convince those women who have taken on leadership roles that 'now you have to go back to this domestic role'?

HsM: Yes. But no matter what, women have to work, still they are fighting. Even if they cannot be a chief, actually they are a chief in their household. They have to manage everything: for their kids and for their education, cooking, look after everything. The men just sit and say, 'I am a leader,' something like that. [laughs] So, sorry for that! I don't want to blame the men. Actually, they have to know that. They abuse the woman's rights. I don't want to talk about broader things, just only my family: my aunt, my grandma. My aunt used to be a village head. My grandfather was a village head, but he got killed by the Burma army. Maybe when you've been to Karen villages you've seen, at the entrance to the village there is a structure. They hung my grandfather there. After he died, my grandma had to take his role.

Then my uncles, they all joined the KNLA. I think they wanted to help their community after what happened to my grandfather. When my uncles all became Karen soldiers, then they cannot come back to the village. If they do they can be killed. So, my grandmother, she is very clever. She wants to take some food for her sons. And then she puts the food under the straw and carries it on her head. And then, when the Burma army saw her walking with the straw, they asked her, 'Where are you going?' She said, 'I will go to my farm.' Then she placed the straw with the food hidden in it near where my uncles were staying. On her way back she sang in Karen (so the Burma army soldiers couldn't understand), 'The food is near here.' It's very clever to do that. That's why I really respect the women's leadership.

TG: So, she was the village chief, she was farming, feeding people … that is so much.

HsM: As the village chief, the villagers, when they need help, they will just come to her and say, 'We have a problem. This is what has happened. What can we do?' She will have to manage that, and encourage them, saying, 'We will look after each other, we are the same community.'

It's very interesting, the women, their talent, no? They know how to deal with the situation. But I feel like the men, they don't recognize it. Or maybe they recognize but they don't want to talk about it. They just thought that this is the woman's job. They have to do it because the men are the people who guard them or protect them. In this way the women's labour, their care work, is naturalized, while the men's labour is seen as 'skilled' (see Hedström 2017).

TG: Something along those lines made a huge impression on me when I was staying in the Peace Park area during my fieldwork. I went to visit the mother of my friend who lives and has a farm there. My friend's mom is in her sixties. She was basically growing the food for all the soldiers who stay there, and there were quite a few. In addition, she was caring for two of her very young grandchildren who had been left to stay with her because their fathers are Karen soldier and their mothers are travelling with them. This woman is extremely brave and has done incredible things in her life, including writing two books, one about Karen history and the other her autobiography.

After visiting my friend's mother at her farm I was thinking a lot about what counts as leadership, as bravery or, like you say, as 'being on the front lines'. I can see how maybe her contribution has not been valued as much as her husband's role as a former soldier.

HsM: Maybe you already read in a KWO report, most of the time at the KNU meetings they ask those of us at Karen organizations to go and help. My friends at KWO, they told about their story, they just have to be at the kitchen and cook for the men. In most of the meetings, the KNU meetings, you can see mostly men. And then for the women's organization they have to cook, and then do the decorations, and cleaning. So next time, they don't want to go.

TG: Ugh, not again! That is awful. This reminds me of what Jenny Hedström writes about women's social reproduction within parastate armed conflict – that, in this context, 'the duty to reproduce both the individual soldier and the army writ-large is placed disproportionally on the shoulders of women'. Because of this, she says, women's work, 'far from being peripheral, carries with it the possibility to both maintain and transform parastate armed conflict' (2020: 2). Therefore, this imbalanced gendered labour can be disheartening for Karen women, but it also presents possibility. Crucially, it shows that Karen women possess the seed of social *transformation*, which has the potential to alter the course of armed conflict. Taking a broader view of things, we can see that women across Myanmar have the power to transform militarized patriarchal and capitalist power in the country, and in its ethnic borderlands, by leveraging the power of their vital labour of social reproduction. In addition, women have the power to shape what a truly just peace might look like for everyone, women as much as for men. I wonder, what would it look like for women across different ethnic groups in Myanmar to withhold or leverage their reproductive labour in acts of solidarity in order to assert their role in defining peace?

'We Have to Acknowledge the Life-Making Aspect'

TG: In this vein, I have been thinking a lot about the word 'care', which is supposedly a very feminine thing. Like what you were saying about your friends at KWO, they want to support the movement, they *care*. Yet, they're asked to always fill this one role when they can do so many things. Whether it's caring for people or caring for the environment, I wonder if you could talk a bit about your relationship to care. Is it something that is important to you? If so, do you also push back against being told that 'this is your role' because of how you are perceived?

HsM: We have to acknowledge the life-making aspect. For women, that includes both paid and unpaid labour. Like I mentioned before, for our Karen community and for the woman, for example, if they are cooking and caring for their family, it's important for a woman, for her family, no? They don't think about other things, they just think about their family: they need to feed their children. It's as important as a woman sitting in the parliament or at the Peace Talk table. The whole narrative of care work that women have been doing, we need to be ready to talk about it. The feminists involved in struggle have to be bold to talk about care work, the social reproduction.

TG: Do you think this message about care work is reaching the leaders, the KNU leaders, for example?

HsM: I think this question we also need to ask the male leaders! [laughs] And then I just want to see what they respond.

TG: Definitely! Thinking about the fraught concept of the 'transition' and the complex changes that have come with it Myanmar's borderlands (see Woods 2011), are there ways you have seen gender roles changing because of the transition? For example, are more women going to work in the formal sector, or has the transition changed relationships within families – including opening up possibilities for women that they didn't have before?

HsM: I don't see so many differences in this transition period. Mostly, in the Karen community the women need to take so many responsibilities: they go to work, they have to care for their children. For example, for the ordinary people from the rural area they go to the farm, gather some vegetables, firewood, and come back, feed their animals, cooking. For the men they don't really do like that. Some go to the farm. But for the women they take more responsibility. So it seems that during the transition period, men get more opportunities while women's already heavy workload gets heavier. For me, I think for the care work we need to have class analysis as well. Nowadays, most feminists they advocate only for gaining entry into the corporate leadership or the patriarchal political setting, but always forget about the women who are at the bottom. So lifting those women up to come up to the corporate or political role is also important.

TG: Mm, yes. And then even if we do have women represented in political roles, is it enough just to have women in those seats, or do we need a more fundamental change? For example, is it enough to aim for representation – to have women in the parliament, in leadership positions, corporate positions – is that the goal? Or is the goal to *change* all those systems, to reimagine them in a more transformative way?

HsM: For me I feel like women and men, we have a different thought. For example, in the parliament and also the communities if we have more women in leadership roles then things will change a *lot*, so that we can go forward equally. For the community representative we always talk about democracy, self-determination. In order to achieve that we need to have women's participation, *fully*.

I know that most of the men don't care about this. But from now on they should care because we women have been contributing to all parts and stages of the betterment of our Karen community, whether at the village, local, national or international level. As women, we know that our involvement in all levels, including decision making, is vital for men in our Karen community and for governing structures. So, while men may act as though they don't need us, deep down they know too well they cannot do a whole lot of things without women. They know that for a fact. Therefore, we have to demand that they care. They will value our work only if they care, or the other way around: if women prove how much we are needed by withholding our labour and contributions. One way or the other, they have to accept that women's participation at all decision-making levels is vital. And the most important thing is they have to *acknowledge* the importance of women's participation and contribution to the betterment of the Karen community. Only if they acknowledge it publicly will we know they care about our contributions and value the product of our work.

However, as women, we don't have to give up. In fact, we have to keep demanding our rights and our visibility so that we are valued like men. In a perfect world, we would not have to do this. But the very sad thing is that there is only the concept that 'all men are equal' but nothing like 'all men and women are equal'. So, for us to get to the equal level, we still have to work very hard. All women, older and younger, we all have to struggle to get to our rightful place. And we won't be able to get there unless we make our voices heard. Men are not going to speak out for us. In particular, those women who have more freedom have to amplify the voice of women who are suppressed. Like here, [holds up t-shirt] 'No Woman, No Peace'.

'As a Woman, You Don't Need to Give Up At All'

TG: Thinking about young women who are just coming up now, maybe in the refugee camps or other places, who are just getting trained: what kind of message do you hope to pass on to them?

HsM: When I was working with the youth doing community radio in the camps, I always tried to encourage them to know their rights to help their community. For people like us, the women in the community, most of the ones in leading roles are men. So I try to encourage them not to get disappointed, not to move back. We have to move forward. I feel like men never need to ask for their rights. But women have to call for their rights, they have to fight to get their role in the community. To get a chance in the place in the leading role, we have to try a *lot*. Even for me, I also have the experience of being discriminated against by male dominance. So I would say to young women, 'don't give up'. As a woman, you don't need to give up at all. Where there is life there is hope.

TG: That is a wonderful message. This is a really unfair question, but now that you are someone in a leadership role do you think your presence or the ways you choose to challenge expectations is helping other people realize the possibilities for themselves?

HsM: I am not really in a leading role. But for them, I think there is always a possible way to do something. You just have to try hard and find a way to make it happen. For me, sometimes I got a chance to do something that other people cannot. Sometimes I feel like that is a privilege, it's not fair for other people. But I try my best enough to do things. So they also, if they do like me they will be successful. They can do like me.

TG: Hsa Moo, I know you are a hard worker because I remember you were working during your own birthday party! We went to sing karaoke and you were working on your laptop the whole time and stepping out to take phone calls. Do you remember that? I think you were doing something for Radio Free Asia (RFA).

HsM: [laughs] Yes. That's kind of what it's like, committed work. When you give a commitment, you commit to do something, you have to do it. You have to do it and you have to do it very well, so people can see your good work. So I live my life always under the commitment, and then I am depressed sometimes.

TG: Yes, this is something important to talk about. I feel like even the little bit that I've done now, trying to write about my research, it's very hard emotionally, because peoples' stories and their situations are so difficult. I can only imagine what it's like for you, doing that work all the time for so much of your life. Is it something that you just accept or have you found ways to make the sadness a little bit less?

HsM: Even if I get stressed or depressed, I try to make myself happy, hanging out with friends, talking to family. But, if you do something that you are happy with, you are not really getting tired. Because you are happy to do this. I live my life under the depressions and the commitment. But this is the way I choose. I think this is something that is really important in my community, so I take it. As you know, people can see things, what can I say in English words? People can see things only on the stage, on the television, for the behind the scenes, they don't see it. That's why, for the women who work behind, nobody recognize them. So I always salute those women. Women like me, because I got a chance, I can be on the television, on the stage, so people can see me. But actually, I'm not that good of a fighter. If you talk to those women, you got a *lot* of ideas, you got a lot of education from them. We see their education, their skills.

TG: Absolutely, you have said it so beautifully. I very much feel that some of the best things I've learned about feminism, about persistence, all the things you've just mentioned, have come from Karen women I have been fortunate to know. I feel incredibly grateful and humbled by that. Thank you so much, Hsa Moo. It's been such a pleasure to get to talk with you about these things. Thank you also for all the ways your work, commitment and joyful tenacity inspire me to keep caring and keep struggling. Have a good day there.

HsM: Thank you. Have a good night. We'll keep in touch!

References

Enloe, Cynthia. 2013. *Seriously! Imagining Crashes and Crises as if Women Mattered.* Oakland: University of California Press.

Hedström, Jenny. 2017. 'The political economy of the Kachin revolutionary household'. *The Pacific Review.* 3 (4): 581–595. Available at: doi.org/10.1080/09512748.2016.1273254

———. 2020. 'Militarized social reproduction: Women's labour and parastate armed conflict'. *Critical Military Studies* 8 (1): 58–76. Available at: doi.org/10.1080/23337486.2020.1715056.

Karen Women's Organization (KWO). 2010. 'Walking amongst Sharp Knives: The Unsung Courage of Karen Women Village Chiefs in Conflict Areas of Eastern Burma'. Mae Sariang, Thailand: KWO. February.

Woods, Kevin. 2011. 'Ceasefire capitalism: Military–private partnerships, resource concessions and military-state building in the Burma–China borderlands'. *Journal of Peasant Studies.* 38 (4): 747–770. Available at: doi.org/10.1080/03066150.2011.607699.

Coming to See Gender Discrimination as Structural

A Scholar's Journey

Ma Khin Mar Mar Kyi and Matthew J. Walton

*D*r. Ma Khin Mar Mar Kyi is a pioneering anthropologist of gender in Myanmar. She was the first female Burmese Senior Research Fellow at Lady Margaret Hall, University of Oxford, and has been the Convenor of that college's International Gender Studies programme. Her dissertation from the Australian National University was given the 'Excellence in Gender Studies' award and her academic career has been characterized by close engagement with a range of different groups in Myanmar, conducting research, organizing seminars and trainings, and generally advocating for greater awareness of and political action on institutionalized gender inequalities. Dr. Matthew J Walton is currently an Assistant Professor of Comparative Political Theory in the Department of Political Science at the University of Toronto. From 2013 to 2018, he was the inaugural Senior Research Fellow in Modern Burmese Studies at St. Antony's College, University of Oxford. His work focuses primarily on Buddhist political thought, as well as on ethnic and political identities in contemporary Myanmar.

Mar and Matt worked closely together during their time at Oxford, convening the Oxford-Myanmar Policy Brief Series, as well as hosting numerous scholars, activists and political figures at seminars and conferences. They were also co-leads of the research project *Understanding 'Buddhist Nationalism' in Myanmar: Religion, Gender, Identity, and Conflict in a Political Transition*, funded by the Economic and Social Research Council of the UK (ESRC). In that capacity, they worked together over several years, conducting interviews and carrying out analysis of sermons, journals and speeches made by monks and laypeople associated with Myanmar's 'Buddhist nationalist' movement.

They are still producing academic outputs from this project, which also had a policy-oriented component, providing regular briefings to NGOs, CBOs, embassies and others to disseminate their findings and help to produce a more nuanced analysis of this recent movement.

Mar and Matt met over Zoom in June 2021 to conduct an interview about Mar's academic and intellectual trajectory, discussing how her ideas on gender and its effects had emerged from her activism and merged with her academic work, dynamics reflected in many of the other contributions to this volume. They also reflected on persistent gaps in robust gendered analysis in Myanmar's current political environment and in scholarship, as well as inspiring changes seen not only in the current generation of researchers featured in the preceding chapters, but in young people taking part in the protest movement against the February 2021 military coup.

Matthew J Walton: Mar, thanks so much for sitting down with me to have this conversation about your research and your personal and intellectual history. We've worked together for several years, from our time together at Oxford to today. It's great to get a chance to ask you about some of these things that I have an implicit understanding of, but we haven't directly discussed before. In your work, you examine a lot of the gender norms in Myanmar that are communicated and enforced across generations through traditions, sayings, practices, and other modes like that. What was your own experience of these things, growing up – in your family, in school and other contexts? And on the other side, were there people who encouraged you to challenge or question those traditions and that received wisdom?

Ma Khin Mar Mar Kyi: So I must say that I grew up in a family that was very progressive and very open. Actually, my father, you could even say that he was very famous for being very accommodating, very tolerant and progressive. After all, he had five daughters as well as a diligent lady of the house!

Growing up in such an environment, I didn't really see or think about those dynamics until the early 1990s, when I accidently met with trafficked children selling tissues or flowers in Khao San Road and the Banglampoo tourist area in Bangkok and later with young girls and women who were sold into prostitution in Thailand. I was interested in their lives, their existence, their struggles, their strength. Really, just the fundamental causes of how they came to be in that position: Why they were there? How did they arrive? Could they return home? What would happen to them? Any possibility for escape? I had already studied education and child psychology and I love children, so I was passionately interested in their lives, and if possible, to help them escape. As I closely investigated, I was in awe and shock to witness their struggle, strength, survival skills and 'success' in their everyday life in the midst of exploitative and structurally violent situations of racism and sexism. Even then, I didn't really know what I was doing was anthropology, ethnography, empirical field work research, but I myself became a participant observer for transformative action and outcomes.

Many were being abused and being smuggled from Burma and many didn't know their families, or the names of the villages that they were from. I also saw how the situation and environment perfectly made them into easy targets. Because there were also many young girls among them, I began to think what would happen to them a few years later. That is when I realized how many young Burmese girls were being trafficked and sold into prostitution. They were desperate to come to Thailand with the hope that they would work in shops and restaurants to send money home. But they ended up being trafficked and sold into downgraded brothels as prostitutes. Many were too young to understand the meaning of 'selling bodies'; they thought they had to 'cut their bodies to sell'. And yet they still felt they were obliged to send money to their families – but were too ashamed to tell them the truth. But they also felt that they needed to protect the honor of the family and themselves by not telling them the truth.

For me, I started to see a very clear pattern of gender-based structural violence experienced by Burmese in general and women in particular. Flower-selling girls or body-selling young women were being exploited in particular ways because of being female. Even in that environment and that situation, they still had to carry out specific 'feminine' responsibilities and were disciplined into 'feminine' traits through concepts of 'shame and fear'. It was even clearer when I began to do research and interviews with young men dying with HIV/AIDS at the Mae Tao Clinic near Mae Sot, along the Thai–Myanmar border. I could see how the patriarchal system and specific cultural patterns were also leading to premature and violent deaths of Burmese men. Even though I was not familiar then with theories of structural violence, based on this empirical evidence I could see a clear pattern and structure of gender and how both genders – but particularly women – were caught up in its pathological nature.

These experiences instilled in me an intellectual curiosity and compelled me to do research with passion and commitment on the root causes of structural violence and for transformative action, for the last 30 years. They grounded me to become a passionate social feminist anthropologist for evidence-based transformative action for social and political change in Myanmar.

MJW: Let me push on this question of your own childhood a little bit more. You grew up in a progressive, open household empowering women; that's still, sadly, relatively rare. But when you look back were there any moments of experience that hinted at structural inequality along gendered lines? Maybe not in your family, maybe not among your parents, but were there moments of tension that maybe you didn't realize then but that looking back now you think of it differently, or through a more explicitly gendered lens? Maybe like a cognitive dissonance that you didn't fully make sense of until later?

MKMMK: Looking back many years later, I was naïve of being in a privileged family and social class. I did not see beyond the surface and also did not have a 'gender lens' back then. Under a determined, ambitious, elegant-looking, cultivating, active, hard-working, disciplined and diligent mother, I saw my soft, tolerant, and accommodating *father* as the victim! Because she just did everything – so perfectly, and it seemed easy for her – I thought she was in control and had power. I did not see then how hard she worked or sacrificed herself to excel at all the tasks, singlehandedly. She was also a sharp, wise and ambitious decision-maker within the family. Then I saw only black and white: strong, ambitious, disciplined mum and gentle and easy-going dad.

I still am in awe to think about my mum's feminine capabilities and capacities. As a young girl, I woke up every morning under her religious prayers. I saw elegant-looking flowers on her head, *thanakha* on her face, a pot of tea in front of her while she read a newspaper, all done after her garden work and playing badminton and all done before I woke up! She looked as if she had everything made available for her. It seemed she had all the power to control everything. I did not realize she was a 'doer', she could not take 'no' for answer. Women can't be daydreaming, they have the responsibility to put food on the table, to manage the finances: even if, for example, their income is lower than the cost of living. By believing education is the only way to change lives, they are willing to sacrifice for their children's education. But my mother always had an even bigger dream compared to many. And so, when my mother said,

'My dream is to send all my daughters to Oxford!' I laughed and screamed out 'MUM!' Even though I laughed, I learned the name of 'Oxford' as a kid; that is how she instilled her ambition and dream in me.

I came to Oxford for my great mother, who would have been studying in Oxford herself if opportunities were given to her and if she could be free from all the feminine-specific burdens she held. But when I arrived at Oxford, my mother was gone, I did not even have a chance to say goodbye to her after not seeing her for so many years. Since I left, or rather escaped, Burma, I could not help but think how much my mother struggled or sacrificed to succeed and to be a well-respected leader in her communities. She rejected all patriarchal social, religious, cultural and political discriminatory ideological-based feminine traits and constraints in her life. Perhaps there was also the contribution of my dad, who was a liberated, progressive, gentle man who did not take patriarchal privilege. But all in all, this was my great mother's achievement. She made me who I am and who I became. Now I am her No. 1 fan even though she is no more. I owe her everything, and every dream that I have, it is for her. Without her, I would not be who I am.

MJW: In encouraging you and your sisters, did your mum urge you just to be the best, to work hard, to go to Oxford, those kinds of things? Or did she talk about it in terms of structural gendered discrimination at all – like, as a woman you're going to have to work harder?

MKMMK: No, not in those terms. She was one of the most knowledgeable people and critical reader and thinker that I know of in my life. She was a very progressive and liberated person even then. She wanted us to stand on our own feet, she wanted us to maximize our capacities based on the equality of being human (not based on gender), whatever we decided in our lives. She would say, 'If you want to be a regent queen, work for it. If you want to be a queen, marry a king. If you just want to be *side car* [trishaw] driver's wife, that's up to you. All are in your hands. So go for it. Get whatever you want. But empower yourself first!'

MJW: How would you say your own feminist perspective developed? Specifically, when did you start to describe and understand it *as* feminist? My assumption is that theorizing about it started well before you were in university and started to work in feminist theory, so I'm curious about how it emerged from your practice, in the initial work you were just describing?

257

MKMMK: I think it started clearly since I was young and when I observed my mum and dad treating each other based on humanity and equality and not based on prescribed gender norms. But working with trafficked girls and women in Thailand helped me to become conscious of gender as a structural issue. This was in the 1990s. Then, when I attended a seminar about women in history and later, I became involved in that project and became a close friend with one of the greatest historians, Prof. Penny Edwards, I began to see how idealized Myanmar women and gender have been politicized and constructed in Myanmar. Reading *The Second Sex*, I saw that when Simone de Beauvoir wrote about the coming into being of 'a woman', that she is 'not born, but rather becomes a woman', it further supported my hypothesis, based on my experience.

I began to be interested in how much influence the ideologies of religion, politics, and society had on the construction of gender identities (both masculinities and femininities) and what were the consequences. Both Penny Edwards and Ma Tin Zar Lwin, who explored how missionaries constructed Karen femininities, had made great contributions for gender studies. They were the prominent and pioneering scholars of gender studies in Myanmar. They had in-depth understanding of gender and structural discrimination.

Recently, I was invited by the National Unity Government (NUG)'s Ministry of Women, Youth and Children to discuss the women's movement in the American and French Revolutions, as part of their campaign against gender-based violence in Myanmar's conflicts. I opened with a question: Why not discuss Burmese women? Was there no revolution in Myanmar? Were no women liberated enough to be involved? Or could we dare ask whether Myanmar women were already liberated that they did not need a revolution like the French and Americans? Why only western feminists? Do we think feminists were here only in our time? Or the fight for women's rights or equality issues emerged only under the influence of Western enlightenment theory?

Feminism for me is the fundamental equality of human beings: the equality of women despite gender, race, religion, and classes. Gender is not just about women's rights or women's issues. It includes variable spectrums of power relations, including intersecting identities such as sexualities, class, political ideology, religion, social identities and so on. Gender inequality is relational. It is rooted in uneven dynamics that give disproportionate power/burden to one group over another based on sex, that creates one-sided, disproportionate suffering, constraints, burdens, discrimination and even violence.

MJW: So part of the challenge is in situating gender contextually, inter-sectionally. But there's also the challenge of simply making gender visible, de-naturalizing our socialized understandings and making space to discuss this critically. We see in Rose Metro's chapter in this volume the ways in which these gender norms are not just reinforced – even in allegedly progressive contexts – but also normalized, in ways that make it more challenging for children to not only notice them *as inequalities* but also name them and speak back against them, to parents, teachers and other authority figures. In doing so, they risk being seen as going against Myanmar traditional values.

MKMMK: When these gender ideologies are being internalized through education, propaganda, religious discourse, cultural prescription, and popular culture, gender inequality is even justified with political and social stereotypes, and gender norms become almost second nature. But this also demonstrates that it isn't just about what girls are learning; in order to fight for equality of women, we also need to understand about men: why they do what they do? How are they learning these norms? And just as importantly, what happens to them under patriarchal privilege and power? Are they better off?

That's why I have been also focusing my research on this subject. In a chapter in my thesis, on 'Men and Masculinities: Construction of man and masculinities from the influence of religion, colonialism, nationalism, militarism, and migrations', I showed that the patriarchal privilege and power was also toxic to Myanmar men, especially the less-educated mass populace (compared to women). It dominated the population through disproportionate prison sentences, rates of substance abuse, and greater premature and violent deaths compared to women. These extreme institutionalized patriarchal power dynamics magnify vulnerabilities and suffering to both genders, but particularly women. That's why I have always argued that gender-based violence has a pathological nature, and solutions based on individuals will not combat gender-based violence. We need proper, comprehensive and anthropologically based research to find solutions for both genders.

But at that time when I started my PhD there were no books on gender [in Burma]. Only Daw Mi Mi Khaing's book (*The World of Burmese Women*, 1984). And that didn't satisfy my curiosity. Earlier a prominent Burmese writer, Saw Mon Nyin, published *Myanmar Amyothami* [*Women of Burma*] in 1976 but that book was only really listing the women figures in history. That was published for the BSPP (Burma Socialist Programme Party). So, when

I started, I had to deploy every type of source I could find: songs, literature, cartoons, Buddhist stories, sayings, popular culture as well as interviews with people ranking from the President to trafficked victims and HIV/AIDS patients.

I started a PhD purely out of intellectual curiosity, to understand the root causes of gendered and structural/cultural violence, because I want to find solutions and transformative outcomes and end the social suffering of women and men. I know the nature of these problems are pathological. Trying to investigate this, I was told that my PhD was not just one simple research, but ten PhDs joined together. I was trying to capture all of these aspects: pre-Buddhist culture, modernity, colonization, militarization, even migration and I was told that this was like ten theses! But what got me through was my promise that I made whenever I had to bury young women who died of HIV/AIDS in Thailand after being trafficked and sold. They died alone in a foreign land and without being willing to tell their families because they were too ashamed or did not want to bring shame to their families. So even now their families may not realize it. Their life stories inflamed me with frustration, anger and desperation.

But I was finding the same evidence from all types of scattered and dusty evidence, hidden in the corners of yellowed pages, tombstones, missionary and ancient travellers' accounts, popular culture outputs (literature, *pwè* [arts], *zat-pwè* [performance arts]), in the education and knowledge system, as well as throughout current issues of human suffering, exploitation and human rights/women's rights such as HIV/AIDS, trafficking and forced migration. This gradually revealed the same structural dynamics.

MJW: And did you feel at that point, what you were putting together in terms of your on-the-ground experiences with trafficked women and others, starting to situate that in the broader context of Burmese socio-religious culture, was it consistent with the feminist theory that you were learning? Did it challenge it? Expand it? Basically, how did the theoretical work you were incorporating integrate with the empirical?

MKMMK: As you know my thesis involved not only women but also men, and not just contemporary but also in pre-colonial, colonial and post-colonial Burma under the influence of religion, colonialism, nationalism and militarism, but also cross border migrations (trafficking and forced migration). For me, comprehensive knowledge can contribute solutions. Like a treatment for cancer, we need to diagnose thoroughly. And also as a researcher, I feel I have moral responsibility to contribute practically, not just doing research for my own interest, for publication, grants or jobs. I also feel I have a responsibility to bring the voiceless and marginalized to speak themselves. [The film that accompanied my PhD thesis] *Dreams of Dutiful Daughters* was designed to make them speak for themselves. The connection from different spectrums made a powerful force, showing how these dynamics were making women who they are, the forces through which Burmese women were being shaped as the idealized 'Burmese woman'. Putting a puzzle together piece by piece, you start to see the pattern, but also how you can dismantle it.

MJW: You've already talked a bit about your research work with trafficked women and children in Thailand. I want to ask more broadly, how has your research and your perspective been influenced by women you've worked with in the field, across different parts of your career: women in ethnic armed organizations, elected MPs, university professors and others in recent years. How have these encounters shaped your views?

MKMMK: First, I think the scarcity of research on women in Myanmar in general, and in history in particular, liberated me in a way, as I had to look at *everything* myself for my PhD. When I started my research on gender, there were then no PhD theses on gender or women in Myanmar. The more difficult it was to find resources, the more desperate I was, the more determined I became. I feel a sense of obligation for my mother, for the women of Myanmar and our ancestors. For me, my mother is an unsung heroine, like many women. I want to do justice for her and for other mothers. I need to put Burmese women on the map and in their original place.

My obsession made every person became my potential informant, every place became my research field site, and I am like a permanent active participant observer, working to analyze and investigate everything that appears. Even Burmese student activists from the 88 Generation who came for protests in Canberra became my field of studies, as many of them would come to stay with me during the protests. There were many female activists who were students, forced into exile, who received military training in the jungles and then moved to Australia and were still actively involved in the democracy movement in Myanmar. These women were courageous and daring soldiers. But as soon as they gathered, the girls would start to organize the food, almost as if it were second nature. Only one male activist was the exception [to this gendered division of labour]. These women were soldiers! They hunted in the jungles! They trained with the men. They were comrades. But in terms of distribution of labour, women would go straight to the kitchen. Distribution of labour is gendered and structured so much so that it became second nature.

MJW: That mirrors the way that Khin Khin Mra and Deborah Livingstone describe the ways in which new opportunities for women's participation in political institutions were still 'nested' within persistent patterns of inequality or gendered norms, perhaps slowing down the pace of reform, because opportunities to participate didn't automatically translate into influence, if women's voices and perspectives weren't being respected and included.

MKMMK: Absolutely. Due to my position as the first senior Burmese female researcher at the University of Oxford, I was able to access to women in the social and political spectrums, that included access to Daw Aung San Suu Kyi, to activists and ethnic women in conflict, or sex workers. But I would see the same patterns, no matter the context. For example, as you know, I organized a *Cooking in Conflict* project, but I found that women living in the midst of armed conflict shared the same patterns across ethnicities, religions and geographical boundaries. In other words, structural discrimination was being internalized and re-enacted as a form of violence all over the country.

MJW: You mention the *Cooking in Conflict* project, and I see that as a creative way of not just recognizing women's work, but of bringing community-oriented conversations out of academic spaces to the locations where women are more comfortable sharing and reflecting. Of course, that's work that some of the groups represented in this volume – such as the KWO, KWAT, WLB – have also been doing for many years. The chapters in this volume on feminist mobilization highlight similar spaces and types of community-building and peacebuilding work that women have done generation after generation, but too often don't get included in political analysis because they're not part of formal institutions, like parliament or the peace process. But even in those places, as Naw K'nyaw Paw relates, women can be constrained by patriarchal practices and traditions.

MKMMK: I agree. Often with regard to femininities, the word 'tradition' is overtly used to justify repression of women. For me, I'm interested in how 'traditions' such as *hpoun* and *pwè* were used to construct, reinvent and politicize femininity and female sexualities. In this way, they measured and obligated women under the fixed and idealized model; women were not born this way, but made to become a new 'Buddhist Myanmar lady'. We saw this especially during the nationalist era, with the construction of the idealized Myanmar woman. The 're-invented' Myanmar woman had to be proper: that meant feminine, submissive, pure, chaste, refined, modest, obliging and thoroughly domesticated, in accordance with imported Victorian feminine values. Myanmar women were never like that! It contrasted with well-documented images of Burmese women in precolonial Burma, before they encountered the Victorian gentlemen. The shock and horror reported by early travellers, missionaries and colonial administrators, seeing Burmese women wearing split skirts, smoking long cigars, managing business, roaming around the village, fighting, suing each other and protecting their interests, unlike their sisters in the West.

The situation in Myanmar since colonization reflects how Myanmar is continuing the battle of imposing ideologies and identities on women. On one level, it says, 'Myanmar women did not need to demand their rights because their traditions already provided for them', and on another level, they still continued the outdated Victorian vision of gender norms and indeed *added to* the antiquated foreign laws of the British, that were developed for India but which are still used in term of dealing with sexual violence today.

MJW: We can see the persistence of these norms in the struggle that women activists have faced to pass the PoVAW [Prevention of Violence Against Women] law. Aye Thiri Kyaw's chapter in this volume examines the challenge activists have faced in even getting the issue of domestic violence to register with the public – and with mostly male legislators – *as a political concern* that needs to be addressed. It's too easy for people to take the confining and biased legal framework as a given, rather than something that can be altered to better address current conditions.

MKMMK: And the additional danger is that if women challenge these norms, they are subject to discipline, abuse, even violence, treated as if they're under influence of Western countries or even as traitors. We also saw that in the death threats that some woman activists faced when they criticized and opposed Ma Ba Tha's 'Race and Religion Protection Laws' in 2014 and 2015. Some gender-related laws in Myanmar are still being developed based on foreign concepts such as the British common laws that overshadow the customary laws. Now you see, today under the influence of modernization, now marriage registration has become fashionable. But Burmese marriage has always been civil; no religious approval or government registration is needed. Same for divorce. We need to find ways to incorporate all traditions of gender liberation, not simply take one method and reject others.

MJW: These patterns that started to come together earlier in your research, do you feel you've continued to see them more recently, in your interactions with women in upper economic classes or social elites such as female MPs, university professors? And similarly, where have you seen these patterns being disrupted or challenged?

MKMMK: Since Burma re-opened after 2011, with the influx of donors, INGOs and NGOs, gender has been in focus. But a rights-based approach has its limits. Gender-based violence in Myanmar has a pathological nature. We need to treat it like cancer. We need a proper diagnosis, painful chemotherapy, then allocate time for recovery and aim to take the root out completely. As I just said, outdated and inappropriate colonial and customary laws (based on India's *Laws of Manu* and applied in Burma as a province of India) are still being used to deal with gender-based violence. That's why we need not just a rights-based approach, but a broader emphasis on social change.

MJW: You and I have written before, with Melyn McKay, about the possible limits of rights-based discourse in fostering a broad-based women's movement in Myanmar. Specifically, we were concerned about the fact that, despite the validity of rights-based critiques of Ma Ba Tha's 'Race and Religion Protection Laws', activists using those arguments were finding limited resonance with women who understood the challenges in their lives in different terms. Throughout this volume, we see the importance of localized understandings and practices, but also a necessary engagement with state institutions and formal processes, such as Hilary Faxon's attention to land use and land legislation in her contribution to this volume. But we also see examples of people not just adapting to, but leading and pushing for the kinds of broader social change you're talking about here.

MKMMK: Social change begins with behaviour change, behaviour changes starts from changes of thinking. Thinking will not change without changing knowledge and education. So, in order to enact social change, we need new knowledge and critical thinking. We need to be critical of our own knowledge and perceptions, about our histories, religions and cultures, because we continue to learn about politics, religion and other spheres from a location within this patriarchal system. And this can't be superficially fixed. We have to go beyond a quick-fix solution and challenge people's thinking, myths, assumptions, values, histories, identities, ideologies and belief systems. And then, when we talk about gender, we have to look at men as well, in order to understand how a patriarchal system messes up everyone, even as it affects women in particular ways.

MJW: The way you discussed that earlier, and in some of your published work, reminds me of some of the foundational work in Critical Race Theory, like the way that W.E.B. Du Bois talks about the 'wages of whiteness'. In his view, White people are benefitting from racial privilege, just as men are benefiting from gender privilege, but at the same time, most men, like most White people, are also being hurt and repressed, or at least limited by these structures in some way, whether that's class-based exploitation of some White groups or the destructive psychological pressures of an idealized, rigid hyper-masculinity.

MKMMK: I agree with you. This is an imbalance of power, where one individual, one system or one group has it over another, and the systems are related in this way. In a way, I'm grateful that, during my PhD, because I didn't have other resources to rely on, I had to dive into everything, to build it all up from nothing. I read extensively, so I was able to encounter some of these things about race and gender together, seeing these comparisons. I studied a lot about Aboriginal communities, and about race and gender together, in the context of gender-based violence and other issues.

This 2021 Spring Revolution is historic and for the first time, we see ideological and identity-oriented revolutions in Myanmar that include gender. I mentioned before how 'traditions' such as *hpoun* and *pwè* have been constructed in support of masculine privilege under patriarchal institutions. As just one example, my previous work on *hpoun* [a type of power or merit reserved only for men in Burmese Buddhist belief] was also related practically to the 'Panty Power' or 'Panties for Peace' movement in 2007 [which involved female activists sending their used underwear to Burmese embassies as a way of antagonizing members of the regime, drawing on beliefs that women's undergarments would sap the *hpoun* of men]. And in the current anti-coup movement, we see the same dynamic in the 'Htamain Alan Htu' or 'Sarong Strike' [where women are hanging out their skirts and undergarments, to challenge the views that women's bodies are 'polluted' and a danger to men]. This activism is really questioning *hpoun*. Belief in *hpoun* is a clear example of how people have internalized a belief system and how traditions can be re-invented; people follow it without question and even attack those who challenge it. At the same time, critical thinking young men who have enjoyed freedom and liberty as a global village's citizen for the last decade or so, also do not accept this. Some of them joined in to support women and challenge these 'traditions', even by wearing the *htamein* as *head* dresses.

MJW: It's interesting that we have seen some deeper discussion of issues such as this recently. It's not only a superficial move to hang up the *htamein* for strategic purposes, but what's surrounding it are conversations between male and female activists challenging these beliefs and structures. Right now, we see those mostly on social media, so we might have reason to be sceptical as to how deep those conversations can go, just because of the conflicting imperatives in the current crisis context. And in a way it might be similar to the movement in 1988, where people really didn't have the time or the bandwidth – in the midst of resisting the military – to address these issues fully. So it's about creating a platform to keep these broader conversations going. And even if these questions aren't fully addressed in the moment of resistance, there are scholars, activists, who are continuing to push it forward.

MKMMK: This is really exciting and I'm hopeful to see the dawn of real social change and turning the tables on these issues.

MJW: I have one final question for you Mar, following on from that. We've seen this exciting proliferation of feminist research – *explicitly* feminist research – related to Myanmar, in the last decade and a half, certainly a far cry from when you were just starting out, when there was just a trickle from scholars like Chie Ikeya and Tharaphi Than. Now there's a whole generation of graduate students and independent scholars and activists who define themselves *as* feminists, doing self-consciously feminist research, some of whom are represented in this volume, but many more of whom are carving out other spaces for their work, in addition to academic channels. I want to ask, what are some of the most exciting developments in this space for you, but also, where are the spaces, the topics that you think still need to receive more attention?

MKMMK: One of the exciting things for me is witnessing how young women and men are debating on social media even without labelling themselves as feminists. It is also exciting to see young men are very active in these debates and we can see that they are interested in structural changes. They are applying theories that they learned in recent years. But they also need to understand their own culture and the root causes of these structures and how they've come into existence. It is still difficult because there is such a limited history of women or social history in Myanmar. If we want values change, social change, we need to go beyond 'partial knowledge'; it has to be comprehensive. Global views, local solutions with transformative action. They are now speaking up, speaking out, and speaking loud on the issue of gender equality.

Their courage is admirable. I am particularly proud of young women and men who are involved in this debate using their progressive ideologies to question patriarchal privilege and power and the structural justification of gender-based violence. That is something significant. That is something historic. This is also a revolution of embodied, sexual politics. If you're going to fight for social change, you need to be able to change behaviour. In order to do so, you need new knowledge and new thinking. It's still change from *within* the culture, but we need to continue to push for this different thinking, to make progress on social change. That's why we need anthropological and social history research focused on transformative action for social change in order to continue to make a difference.

Index

f=figure, n=footnote, **bold**=extended discussion or key reference